T0293959

Bomber Command

Bomber Command

Men, Machines and Missions 1936–68

Gordon A. A. Wilson

AMBERLEY

Frontispiece by H. R. (Rick) Hovey

Jacket illustrations: front: Short Stirling (courtesy of Imperial War Museum); *back:* Avro Vulcan (courtesy of Bill Powderly).

First published 2021

Amberley Publishing
The Hill, Stroud
Gloucestershire, GL5 4EP

www.amberley-books.com

ISBN 978 1 4456 9093 3 (hardback)
ISBN 978 1 4456 9094 0 (ebook)

British Library Cataloguing in Publication Data.
A catalogue record for this book is available from the British Library.

1 2 3 4 5 6 7 8 9 10

Typesetting by SJmagic DESIGN SERVICES, India.
Printed in the UK.

CONTENTS

ACKNOWLEDGEMENTS

My wife Emily for her love and continued support of my writing. My family for their love and encouragement, Grandpa can now come out to play! Shaun Barrington and the team at Amberley Books without whom this book would not have been possible. Gary Vincent for access to his extensive aviation library, and searching for and editing the photographs. Barrie Gabie for his technical assistance, dedicated editing, and grammatical investigations. Syd Leung for his Word support and creating the many tables and charts. John D. (Dave) Birrell, Founding Director, Archivist and Librarian, Bomber Command Museum of Canada, for writing the Foreword and valuable editing. H. R. (Rick) Hovey for creating the frontispiece drawing and the RAF Station Fiskerton map. Deborah Harkin, Marcia Hogg for access to the Grant family papers. Sheila Jakus for the poem on page 283 and Chrissie Egan for the calligraphy. Lynn and Harold Pratsides for Davison and Dawe family information. Colm Egan for website research information. Barrie Laycock for aviation research. Wayne Ralph (author and military historian) for use of his aviation library. Anne Tilbury for IT support. Dr Roy Strang for research support. Donagh and Eddie O'Brien for content support.

Malcolm Barrass – www.rafweb.org – for RAF organisation information.
Surrey Public Library, Inter-Library Loan department.
Bomber Command Museum of Canada, Nanton, Alberta.
Canadian Museum of Flight, Langley, British Columbia.
The International Bomber Command Centre, Lincoln.

I would especially like to thank my friends Gary, Syd, Dave and Barrie, all mentioned above, as they helped me prepare the final manuscript for submission during these very difficult times.

Images: John Allen, Adrian Balch Collection, Bomber Command Museum of Canada, Douglas Bowman (www.archerphotoworks.ca), Ben Budworth, Canadian Museum of Flight, Atsushi 'Fred' Fujimori (Vintage V12s), Deborah Harkin, Maria Hogg, Rick Hovey, Imperial War Museum, Marsham Arms (Jenna), Patrick Martin Collection, Malcolm Nason, No. 75 Squadron RNZAF, William Pearson, Barb Petticrew, Bill Powderly, RCAF Archives, Rolls-Royce Heritage Trust, Richard Vandervord, Jerry Vernon Collection.

Extensive use for research was made of these three books all listed in the Bibliography. They are Middlebrook and Everitt's *The Bomber Command War Diaries*, Moyes's *Bomber Squadrons of the R. A. F. and their Aircraft*, and Falconer's *Bomber Command Handbook 1939-1945*. I am indebted to their work.

My sincere apologies to those I may have missed. Rest assured your contributions were much appreciated.

FOREWORD BY JOHN BIRRELL

Throughout my association with the Bomber Command Museum of Canada since its inception in 1986, I have continuously and increasingly been impressed with the scale, the complexity, the evolution, the profound effect on those who served, and of course, the scale of the losses involved in the huge effort that was Bomber Command.

As I write this foreword, I am working with the museum's archives and have just come across the original documents related to a Bomber Command raid to Leipzig on the night of 19/20 February,1944. No. 431 Squadron RCAF and No. 434 Squadron RCAF, based at RCAF Croft in Yorkshire, participated in this major effort involving 852 bombers. Of the nineteen aircraft dispatched from Croft, five failed to return including three of the nine No. 434 Squadron RCAF Halifaxes.

In No. 434 Squadron's daily diary (ORB Form 540) for the following day, an unknown air force member simply recorded, 'This morning's news is not good ... Three aircraft "O", "V", and "Z" are unreported since take-off and along with the crews have been listed as missing on operations against Leipzig. The missing aircrew include...' The writer then painfully proceeded to type into the document the names, ranks and service numbers of thirty-five young airmen, many of whom he or she likely knew personally. Fully one third lost in a single night; and the young airmen of No. 434 Squadron that returned knew that, given these odds, they would likely not survive the thirty nights required for them to complete their tour of operations.

Through his book, and specifically through the organisation and approach he chose, Gordon focuses on the scale – the numbers of squadrons, bases, aircraft, and personnel, the complexity, the technology and coordination involved – and the incredible changes in equipment and techniques that occurred as the war progressed.

As for the effects on the people involved, Gordon's years as an operational pilot with the Canadian Armed Forces during the height of the Cold War, I'm sure, enabled him to develop an appreciation for the loneliness and fear of flying at night in a military aircraft.

And the losses – the numbers and the sacrifice, we can only learn of examples. It's impossible to adequately comprehend.

John D. (Dave) Birrell is a Founding Director of the Bomber Command Museum of Canada in Nanton, Alberta. He volunteers as the museum's librarian and archivist. He is an accomplished author and has written many books published by the museum on the personalities and aircraft of Bomber Command. He is a retired geophysicist and teacher who specialised in outdoor education centred around the Canadian Rockies.

INTRODUCTION

This is the story of the Royal Air Force's Bomber Command during the Second World War. It explores the organisation, the personnel, and the aircraft that made up this formidable force during that war and its changing role during the ensuing Cold War. It is a story of struggle, heroics, grief, successes and failures during its thirty-two-year lifetime. History continues to debate Bomber Command's mission and how it was carried out. Regardless, without it certainly Great Britain, and possibly the world, would not have the democratic freedom we enjoy today.

The aim of this book is to introduce the reader to a wartime organisation that grew to meet the challenges of the times head-on. The story of its growth from an uncertain beginning under extreme conditions of England's aerial attack into a large and important part of the Allied victory is a unique and powerful one.

Bomber Command in the Second World War was a direct descendant of the First World War strategic bombing forces. Policy and strategic bombing philosophy were subject to the overall political aims of the war effort. Initially as the threat grew it was the junior player in the build- up of arms. As Britain is an island, it was the navy that got priority, followed by the defensive air force. The striking power of Bomber Command in the early years was limited to leaflet dropping, defensive patrols, and a disastrous attempt at daylight raids on the heavily protected German Navy. Bomber Command initially lagged behind in manpower and advanced aircraft but by 1942, under a new Commander-in-Chief, Air Marshal A. T. Harris, the tables began to turn and night-time area bombing by heavier and more numerous bombers began.

Over 1,400 years ago, wooden forts were attacked by fire. In the twentieth century,'Fortress Europe' was attacked and penetrated with explosions, incendiaries and resulting fire, by the Royal Air Force

Bomber Command. As a result of the historic defence of its land by 'The Few' of Fighter Command, Great Britain was able to become the aggressor and defeat Nazi Germany and the Axis powers. The Allied victory was due in no small apart to Bomber Command.

When did civilians first become threatened by explosives dropping from the air? It was in the first few weeks of the First World War that the German Naval Airship Department's Zeppelins dropped bombs on the citizens of Liège and Antwerp, Belgium. This was followed by aerial bombardment of England for the next three years, the airships being joined by Gotha 'G' four-engine bombers in the latter stages of the conflict. The precedence for aerial bombardment had been established not only by airships but also by reconnaissance and bomber aircraft used by both sides in the conflict.

The false sense of peace in the inter-war years was brought to an end by the final realisation by Britain that Germany was undergoing a rebirth of military capability in spite of all the restrictions placed on it. In 1936 the Royal Air Force created Bomber Command to build up an organisation of personnel and equipment to meet *possible* future requirements. The politicians and guardians of the British Government purse still believed that diplomacy could avert the looming crisis. How wrong they were.

Bomber Command eventually increased to thirteen Groups to meet organisational requirements, each with its own headquarters under the command of at least a Group Captain, or an Air Vice-Marshal if a front-line Group. The No. 2 Group was the first group formed in March 1936, a scant three years before its first operational mission in September 1939. Perhaps the most famous of all the Groups was No. 8 Group, the Pathfinder Force. This initiative would raise Bomber Command to new heights of effectiveness through more accurate bombing. Canada eventually formed its own Group, No. 6, later in the war.

If No. 8 Group was the most famous among the Groups, then the Royal Air Force No. 617 'Dambuster' Squadron, flying from Royal Air Force Scampton, Lincolnshire, was the most celebrated squadron for its daring 1943 raid and destruction of dams in the Ruhr Valley. At various times during the war there were over a hundred and thirty active squadrons in Bomber Command. Some of these squadrons could trace their lineage back to the Royal Flying Corps before the formation of the Royal Air Force in 1918.

Owing to its location on the east coast many of the Bomber Command squadrons were stationed in Lincolnshire, and it became known as the 'Bomber County'. Today Lincolnshire is home to the International Bomber Command Centre at Canwick Hill and the Lincolnshire Aviation Heritage Centre at East Kirkby. Both continue to conserve and explain the Second World War history of Bomber Command.

The twenty-one inter-war years saw the development of bomber aircraft from the single-engine biplane, the Hawker Hind (1936) to the single-engine monoplane, the Fairey Battle (1937), and to the twin-engine monoplane, the Vickers Wellington (1938). These aircraft were followed during the war years by the four-engine heavy bomber, the Avro Lancaster (1942) being the most recognised. These aircraft are just a few examples of the many aircraft manufacturers and types that were part of Bomber Command.

Training was an essential part of the success of Bomber Command. The men that looked after the aircraft and the crews that flew them had to be trained to the highest possible standard in spite of the limitations of wartime conditions. The aircrew would start at an Initial Training Wing in England and then many would finish overseas away from the constant danger of enemy bomber attacks. The British Commonwealth Air Training Plan was a cooperatively funded training venture among the Commonwealth countries, Great Britain, Australia, New Zealand, and Canada. The plan was primarily located in the wide-open 'safe from threat' skies of Canada.

There has been some criticism of the extent and scope of Bomber Command operations in the past. However, the German war machine did not hold back from the very beginning with the invasion of Poland. It was a total onslaught, a Blitzkrieg. Negotiation should be met with negotiation, force with force and total force with total force.

Dave Birrell, in his book, *Johnny: Canada's Greatest Bomber Pilot,* quotes from a speech that John E. Fauquier DSO and two Bars, DFC, gave to the Empire Club of Canada on 22 November 1945:

> Does anyone here seriously think that the war would be over now if Germany had been able to maintain her oil and gasoline plants intact, her iron and steel empire working full blast, her internal rail and road communications unimpaired, her canals filled with water and fit for navigation, her factories standing and producing war materials, and her colossal army of civilian workers well housed and organised? No! The war would be on today, and the casualties on D-Day would have been far higher.

The, perhaps belated, guidance to Bomber Command from the Chiefs of Staff in 1943 read: 'Your primary object will be the progressive destruction and dislocation of the German military, industrial and economic system, and the undermining of the morale of the German people to a point where their capacity for armed resistance is fatally weakened.'

Post-war, the role of Bomber Command gradually changed during the Cold War years to a nuclear strike capability and in 1968 it merged with Fighter Command to form Strike Command. The last piston-engine bomber aircraft developed during the war years, the Avro Lincoln, was replaced with the jet engines of the English Electric Canberra and the V Bomber aircraft.

Bomber Command was not perfect, nothing is, but when called upon in Britain's hour of need, it brought the war to the enemy's doorstep and helped to turn the tide of war. Bomber Command was a major part of the final Allied victory.

Author's Note: While every effort has been made to use records and statistics from reliable sources, there are always discrepancies, even in the primary records. Paperwork was inadvertently destroyed, information was wrongly entered or omitted. It was over eighty years ago and in an era prior to the data collection power of the computer. Britain was at war fighting for its very survival; records, though essential, were of secondary importance to 'getting the job done'.

1

PRE-BOMBER COMMAND

The flimsy paper construction slowly rose from the earth and ascended into the sky, defying gravity for the moment. It was 1760 and the Montgolfier brothers had started their experiments with hot air confined within a paper envelope. That envelope would later develop into the cloth hot air balloon. The next step in the evolution of sky travel was to put animals, closely followed by humans, in the balloon for scientific experiments and for man to experience the joy and wonder of flight. On the 19 September 1783 Pilatre de Rozier sent a balloon aloft with a sheep, a duck, and a rooster on board. This flight was quickly followed by the first human hot air balloon flight by de Rozier in a Montgolfier balloon on 21 November from the centre of Paris.

It would follow that the military would quickly see the advantage of aerial observation from a balloon above the battlefield. Seven years later in 1794, during the French Revolutionary Wars, the French used a tethered hydrogen balloon to observe the movements of the Austrian army during the Battle of Fleurus. Extremely valuable intelligence could be gathered from above when you could only see part of the enemy's forces at ground-level. In 1861 Thaddeus Lowe commanded the Union Army Balloon Corps during the American Civil War to gather Confederate Army strength, movements, and location. The Corps was the early forerunner of the United States Army Air Force.

The balloon on a calm day was easily handled; on a windy day it was a challenge or even impossible. The idea was to transport the balloon close to the front, send it airborne, make the observation, and have the ground crew haul it down quickly before it was attacked. Horizontal and vertical stabilisers gave the balloon more control when it was changed to a sausage shape. It would logically follow that adding an engine and a pilot would make it more manoeuvrable.

In late 1911, Italy and the Ottoman Empire were skirmishing over present-day Libya where reconnaissance and crude bombing attacks were directed from Italian dirigibles, an early example of aerial bombing. General Giulio Douhet commanded an Italian aviation battalion in 1912 and had written a report about the lessons learned from the Libya conflict. He went on to expand the report, which became the famous strategic bombing treatise entitled *The Command of the Air*. He was an outspoken advocate of the use of air power and criticised the government and military leaders for not heeding his comments. He was deemed a radical, court-martialled, and subsequently spent a year imprisoned before being reinstated shortly before the end of the war.

This Libyan conflict was only a scant eight years since Orville and Wilbur Wright took to the skies in their epic first flight of a heavier-than-air aircraft. In April 1911 an air battalion of the Royal Engineers was formed with balloons and Bristol Boxkites. In December the Admiralty formed the first naval flying school at Eastbourne. In May 1912 the Royal Flying Corps was formed with naval and military wings. It did not last long, with the navy separating as the Royal Naval Air Service, the military wing retaining the Royal Flying Corps title.

By 1914, the benefits of aerial photo-reconnaissance were fully recognised and, to a lesser extent, bombing was seen as a part of aerial warfare. The scene was set for an epic four-year struggle to control the skies over one's territory to protect resources, and to control the skies over one's enemy's territory to destroy his resources by aerial bombardment.

Deadlocked armies with few ground-based visibility options required aerial intelligence to give them the advantage in future planned movements. Larger aircraft than the fighters with a pilot and observer were assigned to photo-reconnaissance and bombing of supply lines behind the enemy trenches. Being less manoeuvrable, these aircraft were often protected by their own fighters flying top cover. They were not defenceless themselves however, often having forward and rearward facing guns. Attacked from below, these large aircrafts' only escape was to go into a steep dive and so expose the chasing fighter. From early in the war the Royal Flying Corps as a single organisation was dealing with two types of aerial combat, the fighter and the photo-reconnaissance/bomber elements.

As mentioned in the introduction, the first Central Powers' bombing raids took place against cities such as Warsaw and Paris. This was followed closely by Zeppelin raids during 1915 on England. Unlike the free form balloon, the Zeppelin was an airship that had been developed by the German Count Ferdinand von Zeppelin and perfected in the 1890s. It was a rigid metal framework incorporating individual gasbags. It had several engines mounted in gondolas which gave it manoeuvrability unlike the pure balloon which was restricted in movement to the wind direction. Pre-war, the Zeppelin had a checquered history with the German Naval Service but a slightly more successful career with the world's first pleasure cruise airline, DELAG. It did, however, continue to be developed to a higher level of reliability.

The German Army took over the DELAG airships and initiated bombing missions with little success. No suitable bombs were available at the beginning so artillery shells were used as ordinance for initial attacks. Vulnerable to small arms fire at low altitude, the Zeppelins had to be flown at high altitude with resulting loss of bombing accuracy. Air raids were conducted against England and London in 1916. Although there were civilian fatalities, the greatest effect was the propaganda value of bombing the English capital, and the terrorising of English citizens having to deal with death raining down from the skies.

The Zeppelins were supplemented with Gotha G and Zeppelin-Staaken R.VI bombers, which contributed to the later belief that 'the bomber will always get through.' The Gotha could carry 350kg (840lb) and the Zeppelin-Staaken could carry 2,000kg (4,400lb) of bombs, certainly enough to do damage, cause casualties, and divert resources to defence. On 14 June 1917 that is exactly what happened; fourteen Gothas attacked London killing 162 people and injuring 432 people. The army and navy had been bypassed and now warfare would enter a new dimension, defence of the skies above the homeland.

The German Naval Air Service primarily used the airships for reconnaissance missions over the North Sea and Baltic, reporting back on the Royal Navy strength and movements. The Royal Naval Air Service conversely initiated strategic bombing in 1914 by aircraft carrying twenty- pound bombs. They executed a raid on Cologne in September and a successful raid on a Zeppelin shed at Düsseldorf in October. In December, for the first time, a raid was conducted by tender-based Short Type seaplanes against the Zeppelin sheds at Cuxhaven.

Lack of co-ordination of effort by the navy, the Senior Service, and military aviation necessitated the establishment of an Air Committee in 1912 immediately after the formation of the Royal Flying Corps. This committee was comprised of members of the two war ministries and was limited to recommendations to the Admiralty Board and Imperial General Staff, which had to ratify them before presenting them to the War Office. An ineffective committee during the first years of the First World War resulted in the formation of an equally ineffective Joint War Air Committee in 1916. The Royal Flying Corps and the Royal Naval Air Service were at odds, inter-service rivalry affected the supply and design of aircraft, and the defence of Britain. The Air Board, driven by higher-profile members, was slightly more successful in 1917 and specifications were laid down for the Airco DH10 day bomber and the Fairey III and Short N2B floatplane bombers.

In June 1918, long-range bombing missions were flown against industrial targets deep in German territory. They were conducted by the newly formed Royal Air Force, a product of the amalgamation of the Royal Naval Air Service and the Royal Flying Corps on 1 April 1918 under the command of Major-General Hugh Trenchard. These raids were performed by the De Havilland DH9 and Handley Page O/400 bombers ,which dropped twice as many tons of bombs on Germany than had been dropped on England. These aviation company names would rise to fame again in the Second World War with the De Havilland Mosquito and the Handley Page Halifax, both prominent in the victory effort.

German Generals Ludendorf and Hindenburg are reputed to have opined that it was 'the defeatism of the civilian population that had made defeat inevitable'. That is certainly a statement that contributes to the area versus strategic bombing discussion, and the total war versus limited war argument.

Jonathan Falconer, in his book *Bomber Command Handbook 1939-1945*, stated in the prologue: 'The cult of the bomber was very much a phenomenon of the interwar period. Its new mass destructive role witnessed during the closing stages of the First World War strongly affected military thinking in the years that immediately followed.'

The euphoria of victory would soon fade in the shadow of the human cost and the realisation of the financial impact of the war on the economy of the country. Three main issues were predominant in the inter-war years of 1918-1936 prior to, and responsible for, the formation of the Royal Air Force Bomber Command in 1936: the changing political scene at home in Britain and in Europe, the development of the British civil aviation industry and its resulting aircraft, and the growth of the Royal Air Force in peacetime. We will look at these three factors individually in incremental three-year time-periods as they ultimately resulted in the formation of Bomber Command.

The British civil aviation industry and car manufactures, seconded into wartime production, contributed enormously to the production of aircraft and aero engines during 1914-1918. Some companies survived the lean 1920s and some did not. Some would rise again to the challenge of the Second World War and provide the famous aircraft and engines of this conflict.

There were several main aircraft manufacturers that were successful commercially but there were many inventors and small companies that took on the challenge of heavier-than-air flight and were not to survive. Some used established engines such as the Rolls-Royce Eagle in their airframe and others designed their own engine, all trying for maximum horsepower from the lowest engine weight with the lowest fuel consumption.

These are a few examples of the British aircraft manufacturers of the pre-Bomber Command period, including a few lesser known companies, that the reader may wish to further investigate. It is not within the scope of this chapter, for example, to fully describe the multitude of aircraft produced by the De Havilland aircraft company.

Aircraft Manufacturers

1931–1951 AIRSPEED LIMITED Founded in York, later moved to Portsmouth, by A. H. Tiltman and the famous novelist Nevil Shute Norway. In 1932 the ten-seat AS4 Ferry was produced. The biplane was unusual in that the third engine was mounted in the upper wing of the biplane. In 1933, the AS5 six-seat Courier was built at Portsmouth. It was the first British aircraft with retractable landing gear to go into production. The AS6 Envoy was a twin-engine version of the Courier introduced in 1934.

1912–1961 ARMSTRONG WHITWORTH Founded in Newcastle-upon-Tyne it hired the Dutch engineer Frederick Koolhoven, which gave rise to a series, 1 to 10, of aircraft with the FK designation. The company had a succession of mergers and acquisitions with Siddeley, Vickers, Hawker and Gloster building various fighters, bombers, and airliners.

1910–1963 AVRO (A.V. Roe and Company) Founded in Manchester by Alliott Verdun Roe, it was one of the world's first aircraft builders. AVRO built the first aircraft with an enclosed crew cockpit in 1912, the Type F, although it never reached production. The Avro 504 trainer was the most produced of any trainer that served in the First World War. It also had the distinction of being the first British aircraft shot down in the war on 22 August 1914.

1917–1919 BRITISH AERIAL TRANSPORT Founded at Willesden, London, it also used the talents of the Dutch designer Frederick Koolhoven. It produced six aircraft in the series FK22 to FK28.

1927–1936 BRITISH AIRCRAFT MANUFACTURING Founded at Hanworth, Middlesex, it was originally a dealership for the German manufacturer Klemm and in 1933 the first British Klemm BK Swallow flew. In 1936 the last aircraft produced was the BA IV Double Eagle, a six-seat twin-engine high wing monoplane. The company ceased operations due to, I suspect, the growing concern of being associated with the German political situation.

1887–1983 WILLIAM BEARDMORE AND COMPANY Founded in 1887 in Glasgow, it was primarily a steelmaking and heavy industry company. In 1913 it became involved in aviation by acquiring the rights for the Austro-Daimler aero engines. A shipboard version of the Sopwith Pup for the Royal Naval Air Service was very successful for them. The company built and ran the Inchinnan Airship Construction Station, which produced the famous R36 of transatlantic fame.

1914–1960 BLACKBURN AEROPLANE & MOTOR COMPANY Founded in 1914 in Brough, East Riding of Yorkshire, by Robert Blackburn, who had built his first aircraft at Leeds in 1911. The company in the inter-war years was quite prolific and specialised in reconnaissance and torpedo bombers for the Navy.

1905–1934 BOULTON & PAUL Founded as a construction engineering division in 1905. In 1905 it constructed the Royal Aircraft factory FE2b under licence, powered enclosed machine gun turrets for bombers, and built the structure for the R101 airship. In 1934 the division was sold off as Boulton Paul Aircraft and moved to Wolverhampton.

1910–1959 BRISTOL AEROPLANE COMPANY Founded in 1910 at Filton, Bristol, it was the most important of British aviation companies at that time. It manufactured airframes, aero engines, and established flying schools, which by the beginning of the war had issued nearly half of the Royal Aero Club certificates. The Bristol Boxkite, an improved Henri Farman design, flew in 1910 and was a commercial success. The Bristol F2B was a highly successful First World War fighter. The Bristol Bulldog was the mainstay of fighters and the Bristol Blenheim the mainstay of the bombers in the Royal Air Force in the inter-war years.

1916–1926 CENTRAL AIRCRAFT COMPANY Founded in 1916 at Kilburn, London, it was the subsidiary of a woodworking company performing subcontract work for aircraft components.

1920–1963 DE HAVILLAND AIRCRAFT COMPANY Founded in Stag Lane Aerodrome, North London, in 1920 by Geoffrey de Havilland. So began the list of 'DH' models with the Moth, Gipsy Moth, Tiger Moth, and Dragon Rapide prominent in the inter-war years.

1915–1960 FAIREY AVIATION COMPANY Founded in Hayes, Middlesex, with flight testing initially at Northolt Aerodrome, it designed several naval aircraft, the Fairey Swordfish being a well-known torpedo bomber.

1917–1963 GLOSTER AIRCRAFT COMPANY Founded in Hucclecote, Gloucestershire, it produced the Bristol Fighter under licence. Its inter-war claim to fame was the Gloster Gladiator biplane fighter, first flight in 1934.

1911–1920 GRAHAME-WHITE AVIATION COMPANY Founded by Claude Grahame-White at Hendon, London, in 1911. It produced the Type XV so-called 'Box-kite', which was used for training and the first trials of firing an airborne machine gun at targets on the ground.

1921–1924 HANDASYDE AIRCRAFT COMPANY Founded in 1921, it produced a glider for the 1922 Itford gliding competition followed the same year by the H2 six-seat airliner.

1909–1970 HANDLEY PAGE LIMITED Founded in 1909 by Frederick Handley Page, this was the first British public company to build aircraft. It built heavy bombers for the Royal Naval Air Service. Aerodynamically, Handley page designed the slat, an auxiliary aerofoil at the leading edge of the wing to improve airflow at high angles of attack. The HP52 Hampden first flew in 1936.

1920–1963 HAWKER AIRCRAFT LIMITED Founded by Sopwith test pilot Harry Hawker in Kingston-upon-Thames it survived by mergers and acquisitions with Armstrong Siddeley and AVRO. Sydney Camm designed the successful Hawker Hind and Hawker Hart, the most produced aircraft of the inter-war years. The Hawker Hurricane first flew in 1935.

1908–1922 MARTINSYDE LTD Founded by H. Martin and G. Handasyde its 1914 biplane, the S1, turned the company into a successful concern with flight sheds at Brooklands and a factory at Woking.

1930–1947 PHILLIPS & POWIS AIRCRAFT Founded by Jack Phillips and Charles Powis, the company was based at Woodley Aerodrome, Berkshire, from 1932. The Hawk Trainer supplemented the Tiger Moth as it had dual controls and blind flying instruments which allowed the pilot to fly without reference to the horizon.

1912–1918 ROYAL AIRCRAFT FACTORY Founded at Farnborough Airfield, Hampshire, it started life in 1904 as the Army Balloon Factory. One of its original designers was Geoffrey de Havilland. The FE2 was one of its famous aircraft. Designations are confusing; there were three FE2s, and it was the FE2 (1914) that was the star.

1929–1964 SARO (Saunders-Roe Limited) Founded at East Cowes, Isle of Wight, was a flying boat business with Alliott Verdun Roe among its founders.

1908-present SHORT BROTHERS Founded by Eustace & Oswald Short in Battersea, London, who six years previously started a balloon business. Short Brothers was the first company in the world to make production aircraft and shifted its workshop close to the Royal Aero Club on the Isle of Sheppey. Seaplanes at Rochester, Kent, and airships at Cardington, Bedfordshire, were part of the Short expansion followed by large flying boats in the 1920s and 1930s. Twenty-eight Short aircraft were produced between 1919 and 1936.

1913–1920 SOPWITH AVIATION COMPANY Founded at Brooklands by Tommy (later Sir Thomas) Sopwith the company produced the very successful Sopwith Scout, nicknamed the Pup, biplane fighter which was followed closely by the twin-gun Camel fighter.

1913–1960 SUPERMARINE AVIATION WORKS LTD Founded as Pemberton-Billing Ltd at Woolston, Southampton, specialised in flying boats. R. J. Mitchell was on staff during the Schneider Trophy era, won outright in 1931 by Britain. The same year Supermarine was working on the Type 224 which became the Type 300 and was given the name Spitfire.

1828–1999 VICKERS LIMITED was the parent company founded in Sheffield as a steel foundry by Edward Vickers and his father-in-law. Ship and ammunition production were followed in 1911 by an aviation department and flying school at Brooklands. Supermarine was acquired in 1928.

1915–1961 WESTLAND AIRCRAFT WORKS Founded in Yeovil, Somerset, to build aircraft under licence for the war effort. Within two years it was designing its own aircraft.

The following are examples of some of the engine manufacturers of the pre-Bomber Command period.

Engine Manufacturers

1912–1951 ABC MOTORS LIMITED of Hersham, Surrey.

1919–1967 ALVIS CAR AND ENGINEERING COMPANY LIMITED of Coventry initially built Gnome-Rhone radials under licence before designing their own fourteen-cylinder Alvis Pelides engine in 1936.

1919–1960 ARMSTRONG-SIDDELEY of Coventry built a range of radial engines named after big cats. It started with the Lynx and continued to the Cheetah engine in 1935.

1887–1983 WILLIAM BEARDMORE AND COMPANY of Glasgow built one aircraft engine, the Beardmore Adriatic.

1916–1918 BHP (Beardmore Halford Pullinger) the 230 hp six-cylinder engines were given to Siddeley-Deasy for production.

1914–1960 BLACKBURN AIRCRAFT LIMITED of Brough, Yorkshire, built aircraft engines as part of their Cirrus division.

1910–1959 BRISTOL AEROPLANE COMPANY built radial engines such as the Pegasus for the Fairey Swordfish and the uniquely designed sleeve valve engines such as the Perseus for the Blackburn Skua.

1920–1963 DE HAVILLAND of Stag Lane Aerodrome, North London, is famous for its own line of Gypsy four, six, and twelve piston engines for its airframes.

1808–1942 D. NAPIER & SON of London initially built aircraft and engines, such as the RAF 3, under contract but designed and produced their own very successful Lion engine in 1916. The Lion engine went on to set land and water speed records.

1928–1935 POBJOY AIRMOTORS AND AIRCRAFT of Rochester, Kent, designed seven- cylinder radial air-cooled engines.

1912–1918 ROYAL AIRCRAFT FACTORY at Farnborough released a series of engines numbered RAF 1 to 8 omitting 6 and 7. Some engines were built in-house and others were subcontracted out; for example, the RAF4 was built by Siddeley-Deasy.

1904-present ROLLS-ROYCE founded in 1904 by Charles Rolls and Henry Royce initially was a luxury car production company that added aero engines to its portfolio. In 1915 the first of its many engines appeared; it was the twelve-cylinder Eagle engine used in the Vickers Vimy among many other aircraft. The Merlin first ran in 1933 and would be the powerplant of choice for many fighters and bombers of the Royal Air Force in the Second World War.

1912–1919 SIDDELEY-DEASY MOTOR CAR COMPANY LIMITED at Kenilworth transitioned to aero engines and in 1917 its Puma engine powered the Airco DH9 bomber.

1905–1934 SUNBEAM MOTOR CAR COMPANY LIMITED in Wolverhampton manufactured aero engines in 1912, such as the Sunbeam Maori for the Handley Page O/400 bomber aircraft, under the engineering leadership of Louis Coatalen.

1901–1975 WOLSELEY MOTORS LIMITED of Birmingham built aircraft and aero engines under licence for the war effort. It withdrew from the aero engine market in 1936.

After The Great War

The imperial power of Britain, after two hundred years of the 'sun never sets on the British Empire', was coming to an end. Territorially it still existed. In fact, it was slightly larger once the Ottoman Empire had been divided up between France and Britain. However, Britain now had astronomical war loans owed to the United States which were due immediately, nine million pounds' worth. Britain could no longer defend its far-flung colonies effectively due to lack of funds.

In spite of this situation the Royal Air Force still 'flew the flag' in far flung corners of the British Empire, but with aircraft that were quickly becoming obsolete. The bravery of the aircrew and the dedication of the ground crew, both in very trying conditions, can never be overstated during these inter-war years. The following chart shows the Royal Air Force commitment overseas before the Second World War; the majority of the twenty-six squadrons were flying obsolete biplanes.

In the inter-war years Britain and the Royal Air Force were committed to full warlike operations every day of the year somewhere around the globe. The list of main bases below indicates some of the areas. These conflicts varied from local policing to full-scale operations to maintain the peace. Five Victoria Crosses, three posthumously, were awarded during this era to Army personnel in Mesopotamia and India. The Royal Air Force would have been involved in these operations. The force was under constant threat from politicians, the army and navy of being absorbed into the other services. It was certainly not anything to waste money on; it was the 'junior service'.

Royal Air Force Overseas 1919–1938

MAIN BASE	SQN	DATE DEPLOYED	AIRCRAFT
Risalpur India	5	February 1920	Westland Wapiti
Ramleh Palestine	6	April 1919	Hawker Hardy
Khormaksar Aden	8	October 1920	Vickers Vincent
Risalpur India	11	December 1928	Bristol Blenheim
Amman Transjordan	14	February 1920	Vickers Wellesley
Peshawar India	20	May 1919	Hawker Audax
Kohat India	27	April 1920	Westland Wapiti
Ambala India	28	February 1920	Hawker Audax
Habbaniya Iraq	30	February 1920	Bristol Blenheim
Drigh Road India	31	1916	Westland Wapiti
Heliopolis Egypt	33	October 1935	Gloster Gladiator
Seletar Singapore	36	December 1930	Vickers Vildebeest
Risalpur India	39	January 1929	Hawker Hart
Khartoum Sudan	47	February 1920	Vickers Vincent
Habbaniya Iraq	55	February 1920	Vickers Vincent
Kohat India	60	April 1920	Westland Wapiti
Habbaniya Iraq	70	February 1920	Vickers Valentia
Shaibah Iraq	84	August 1920	Vickers Vincent
Seletar Singapore	100	September 1933	Vickers Vildebeest
Heliopolis Egypt	113	August 1938	Hawker Hind
Kalafrana Egypt	202	January 1929	Sar London
Basra Iraq	203	February 1929	Short Singapore
Seletar Singapore	205	January 1929	Short Singapore
Mersa Matruh Egypt	208	February 1920	Hawker Audax
Heliopolis Egypt	216	July 1919	Vickers Valentia
Seletar Singapore	230	October 1936	Short Sunderland

1918 – 1921

POLITICAL

The Treaty of Versailles was signed six months after hostilities ceased at the Paris Peace Conference in June 1919. One of the provisions of the treaty has been debated extensively over the years: that 'Germany accept the responsibility of Germany and her allies for causing all the loss and damage'; it became known as the 'War Guilt' clause. Reparations amounted to approximately seven times the amount that Britain owed in war loans. It has been debated ever since whether or not this was too harsh and counter-productive and sowed the seeds for a future war.

The treaty required Germany to disarm, make territorial concessions, and make reparations to the Entente Powers (Britain, France, and Russia). It is interesting to note that Britain's Prime Minister Lloyd George, behind the scenes, did not want to totally cripple the German economy so that it would become a viable trading partner in the future and would balance the power in Europe, ensuring that France would not become the dominant player.

Militarily, Germany would greatly reduce its standing army and navy, dissolve its General Staff, and greatly limit training schools. It was prohibited from having an air force, including a naval air force, and had to hand over all aerial related materials. Germany was also forbidden to manufacture or import aircraft for a period of six months after signing the treaty. It is important to note the importance in 1919 given to the air force; it was prohibited, not reduced, like the army and navy. Sixteen years after the Wright's first flight, political and military thinking was rapidly coming to acknowledge the role and growing importance of aerial combat.

The League of Nations, a product of US President Woodrow Wilson and the Paris Peace Conference, was the first intergovernmental organisation after the First World War to attempt to maintain world peace through negotiation and arbitration. It also focused on labour conditions, human and drug trafficking, arms trade, global health, and protection of minorities in Europe. At its zenith in 1935 it had fifty-eight member states, but it was weakened by the fact that the United States failed to join. It eventually failed in its primary purpose – to prevent war.

Post-war universal manhood suffrage at age twenty-one was introduced in Britain, to be followed within ten years by women suffrage with the same parameters. Millions of women had joined the workforce with the men away at war, and they kept the country going in all occupations. The labour movement grew out of this mixing of resources and the idea of social welfare for everyone took hold. Deference to established authority began to fade.

The Housing, Town Planning Act of 1919 and the Unemployment Insurance Act of 1920 gave some stability to the working class during this post-war recovery period. The former promised government subsidies to help finance the construction of 500,000 houses within three years. As the economy rapidly weakened in the early 1920s, however, funding had to be cut, and only 213,000 homes were completed under the Act's provisions The economy was generally lacklustre. There were significant declines in heavy industry and coal due to the industries not keeping up with modern practices. Shipping, the previous backbone of heavy industry, remained in the doldrums. Britain had fallen behind the US as an industrial power.

The 'Ten Year Rule' of August 1919 was a British Government guideline to the armed forces that they should base their budget requests on the assumption 'that the British Empire would not engage in any great war during the next ten years'. This guideline would have a great effect on the Royal Air Force, as it spread its resources among the coastal, reconnaissance, fighter, and bomber requirements. After the war, the RAF was greatly reduced in size and during the immediate inter-war years was used mainly to 'police' the British Empire in such locations as India, Mesopotamia, and Singapore. At the end of the war the Royal Air Force was the largest air force in the world with 263 squadrons and nearly 300,000 personnel; these were immediately reduced to seventeen squadrons and 31,000 personnel, seven per cent of its former strength.

The Army and the Navy had the inside track to what money was available. That situation would change, but it would take fifteen years. The re-organisation of the RAF by the Air Ministry was based upon the premise that Britain just had won the 'war to end all wars' and it could not possibly happen again. This thinking, and the memory of the horror of First World War casualties, would influence government military decisions right up until the moment in the mid-1930s that it was realised that yes, it could happen again, and probably would.

The Air Ministry was formed in January 1918, which promised better results under the leadership of the Prime Minister Lloyd George and General Smuts. It was created following the sequential failures of the Air Committee, Joint War Air Committee, and the First and Second Air Boards. Sir Hugh Trenchard was a member of the original Air Ministry. It issued specifications for prototype aircraft to British manufacturing companies. It would assign names to these aircraft and if found suitable, subsequently ordered them into production – 'Intention to Proceed'. In 1919 the Air Ministry took control from the Ministry of Munitions of supply, design, and inspection of all aircraft.

Following the forced abdication of Kaiser Wilhelm II in November 1918 and peace two days later, Germany became the Weimar Republic. Many in the German Army felt that they had been let down by the civilian home front who had forced the abdication of the monarchy. Perhaps this feeling was evoked by lost pride rather than actual events. We have mentioned the Treaty of Versailles and its immediate repercussions for Germany. There was internal unrest over the Treaty. Significant numbers believed that too much had been given away.

In Germany, those immediate post-war years were about survival; growth would come later. Food, housing, and employment were the social priorities of a government also dealing with the loss of colonies and lands, the Rhineland occupation, reparation payments, hyperinflation, and re-establishing industry. The military, for now, was a mere shadow of its former self.

To say that Germany, using the commonly used name for the country, was in political and social turmoil is an understatement. The Independent Social Democratic Party of Germany, the Social Democratic Party of Germany, the communist Spartacist League, the 'Workers' and 'Soldiers' Councils, sundry political splinter groups, and the remnants of the monarchy all struggled for representation in the National Assembly. Adolf Hitler, involved with the army's political instruction program, worked with veterans to keep a patriotic and military spirit alive. He eventually became the leader of the National Socialist German Workers' party, the Nazis. In 1920 he published its twenty-five-point program.

However, the immediate transfer of power from aristocracy to democracy was not a violent transition. It left the 'old guard' with their position and possessions in place until the 1930s. The Assembly had to maintain law and order in the face of communists and reactionary or antidemocratic agitators. One of these agitators, Adolf Hitler, four years later in 1923, would stage an abortive revolt in Munich. Sentenced to prison he wrote his infamous *Mein Kampf* (My Struggle) which sold widely and brought Hitler to national attention. This was the start of his meteoric rise.

CIVIL AVIATION

Transport flying began immediately after the First World War when the Civil Aviation Department of the Air Ministry was formed in February 1919. Air traffic regulations, airworthiness, and registrations requirements were issued by the Secretary of State for Air. By 20 April 1919 civil aviation in Britain had officially begun, mainly using surplus military aircraft, such as the Handley Page O/400, hastily adapted for the purpose. Until 1929 civil aviation was under military influence but this gradually changed until the Air Navigation Act of 1936, which resulted in the 1937 establishment of the autonomous Air Registration Board.

The growth and development of the civil aviation industry during these three-year time periods leading up to the formation of bomber

Command can be monitored by looking at significant aircraft of each period. Bigger, faster, higher, and longer range are adjectives that come to mind.

1919 14/15 June	First non-stop Atlantic crossing
1919 02 July/13 July	Scotland to New York return airship R34
1919 12 November/10 December	First flight Britain to Australia
1920 04 February/20 March	First flight Britain to Capetown, South Africa

YEAR	AIRCRAFT TYPE	SEATS	WEIGHT lb/kg	CRUISE mph/kmh	RANGE m/km
1919	Vickers Vimy Commercial	10	12,500/5670	84/135	450/724
1919	Westland Limousine	3	3,383/1535	85/137	290/467
1919	Handley Page W8	12	12,250/5557	90/145	500/805
1919	Avro 504k	4	1,829/830	75/121	225/362
1919	Central Centaur Iv	2	1,600/726	70/113	210/338
1920	De Havilland DH18	8	6,516/2956	100/161	400/644
1920	Avro 547	5	3,000/1361	80/129	230/370
1921	De Havilland DH9c	3	3,667/1663	95/153	490/789

Vickers Vimy Commercial, constructor's number K-107, first flew on 13 April 1919. The wing and tail unit were standard from the Vimy, but the fuselage had changed to an oval monocoque plywood section with seating for ten passengers. The engines were two 360hp Rolls-Royce Eagle VIIIs. The entry door was on the port side with the pilots sitting in an open cockpit high in the nose section. G-EAOU achieved immediate celebrity by winning the Australian Government's prize for the first England to Australia flight. 11,340 miles (18,250km) in twenty-seven days and twenty-one hours from Hounslow to Darwin, Northern Territory. S. Instone and Co. Ltd operated the forty-first Vimy Commercial on a schedule from Croydon to Brussels, Paris, and Cologne routes starting May 1920.

The Handley Page W8 had two pilots in an open cockpit forward of a glazed cabin with seating initially for fifteen and later reduced to twelve passengers. The first flight was on 4 December 1919 at Cricklewood. It established a weight 3,690lb (1,674kg) to altitude 14,000ft (4,427m) record for its class on 4 May 1920. In August it won the Air Ministry's heavy commercial aeroplane competition for comfort and appearance with the added bonuses of reliability, handling, and superior speed. Three aircraft maintained the Paris and Brussels service by Handley Page until absorbed into Imperial Airways on 1 April 1924. The W8e had a third engine mounted in the nose, a Rolls-Royce Eagle IX, in conjunction with two Siddeley Pumas in the outboard nacelles. This modified model was supplied to Sabena, the Belgian airline.

The De Havilland DH18 was a single-engine two-bay biplane with plywood-covered front fuselage and the passengers accommodated amidships. The pilot sat in an open cockpit behind. The engine was a 450hp Napier Lion. Aircraft Transport & Travel Ltd operated the aircraft from 8 September 1919. The Air Council later purchased the AT&T aircraft and leased them to S. Instone and Co. Ltd. On 2 May 1924 a DH18b took part in ditching testing and floated for twenty-five minutes – enabling removal of the Lion engine!

ROYAL AIR FORCE 1918-1921

Just before the beginning of the First World War the Royal Flying Corps consisted of five aircraft squadrons, Nos. 2, 3, 4, 5 and 6. No. 1 squadron was in the process of converting from balloons to aircraft and No. 7 had been formed and disbanded until formed again in September 1914. At the outbreak of war, the strength of the Royal Flying Corps was of course minimal. It was comprised of approximately 180 aircraft supported by 140 officers and 1,000 airmen. By November 1918 it was the largest independent air force in the world with approximately 3,300 aircraft and 100 airships supported by 27,000 officers and 300,000 non-commissioned airmen and airwomen. 1920 saw the drastic demobilisation of the Royal Air Force with the force reduced to 1,000 officers, 70,000 airmen, and a handful of squadrons, twenty-five.

The Royal Air Force bomber force at the end of the First World War was comprised of the ex-Royal Flying Corps De Havilland DH4 and DH9 and the ex-Royal Naval Air Service Handley Page O/100, O/400, and V/1500. All these aircraft were biplanes and the De Havillands were single engine.

At the beginning of 1919 Winston Churchill was appointed Secretary of State for War and Air. He immediately re-appointed Hugh Trenchard to be the new Chief of Staff as recommended by Lord Weir, his predecessor at the Air Ministry. Trenchard had the reputation for doing a lot with very little and was confident operating on his own. This was vitally important as the funds were drying up and the 'Ten Year Rule' belief was firmly entrenched. True as it turned out, but it did leave

Britain in a militarily vulnerable position with less than thirteen years to recover its military might before the next conflict in 1939.

In September 1919, Trenchard drew the proverbial line in the sand and wrote what became known as 'Trenchard's Memorandum', which was presented as a White Paper in Westminster. The Royal Air Force must remain a separate service, which could be done economically, Regarding training, the Royal Air Force College for Officer Cadets was to be established at Cranwell (5 February 1920), the Air Staff College at Andover (4 April 1922) for senior officers, and a Royal Air Force Aircraft Apprentice school of technical training at Halton (1920).

Other proposals were a Short Service Commission to keep the force young with a reserve force commitment after leaving the regular force. Trenchard also proposed sending many squadrons overseas to help protect the far-flung territories of the Empire (see page 24). In 1920 the Royal Air Force was sent to Somaliland to fight against the 'Mad Mullah' and defeat his Dervishes. This exonerated Trenchard's views about the Royal Air Force being able to deploy to trouble spots and regain control. The theory of 'air control' was gaining momentum.

Once again, in Iraq, the validity of air control was demonstrated by the eight squadrons in the field. Finally, on 1 October 1922, a momentous date for the Royal Air Force, control of all the forces in Iraq was given to Air Vice-Marshal John Salmond. The mere presence of the air force was enough to quell lawlessness among the Arab tribes, deterrence at its finest. The aircraft were also used for mercy flights on occasion, which impressed the citizens.

The main thrust of 'The Douhet Theory', completed in 1921, was that aircraft operating in the vastness of the skies could roam at will and destroy the enemy's resources, military and civilian. Command of the air would be achieved by bombing the enemy's air force while it was on the ground, lending credence to the theory that the best defence was offence. Military targets would be supplemented with industrial, transportation, communications, government, and civilian population targets. Terrorise the population and so destroy the will of the people to continue to fight. Douhet's theory was one of total war and was read worldwide by military commanders, some supportive and others not so. Interesting to note that Douhet and Major-General Trenchard, Chief of the Air Staff, often called 'Father of the Royal Air Force', were of similar ages and Trenchard would have been aware of, if not studied, Douhet's theory of air warfare.

Great Britain, an island nation, initially devoted the greater part of its post-war limited resources to the Royal Navy and Army for defence purposes. One of the philosophies of those times was that the large bombers with their heavy bomb loads 'would always get through', so the country's defences would have to be built up. The opposing philosophy was that the First World War had been 'the war to end all wars' and it could not possibly happen again. It was this latter philosophy that influenced the re-organisation of the Royal Air Force, including the integral bomber force, which was now controlled by the Air Ministry of the British Government and subject to defence cuts. The fighter force would overshadow the bomber force for some time until the European political scene changed.

MILITARY AIRCRAFT

YEAR	BOMBER AIRCRAFT	MAXIMUM SPEED mph/kmh	SERVICE CEILING ft	RANGE mi/km
(1917)	Vickers Vimy	185/298	22,800	430 /692

1922 – 1925

POLITICAL

By 1921 over 2 million unemployed were receiving benefits from the 1920 Unemployment Insurance Act. The inability of British manufacturing to modernise many industries coupled with tariffs and customs barriers from emerging economically aggressive nations combined to slow down the economy. The addition of benefits such as pensions, medical aid, and subsidised housing helped prevent a drastic decline in living conditions for the 'working man' and now the working woman. These would come at a cost to the government. The Labour party took over from the Liberals as the official opposition in 1922. In fact, it governed the country under a coalition with the Liberals in 1924. The short-lived Labour government succumbed to some overtures from Communist International that became public knowledge. It had already diplomatically recognised the newly formed Soviet Union, which was a move too fast, too far.

In 1923 The Hague Rules of Aerial Warfare stated that aerial bombardment is only legitimate

- against a military objective,
- exclusively against that objective,
- objective is enumerated and defined,
- bombardment of civilian housing outside the objective is forbidden,
- if unable to bomb the objective without civilian collateral damage it will not be attacked,
- bombardment of civilian housing only legitimate if military concentration warrants attack,
- that the attacker is liable for compensation if violating the rules.

These Rules, although proposed, never became legally binding.

At this same time the German economy went through a massive inflation crisis. Great to pay off internal loans as the paper money was printed in excess but it had consequences. The United States assisted financially with the Dawes Plan, a series of loans, which enabled Germany to start paying back reparations. In 1925 Germany joined the League of Nations. For a period of five years the Allies and Germany saw relative prosperity until the looming depression of 1929.

CIVIL AVIATION

1924 Apri l – September	First circumnavigation of the globe.
1924 April 26	Imperial Airways was created with a daily London–Paris route using a De Havilland DH34 cruising at 105mph/169kmh for a range of 365mi/586km.

YEAR	AIRCRAFT TYPE	SEATS	WEIGHT lb/kg	CRUISE mph/kmh	RANGE mi/km
1922	De Havilland DH34	10	17,200/7,802	100/161	365/587
1922	Vickers Vulcan	8	6,150/2,790	90/145	360/579
1923	De Havilland DH50	4	4,200/1,905	110/177	375/604
1925	De Havilland DH54	12	11,250/5,103	100/161	400/644
1925	Avro 563 Andover	12	10,685/4,847	90/145	460/740

The De Havilland DH34 was the result of trying to improve the DH18 performance. It resulted in the ten-passenger DH34 using the 450hp Napier Lion engine, this time with inertia starting, no more hand swinging of the propeller. The cabin was designed with a spare engine carrying capability to rescue unserviceable aircraft. The pilots sat ahead of the wings and passenger cabin. The aircraft entered service with Daimler Airway on 2 April 1922 flying the Croydon to Paris route.

The Vickers Vulcan was first flown in May 1922 at Brooklands. Based on the Vickers Vimy it did not resemble it at all. The fuselage was larger, taller, and carried a single Rolls-Royce Eagle VIII engine to save operating costs. It got the nickname 'Flying Pig' and the Type 74 changed to a Napier Lion engine to improve performance.

The De Havilland DH54 Highclere was designed to replace the DH34 using the Rolls-Royce Condor IIIA 650 hp engine to carry twelve passengers. Both biplanes had their construction and layout in common: two-bay with fabric covered wings and plywood-covered fuselage. The Highclere did not have staggered wings and the upper wing was joined to the fuselage by struts. The landing gear could be jettisoned to reduce the hazards of ditching. The passengers sat in three rows of seats, single to the left and double to the right facing forward. Test flown in June 1925 it did not proceed to production.

ROYAL AIR FORCE 1922–1925

1922	Instant mobility exercise, Chanak crisis, Nos. 56 & 208 Squadrons deployed
1925 27 Oct/19 Nov	Helwan, Egypt to Kaduna, Nigeria return, three De Havilland DH9A

By 1925 Trenchard's defensive work for the Royal Air Force had yielded results; it was still in existence as a separate unit. He could now concentrate on his front-line squadrons, personnel, equipment, and materials. His opportunity was short-lived. Britain returned to the gold standard which had been suspended during the war. A reduction in allotted finances to the Royal Air Force put paid to any meaningful expansion at this time.

The Air Defence of Great Britain Command was created in 1925, the responsibility being transferred from the War Office to the Air Ministry. The main components were the Royal Air Force's Metropolitan Air Force which expanded to fifty-two squadrons, searchlights and heavy anti-aircraft guns, and the volunteer part-time Observer Corps.

The three defensive zones were the Inner Artillery London zone, the Air Fighter Zone, comprising the Wessex Bombing Area and the Fighting Area, and the Outer Artillery Zone along the coast.

MILITARY AIRCRAFT

YEAR	BOMBER AIRCRAFT	MAXIMUM SPEED mph/kmh	SERVICE CEILING ft	RANGE mi/km
1922	Avro 549 Aldershot	110/177	14,500	625/1006
1922	Vickers Virginia	108/173	13,800	985/1585
1923	Vickers Valparaiso	136/219	19,500	550/886
1923	Vickers Vixen	134/215	20,000	764/1230
1923	Fairey Fawn	114/183	13,850	650/1046
1923	Handley Page HP24 Hyderabad	109/175	14,000	500/805
1925	Hawker Horsley	125/201	14,000	900/1449

1926 – 1929

POLITICAL

Oil was the new fuel of choice and the old coal seams were becoming exhausted. Tension in the industry led to the lock-out of the coal miners as they had refused to work longer hours for less pay. The labour unions were adamant about not giving up wage gains and other concessions won when Britain needed the workers to support the war effort. A General Strike in 1926 of 1.3 million railwaymen, transport workers, printers, dockers, iron workers, and steelworkers supported the coal miners. The general strike was made illegal in 1927. Although unemployment figures continued to grow, Britain did not suffer generally as badly as the US in the 1929 global economic crisis. Britain did not have as far to fall.

The turning point for the world economy occurred with the crash of the New York Stock Exchange in October 1929. Stock worth tumbled seventy-five per cent over the next three years and the domino effect was felt throughout Europe and the world. Unemployment was everywhere and so was despair, anger, and frustration among the world's civilians. This was a breeding ground for new take-action political ideas. Tariffs were established to try and establish an island of security for individual countries. Eighty-seven years later President Trump attempted the same thing in 2019.

Democracy, it has been said, is only good for countries that can afford it. Germany could not afford anything. The depression turned the populace to the idea of a 'white knight' to rescue them from this social and financial nightmare. A leader who was decisive, who would inspire confidence, an orator, and one who would restore national pride. In 1928 the Nazis won twelve seats in the Reichstag.

CIVIL AVIATION

1926 08/09 May	First flight over North Pole
1927 20/21 May	First non-stop solo flight from New York to Paris
1928 06/22 February	First solo flight England to Australia
1929 April	First non-stop flight England to India
1929 08 August/29 August	Graf Zeppelin: the first lighter than air flight around the world
1929 28/29 November	First flight over South Pole
1929 March	Imperial Airways London to Karachi

YEAR	AIRCRAFT TYPE	SEATS	WEIGHT lb/kg	CRUISE mph/kmh	RANGE mi/km
1926	Armstrong-Whitworth Argosy	20	19,200/8,709	90/145	405/652
1927	De Havilland DH61 Giant Moth	6	7,000/3,175	110/177	650/1046
1928	Short S8 Calcutta	15	22,500/10,206	97/156	650/1046
1929	Avro 618 Ten	8	10.600/4,808	100/161	400/644

The Armstrong Whitworth Argosy II was a large three-engine biplane seating twenty passengers in a more comfortable, roomier, and square-sided fuselage. In 1926 the pilots were still sitting outside in the nose of the aircraft. The Argosy was the company's first airliner and it used the technology of the successful Siskin III, namely a steel tube fuselage joined to all steel wings. Three Armstrong Siddeley direct drive Jaguar IVA engines provided power, one in the nose and the other two mounted in inboard struts. The Argosy appeared in public for the first time at the Hendon Royal Air Force Display on 3 July 1926. On 1 May 1927 the world's first 'luxury' air route, the London to Paris 'Silver Wing' lunch service, was flown with a buffet and steward replacing the rearmost seats. A year later the Argosy raced against the Flying Scotsman train and won by fifteen minutes.

The Short S8 Calcutta was a civil biplane airliner flying boat. It was the first commercial service flying boat to have a stressed skin metal-hull. The three Bristol Jupiter IXF engines were mounted between the wings. The fuel was located in the upper wings allowing smoking in the cabin. Airworthiness and sea handling checks were done during the summer of 1928. The aircraft, G-EBVG, was landed on the Thames River near Westminster on 1 August 1928. A three-day visit enabled Members of Parliament, including Winston Churchill, to view the aircraft that would establish links throughout the Empire.

ROYAL AIR FORCE 1926–1929

The Royal Air Force expansion plans ground to a halt between 1926 and 1928. Then the unending extension of the restrictive 'Ten Year Plan' put another nail in the coffin. Of the 600 million pounds allotted for the armed forces during the years 1924 to 1929, the Royal Air Force was allotted just thirty-six million, a mere six per cent of the total. It was indeed the poor junior service.

It is interesting to note that in 1928 Sir Hugh Trenchard observed that bombing civilians contravened the rules of warfare, but it would be different to terrorise civilians who worked in an ammunition factory and cause them to stay away from work for fear of an attack on the factory. Once again, the spectre of total war was a topic of deliberation during this time mid-way between the First and Second World Wars.

1926 01 March/ 27 May	Heliopolis, Egypt to Capetown, South Africa, return. Fairey IIIDs
1927	Mobility exercise, Shanghai under threat
1927 14 Oct/1928 28 Feb	Four Supermarine Southhampton MKIIs deployed to Singapore
1928 21 May/!5 September	Southamptons then circumnavigated Australia
1928 01 November/11 December	Southhamptons deployed to Hong Kong as No. 205 Squadron

MILITARY AIRCRAFT

YEAR	BOMBER AIRCRAFT	MAXIMUM SPEED mph/kmh	SERVICE CEILING ft	RANGE mi/km
1926	Boulton Paul P29 Sidestrand	139/224	20,800	520/873
1927	Handley Page Hinaidi	123/197	14,900	850/1370
1928	Hawker Hart	185/298	22,800	430/692

1930 – 1933

POLITICAL

In the German election of 1930, the Nazis had 107 seats and 230 seats in 1932, dropping to 196 seats in an autumn election. In spite of this drawback, and with several quick changes of leaders, Hitler was nominated to be Chancellor of the German Republic with a coalition cabinet, Nationalists and Nazis, in 1933. The burning of the Reichstag building allowed Hitler to declare a national emergency and assume dictatorial powers. The Nazi rise to political supremacy was complete. The world would never be the same.

Germany would now become a unitarian state: no variance from the party line was allowed. In fact no variance from Hitler's line was allowed. Jewish people were considered as un-German. By 1933 Germany had withdrawn from the League of Nations: the writing was on the wall. In 1934 the Nazi party itself was cleansed of dissidents. Churches and Labour Unions were 'co-ordinated' with the government. Infrastructure projects were initiated, industry revitalised under government control, and a rearmament program was introduced, a scant fifteen years after the Treaty of Versailles.

In Britain peace was the operative word. Some students in Oxford publicly resolved in 1933 to never take up arms for their country under any conditions. Against this was the fear of communism, which might mean sympathy for the fascist dictators as a bulwark against it, and appeasement was attractive as Britain needed time to catch up militarily, not least in terms of aviation and air defence. Hitler manipulated the governments of Europe and started private alliances and treaties of his own, ignoring clauses in the Treaty of Versailles. Appeasement of Germany was the government's policy until early 1939, aptly illustrated later when Britain and France sacrificed Czechoslovakia to Hitler's demands at the Munich Agreement of 1938.

CIVIL AVIATION

1930 September	First non-stop flight Paris to New York
1930	Amy Johnson flew solo to Australia
1930	Airship R100 England to Canada return in seventy-eight hours
1931 June/July	Around the world in fewer than nine days
1931	Britain wins Schneider Trophy
1932 20/21 May	First women's solo flight across the Atlantic
1932 24 September	Aeroplane altitude record of 43,976 ft (13,404 m)
1933 03 April	First flight over Mount Everest

YEAR	AIRCRAFT TYPE	SEATS	WEIGHT lb/kg	CRUISE mph/kmh	RANGE mi/km
1930	Handley Page HP42e	24	28,000/12,701	100/161	500/805
1930	Blackburn Segrave	4	3,300/1,497	112/180	450/724
1930	Vickers Viastra	10	11,850/5,375	90/145	360/579
1931	Armstrong-Whitworth 15 Atalanta	10	21,000/9,525	130/209	400/644

YEAR	AIRCRAFT TYPE	SEATS	WEIGHT lb/kg	CRUISE mph/kmh	RANGE mi/km
1932	De Havilland DH83 Fox Moth	4	2,070/939	96/155	360/579
1932	De Havilland DH84 Dragon	6	4,500/2,041	114/184	545/877
1932	Airspeed AS5 Courier	6	3,900/1,769	132/212	635/1022
1933	Short S16 Scion	5	3,000/1,361	102/164	360/579

The Blackburn Segrave was named after Sir Henry Segrave, a First World War fighter pilot, famous race car driver, and holder of the world's land speed record. He drew up the plans for a revolutionary luxury touring aircraft featuring two De Havilland Gipsy Major engines that, because of airframe streamlining, could safely fly on one engine. It was a cantilevered monoplane. Blackburn took the wooden fuselage and converted it to an all-metal stressed skin version. Further development was affected by the death of Sir Henry in the speedboat *Miss England II* on Lake Windermere on 13 June 1930.

The Airspeed AS5 Courier was notable for being the first British aircraft with retractable landing gear to go into production. The landing gear was operated by a hydraulic hand pump. It was built in 1933 by Airspeed at York for an attempt by Sir Alan Cobham to fly non-stop to India using inflight refuelling. The attempt was abandoned when a throttle linkage failure necessitated a wheels-up landing. In 1934 the clean lines represented the advanced aerodynamics of the time. London, Scottish, and Provincial Airways Ltd. operated the Courier for a short time. The AS5A had one Armstrong Siddeley Lynx IVC engine.

ROYAL AIR FORCE 1930–1933

1930	De Havilland DH9A began to retire from operational use
1933 15 October	Rolls-Royce Merlin engine first ran

On 1 January 1930 Hugh Trenchard relinquished control of the Royal Air Force to Air Chief Marshal John Salmond of Iraq fame. He left a legacy of 'quality before quantity' and Salmond inherited an organisation that was built on a very sound foundation. The Royal

Air Force had fifty-seven squadrons, twenty-two were overseas, plus nine Special reserve squadrons. In 1932 the Geneva Conference on disarmament was ineffective and the government reversed policy and started to expand and re-arm it forces.

MILITARY AIRCRAFT

YEAR	BOMBER AIRCRAFT	MAXIMUM SPEED mph/kmh	SERVICE CEILING ft	RANGE mi/km
1930	Fairey Hendon	152/245	21,400	1,360/2,190
1930	Handley Page Heyford	142/229	21,000	920/1481
1931	Fairey Gordon	145/240	22,000	600/966
1933	Boulton Paul P75 Overstrand	148/238	21,300	545/872

1934 – 1936

POLITICAL

In 1934 the British Army's allocation of funds was halved as the rearmament program called for the deterrent of a larger air force. The Royal Air Force was now to receive forty per cent of the combined budget and expand to forty-one bomber squadrons. These figures were part of Expansion Scheme 'A' of the Royal Air Force approved by cabinet. They would be revised many times until 1939 as parliament received intelligence reports.

In March 1936 Hitler's troops re-occupied the Rhineland de-militarised zone. The French talked about action but not without British support. The British did not want to risk another war over the German troops occupying German soil. In July 1936 the Spanish Civil War began, with Germany sending air and ground support, a test of military readiness that we now know in retrospect for what was ultimately planned. This was the political state of Europe that influenced the formation of Bomber Command. The time had been right for a while. Now, in July 1936, it was an imperative. The politicians and Royal Air Force hierarchy finally created Bomber Command to meet the now perceived threat.

CIVIL AVIATION

1934 October Unofficial speed record 441mph/710km/h

1935 Australian and Cape Town records broken

YEAR	AIRCRAFT TYPE	SEATS	WEIGHT lb/kg	CRUISE mph/kmh	RANGE mi/km
1934	De Havilland DH86	10	10,000/4,536	170/274	760/1,223
1934	De Havilland DH89 Dragon Rapide	8	6,000/2,722	132/212	578/930
1934	BA Eagle	2	2,400/1,089	130/209	650/1,046
1935	Percival Vega Gull	3	2,750/1,247	160/258	620/998
1936	Short S23 Empire	17	40,500/18,370	165/266	760/1,223

The De Havilland DH89 Dragon Rapide was a scaled-down version of the DH86 Dragon Express. A twin-engine De Havilland Gipsy Six was a more efficient and comfortable version. It still retained the tapered mainplanes and the engine cowling 'trousered' main landing gear combination. The start of a ten-year production run commenced with the first successful flight on 17 April 1934 at Stag Lane. It commenced commercial service with Hillman Airways. One aircraft also joined the King's Flight at No. 24 Squadron, Hendon. By the outbreak of the Second World War two hundred and five aircraft had been delivered throughout the world. This included Ireland (Aer Lingus), land of my birth, and Canada (Canadian Airways, the DH89 was on floats) where I live now.

The Percival Vega Gull was a low-wing three-passenger fast touring aircraft that first flew in November 1935. A Vega Gull won the 1936 King's Cup race in July and followed up by being the only finisher in October of the Schlesinger Race to Johannesburg. Ninety aircraft were built before the production ceased at the onset of war.

ROYAL AIR FORCE 1934–1936

1934	Royal Air Force had grown to ninety squadrons, including Fleet Air Arm
1935 July	HM King George V reviewed the Royal Air Force at RAF Mildenhall: thirty-seven squadrons with 356 aircraft. Impressive? Not really, they were all biplanes. This is four years before the beginning of the Second World War!

1935 October	Italy invaded Abyssinia. Eleven squadrons responded by deploying.
1935 November	First flight of the Hawker Hurricane with a Rolls-Royce Merlin engine
1936 March	First flight of the Supermarine Spitfire with a Rolls-Royce Merlin engine

MILITARY AIRCRAFT

YEAR	AIRCRAFT	MAXIMUM SPEED mph/kmh	SERVICE CEILING ft	RANGE mi/km
1934	Hawker Hind	185/298	26,400	430/692
1935	Avro Anson	188/302	19,000	790/1,271
1935	Vickers Wellesley	228/369	25,500	1,220/1,963
1935	Bristol Blenheim	266/428	27,260	1,460/2,351
1936	Armstrong Whitworth AW38 Whitley	230/370	26,000	1,650/2,650
1936	Vickers Wellington	235/378	18,000	2,550/4,106
1936	Fairey Battle	257/413	25,000	1,000/1,610

These striking words in tribute to the first Chief of the Air Staff, Hugh Montague Trenchard, came from Marshal of the Royal Air Force and wartime leader of the Royal Air Force Bomber Command, Sir Arthur Harris, and provide an excellent summary of the importance of the one man who so effectively led the Royal Air Force throughout its infancy: 'For nearly 20 years I watched the Army and the Navy... engineer one deliberate attempt after another to destroy the Royal Air Force ... time after time Trenchard, and Trenchard alone, saved us.'

British politics, civil aviation, and the RAF of the inter-war period influenced and shaped the formation of Bomber Command on 14 July 1936. The Royal Air Force, for the first ten of the inter-war years, gave up its previous wartime position in the limelight to civil aviation's highly visible desire to fly faster, longer, and higher and get the general public's attention through the media of the day, radio and newspapers. In the 1930s the RAF came slowly out of the shadow of the Royal Navy and the British Army, albeit with outdated aircraft. By 1936 the Royal Air Force was back on track with political and financial recognition, national annual air displays, long-distance deployment proving formation flights, and most importantly, with the advent of the performance monoplane aircraft.

2

BOMBER COMMAND ORGANISATION 1936–1945

Chain of Command

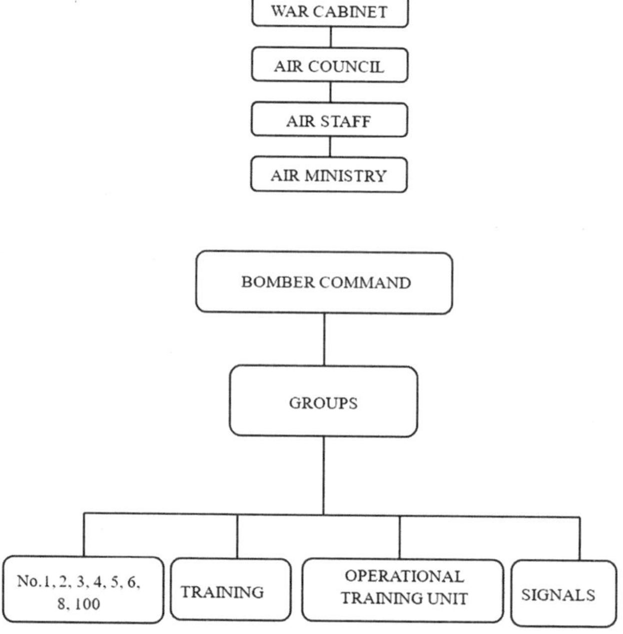

SPECIAL GROUPS
No. 6 Royal Canadian Air Force
No. 8 Pathfinder Force
No. 100 Bomber Support

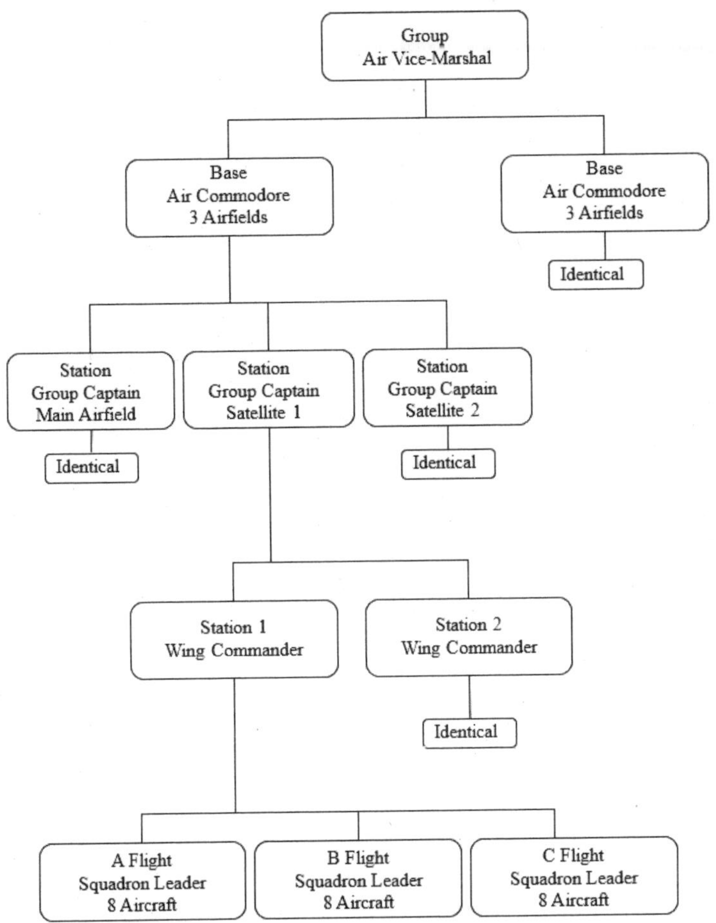

Bomber Command did not, and could not, act alone. It was responsible to the Royal Air Force of which it was a part. The Royal Air Force in turn was responsible to its political masters who could establish, or rescind, policies and directives, according to the political winds of the day. The government set up various boards, committees, cabinets, councils, and ministries to run the British Army, Navy, and Air Force which varied depending on the level of threat. The titles of the members of these groups could change as per the requirements, so a general sample will be used to indicate the essence of them. The tone and efficiency of these organisations were the ultimate responsibility of the incumbent Prime Minister.

The Prime Minister would appoint the Secretary of State for Air who oversaw the Air Ministry. The Air Ministry was a government department responsible for the Royal Air Force and had an Air Council, presided over by the Secretary of State for Air, its members including the Royal Air Force Chief and Deputy Chief of the Air Staff. This latter position, and many others, were abolished in 1964 when it came under the auspices of the Secretary of State for Defence.

During the Second World War the Prime Ministers Neville Chamberlain and Winston Churchill established a War Cabinet comprised of both military chiefs and opposition party politicians. As in peacetime, the members of the cabinet would change and there were casual attendees who would be brought in for consultation. As an example, the initial War Cabinet under Neville Chamberlain was comprised of the following officers: the Lord Privy Seal, Chancellor of the Exchequer, Foreign Secretary, Secretary of State for War, Secretary of State for Air, First Lord of the Admiralty, Minister for the Coordination of Defence, and a Minister without Portfolio.

The War Cabinet met beneath the present Treasury Building in the Whitehall area of Westminster. The Cabinet War Rooms had two more important rooms in the complex: the Map Room, which produced a daily intelligence report for the King, Prime Minister, and military Chiefs of Staff and the Cabinet Room, where Winston Churchill directed the war and had many cabinet meetings. The political decisions and directives would be passed on to the Air Staff for action, before 1943 to the Air Officer Commanding-in-Chief of Bomber Command, and after January 1943 the plans became subject to the authority of the Combined Chiefs of Staff. The Commander-in-Chief would interpret the directives and decide on the means and timing of operations.

The Commander-in-Chief would attend a morning conference and briefing in the operations room at Command Headquarters. The Meteorological Officer would give a briefing on the expected weather conditions over enemy territory and the home bases. The Intelligence Officer then briefed on what target objectives were available in the weather-suitable area. The targets would be on a priority list which had them grouped under such headings as rail transport, oil, airfields, industrial areas etc.

Once the targets were selected, and the nature of them understood, the number of aircraft and type of bomb load were calculated and decided upon. The number of available aircraft varied daily as per serviceability, attrition from last operations, and delivery of new aircraft off the production line. The Deputy Commander-in-Chief was responsible for the planning details while the Senior Air Staffing Officer was responsible for the operational side. The Commander-in-Chief made a decision about 'H hour', the time over the target, considering such variables as the weather, distance to target, hours of darkness, and coordination of effort with other operations. The Groups concerned were now given 'Warning Orders' of the impending raid.

Routes, aiming points, enemy defence activity, and electronic countermeasures details were all planned and sent out to the Groups as Operational Orders. Upon acceptance by the Group, there was room for negotiation; the Orders would be passed on to the various Stations. The individual Squadrons would then be passed their details of the planned raid. A further confirmation would be made by Bomber Command during the afternoon and the operational side would continue to prepare itself for the planned departure times (the headquarters work was done and now it was the turn of 'the pointy end', the squadrons and their aircraft, to get the job done).

The word 'command' when applied to the military is an organised unit which is the responsibility of a specific commander. The organised unit under the commander is an assembly of personnel working together to achieve a particular purpose. Characteristics of an effective unit of individuals and groups working together for a purpose are leadership, teamwork, morale (pride), performance, and effective structure. The organisation will be as good as the leadership provided to the middle managers who put into operation the goals and functions of the unit. By the time Bomber Command was formed in 1936 there had been twenty-four years of air environment leadership with the Royal Flying Corps and hundreds of years of military leadership. The leadership foundations had already been established; the Second World War would test if it was good enough.

As we have described, at the turn of the twentieth century balloons and aircraft were changing the way the military thought of waging war. There was now a third dimension to consider, airborne offensive measures and the responding threats. The political Committee of Imperial Defence, a military strategy research committee, recommended that a flying corps be formed and consist of a naval wing, a military wing, a central flying school, and an aircraft factory. On 13 April 1912 the Royal Flying Corps was established. A month later the Air Battalion of the Royal Engineers became the military wing of the Royal Flying Corps.

The Royal Flying Corps' motto was *Per ardua ad astra* (through adversity to the stars) which remains the motto of the Royal Air Force to this day. Major Frederick H. Sykes commanded the military wing and by the end of 1912 it consisted of manned balloons and aeroplanes assigned to squadrons. The naval wing broke away from the Royal Flying Corps and formed the Royal Navy Air Service on the 1 July 1914 under Commander C. R. Samson. One month later, on 4 August 1914, German troops crossed the border into Belgium and, in the first battle of the First World War, attacked the city of Liège. On 5 August 1914 Major General Sir David Henderson had command of the Royal Flying Corps in the field and so began a continuous string of leaders with the Royal Flying Corps, the Royal Air Force, and finally, Bomber Command, after it was separated from the main force. These leaders would guide these organisations through the challenges of war and peace.

The following is a list of the individuals who provided executive military leadership and includes some brief personal histories to illustrate the depth of their military experience. First a brief introduction to the senior Royal Air Force rank structure will give some background to the organisation after 1 April 1918; these ranks continued to be used in Bomber Command after its founding in 1936. The Royal Flying Corps used military ranks, an example being Major, which would become a Squadron Leader in the Royal Air Force. Some earlier serving individuals had Royal Flying Corps ranks initially, to be superseded by Royal Air Force ranks later.

Marshal of the Royal Air Force	Wartime/honorary only	Chief of Air Staff
Air Chief Marshal		Chief of Air Staff
Air Marshal		Chief of Command
Air Vice-Marshal		Chief of Group
Air Commodore		Chief of Base/ Post 1943
Group Captain		Chief of Station
Wing Commander		Chief of Squadron

Field Commanders of The RFC

Lieutenant General Sir David Henderson, KCB, KCVO, DSO

05 August 1914 – 22 November 1914 and 20 December 1914 – 19 August 1915.

Following graduation from the Royal Military College, Sandhurst, he served in the British Army during the Nile Expedition and the Boer War in South Africa as Director of Military Intelligence. He wrote two works, *Field Intelligence: Its Principles and Practice* and *The Art of Reconnaissance*, which solidified his reputation as being an expert on military tactical intelligence.

In 1911 Henderson was part of a sub-committee of the Air Ministry that was instrumental in the formation of the Royal Flying Corps. That same year he also learned to fly at the age of forty-nine. Appointed Director of the Department of Military Aeronautics, he was appointed the commander of the Royal Flying Corps upon the outbreak of war. A less than one-month appointment in November 1914, as General Officer Commanding the 1st Infantry Division, was reversed by Lord Kitchener with whom he had served in the Boer War and he returned to command the Royal Flying Corps.

In 1915 he returned to London as the Director-General of Military Aeronautics and assisted General Smuts with his 1917 review of the British Air Services. It has been suggested by some historians that Henderson had better claim to the informal title of 'Father of the Royal Air Force' than Sir Hugh Trenchard, surely a topic for debate. Disappointed at not being made Chief of the Air Staff of the newly formed Royal Air Force in April 1918, Henderson resigned from the Air Council and returned to France until the Armistice.

Air Vice Marshal Sir Frederick Hugh Sykes, GCSI, GCIE, GBE, KCB, CMG
22 November 1914 – 20 December 1914

Sykes served as a trooper in the Boer War and subsequently in Lord Roberts' bodyguard detail where he was wounded and repatriated to Great Britain. He developed an interest in aviation and obtained a ballooning certificate while with the Balloon Section of the Royal Engineers. Upon returning to England, after serving in India, he commenced flying lessons and obtained Royal Aero Club certificate No. 96 in June 1911.

He served on the same sub-committee as Henderson that recommended the formation of the Royal Flying Corps and on 13 May 1912 served as its first Officer Commanding the Military Wing of the Royal Flying Corps. Sykes was responsible for the recruitment and training of pilots. In August 1914 the Royal Flying Corps deployed to France under his leadership. His not being a senior officer resulted in Henderson becoming the Officer Commanding in the Field in November 1914 and Sykes serving as his Chief of Staff. Sykes did serve for one month in the leader's role, from 20 November 1914 to 20 December 1914, until reversed by Lord Kitchener upon the appeal of Trenchard not to work for him; such are the vagaries of war.

Sykes career culminated with being appointed Chief of the Air Staff on 13 April 1918, but he fell out of favour with Winston Churchill, Secretary of State for Air, who was focusing on post-war defence cuts, and retired on 31 March 1919.

Marshal of the Royal Air Force Hugh Montagu Trenchard, 1st Viscount Trenchard, GCB, OM, GCVO, DSO
25 August 1915 – 03 January 1918

There are some names which are very prominent in the history of the Royal Air Force and Trenchard is certainly one of them. He is noted for securing the future of the RAF when it was under threat from the senior services and continued to advocate for it after he retired, a true stalwart of the 'blue' uniform. It is interesting to note that he reputedly favoured strategic bombing rather than area bombing.

He served with the Royal Scots Fusiliers in India and South Africa where he was critically wounded. Determined to return to service, he once again took part in the Boer War and when it ended, he went to the Southern Nigeria Regiment and spent six years on interior patrols. In 1910 he rejoined the Fusiliers in Derry, Northern Ireland. In 1912, on three months of paid leave, he attended Thomas Sopwith's flying school at Brooklands and was awarded the Royal Aero Club's certificate No. 270. Somewhat lacking in flying proficiency, he found an opportunity in training administrative duties with the Central Flying School where he was promoted to Assistant Commandant in 1913.

On the outbreak of the First World War Trenchard was initially appointed Officer Commanding the Military Wing of the Royal Flying Corps. One of his priorities was to raise new squadrons for service in mainland Europe and in October 1914 No. 6 Squadron deployed to Belgium. Under restructuring plans the Military Wing was disbanded and Trenchard assumed command of the Royal Flying Corps First Wing at Merville, France. The Wing provided support for the army by photo-reconnaissance, artillery co-ordination, and payload limited bombing flights.

In August 1915 Trenchard was appointed Officer Commanding the Royal Flying Corps in the Field and by March 1916 promoted to major-general. There followed a period of military and political intrigue and manoeuvring which influenced his career. By January 1918 he had been repatriated to Britain and appointed Chief of the Air Staff in the newly formed Air Ministry. Disagreements with Lord Rothermere, the Air Minister, led to his resignation coincidental with the forming of the Royal Air Force on 1 April 1918. A short time later he was named General Officer Commanding of the Independent Air Force in Nancy, France, which supported the army and provided strategic bombing raids on German railways and airfields. At the Armistice Trenchard had his forces returned to British command.

Marshal of the Royal Air Force Sir John Maitland Salmond, GCB, CMG, CVO, DSO & Bar
18 January 1918 – 01 April 1918

Upon graduation from the Royal Military College, Sandhurst, he served with the King's Own Royal Lancaster Regiment in Africa. Returning to England he learned to fly at the Central Flying School and was awarded the Royal Aero Club certificate No. 272, two numbers after Trenchard. He became a Squadron Commander at the Central Flying School, and then assumed command of No. 3 Squadron on the Western Front.

Returning to England in 1915 he assumed positions in the Training Division, eventually reaching General Officer Commanding Training Division. Salmond subsequently became the General Officer Commanding the Royal Flying Corps in January 1918 and continued his military career with the RAF after the armistice.

Inter-war RAF Commanders

Marshal of the Royal Air Force Hugh Montagu Trenchard
31 March 1919 – 01 January 1930

Winston Churchill requested Trenchard accept the post of Chief of the Air Staff, which he accepted in March 1919. His priority was demobilisation of the Royal Air Force to ten per cent of its wartime size, approximately thirty squadrons. It was during these difficult financial and social times that he established the foundation of the new force. He founded a military academy, Royal Air Force (Cadet) College, at Cranwell, inaugurated an Aircraft Apprentice system, and established the Royal Air Force Staff College at Andover, England. Trenchard was now an Air Marshal under the new rank structure.

In the early 1920s the Royal Air Force was under constant political and military attack, by the Navy in particular, to justify its worth. He advocated using the it to police the British Empire and it proved its worth in many areas including India, Afghanistan, and Somaliland. He also created the Auxiliary Air Force, short service officer commissions, and the University Air Squadron scheme. Trenchard supported Britain's effort to win the high-speed flight Schneider Trophy. In January 1927 he was promoted to Marshal of the Royal Air Force, the first person to hold the highest rank. He resigned from his position as Chief of the Air Staff in January 1930.

Air Chief Marshal John Salmond
01 January 1930 – 22 May 1933

During that period his brother Sir Geoffrey Salmond held the position before dying in office after twenty-six days. John Salmond took over until a permanent replacement was found. He was subsequently promoted to Marshal of the Royal Air Force.

Marshal of the Royal Air Force Sir Edward Leonard Ellington, GCB, CMG, CBE
22 May 1933 – 01 September 1937

He attended the Royal Military Academy, Woolwich, and was commissioned in the Royal Field Artillery. Posted to the War Office in August 1909, he learned to fly in 1912 and was awarded the Royal Aero Club certificate No. 305. He served as a staff officer in the Directorate of Military Aeronautics and was under training at the Central Flying School when the First World War started. A lifelong staff officer, he was in France with the British Expeditionary Force as Deputy Assistant Quartermaster-General, serve with the 2nd Army, Department of the Imperial General Staff, Deputy Director and Director-General of Military Aeronautics, and Controller-General of Equipment in April 1918.

Further service as the Director-General Supply and Research preceded Air Officer Commanding Royal Air Force Middle East (1922), Air Officer Commanding Royal Air Force India (1923), Air Officer Commanding-in-Chief Air Defence of Great Britain (1929), Principal Air Aide-de-Camp to the King (1930), and Air Member for Personnel (1931). Ellington was appointed Chief of the Air Staff and initiated plan 'Scheme F' to increase the size of the RAF within three years to counter the mounting threat from Hitler's Germany.

The plan was for a total of 187 squadrons with a ratio of five bomber squadrons to two fighter squadrons. The emphasis was on offence with a bombing strategy. To achieve this, Ellington reorganised the Home Royal Air Force squadrons into new commands forming Bomber Command, Fighter Command, Coastal Command, and Training Command on 14 July 1936. His previous extensive staff officer service prepared him for the leadership role.

Commanders Bomber Command

Air Chief Marshal Sir John Miles Steel, GCB, KBE, CMG
14 July 1936

Steel had the distinction of being the initial Bomber Command leader. A Royal Navy officer, he was chosen to command the Royal Naval Air Station Eastchurch, Isle of Sheppey, Kent. Nearby at Leysdown the Aero Club of Great Britain established their first flying ground. Close by, the Short brothers established the first aircraft factory in Great Britain. In 1910 the Royal Aero Club had moved to Eastchurch and began training naval pilots; Steel became the Officer Commanding No. 58 Wing where he qualified as a pilot. By 1925 Steel had become Air Officer Commanding the Wessex Bombing Area. He subsequently was promoted to Air Marshal in 1932 and appointed the Air Officer Commanding-in-Chief Air Defence of Great Britain in August 1935. He assumed the leadership of Bomber Command on 14 July 1936.

Air Chief Marshal Sir Edgar Rainey Ludlow-Hewitt, GCB, GBE, CMG, DSO, MC, DL
12 September 1937

Ludlow-Hewitt would lead Bomber Command into the Second World War. A graduate of Sandhurst he was commissioned in the Royal Irish Rifles and transferred to the Royal Flying Corps. In September 1914 he attained the Royal Aero Clubs Certificate No. 886. He served as a pilot with No. 1 Squadron and Officer Commanding of No. 15 and No. 3 Squadrons. Ludlow-Hewitt then assumed positions in the Training Division. In 1922 he was appointed Air Secretary followed by Commandant of the Royal Air Force Staff College in 1926. Further senior appointments included the Iraq Command and Royal Air Force India before his promotion to Air Chief Marshal and Air Officer Commanding-in-Chief of Bomber Command. He was a firm believer in training, which was not surprising considering his previous experience.

Marshal of the Royal Air Force Sir Charles F. A. Portal, 1st Viscount Portal of Hungerford, KG, GCB, OM, DSO & Bar, MC, DL
03 April 1940

Portal left his studies at Christ Church, Oxford, to join the British Army in 1914. He quickly gained notice and was commissioned in, and given command of, the 1st Corps headquarters Signals Company's dispatch riders. Transferring to the Flying Corps initially as an observer, he obtained his pilot's wings and served with No. 60 Squadron, eventually commanding No. 16 Squadron. By the end of the war he commanded No. 24 (Training) Wing. Chief flying instructor at Royal Air Force College, Cranwell, was followed by Royal Air Force Staff College in 1922. In 1926 he commanded No. 7 Squadron and one of his ambitions was to achieve bombing accuracy. By 1930 he was Deputy Director of Plans in the Directorate of Operations and Intelligence at the Air Ministry. Commander of British Forces in Aden was followed in 1935 by appointments at the Imperial Defence College and Air Ministry where he was Director of Organisation. Portal's work as Air Member for Personnel on the Air Council preceded his command of Bomber Command. Portal's history-changing decision, on 25 August 1940, to initiate bombing of German cities in retaliation for the 'accidental' bombing of London, altered the course of the war. The idea was to not only destroy the factories but also the people working in them. The German High Command responded by abandoning some military targets in favour of retaliatory raids against British cities. This allowed Fighter Command, and its stations, time to recover and go on to win the Battle of Britain.

Air Chief Marshal Sir Richard Edmund Charles Peirse, KCB, DSO, AFC
05 October 1940

Peirse was educated at King's College, London, and joined the Royal Navy Volunteer Reserve and then served as a pilot with the Royal Naval Air Service. He commanded No. 222 Squadron in 1918 at Royal Air Force Station Gosport and Royal Air Force Station Heliopolis in 1929. In 1930 he was Deputy Director of Operations and Intelligence in the Air Ministry. In 1933 he was Air Officer Commanding Palestine Transjordan Command and by 1936 was Deputy Chief of the Air Staff. He assumed command of Bomber Command at a time of massive expansion with very high losses of aircraft and crews. He was relieved of his command at the beginning of 1942 because of the no apparent significant effect of the bombing on Germany after two years.

Air Marshal Sir John Eustice Arthur Baldwin, KBE, CB, DSO DL
08 January 1942

Educated at Rugby School and the Royal Military College, Sandhurst, Baldwin was commissioned into the 8th (King's Royal Irish) Hussars in 1911. He was awarded the Royal Aero Club's Aviator Certificate No. 971 in November 1914 and became a pilot in the Royal Flying Corps. He commanded No. 55 Squadron in 1916 and No. 41 Wing in 1917. In 1928 Baldwin was Commandant of the Central Flying School, 1931-32 he was Aide-de-Camp to King George V, Air officer Commanding No. 1 Group in 1934, Director of Personnel Services in 1935 followed by Commandant of the Royal Air Force College Cranwell, and Air Officer Commanding No. 21 group in 1938. He retired in 1939. He was recalled to service as Air Officer Commanding No. 3 Group at Royal Air Force Bomber Command and served as (Acting) Commander in Chief, Bomber Command, for a short period on the removal of Peirse from the position.

Marshal of the Royal Air Force Sir Arthur Travers Harris, 1st Baronet, GCB, OBE, AFC
22 February 1942

Having written three previous books connected with Bomber Command, two on the Lancaster and one on the Merlin engine, all published by Amberley Books, I am very familiar with 'Bomber Harris'(as he was known to the press) and his faults and attributes, his failures and successes. I look across at my bookshelf and see *Bomber Harris: His Life and Times* by Henry Probert among many books written about him and the Royal Air Force Bomber Command. His appointment coincided with the introduction of the Avro Lancaster heavy bomber to active service with Bomber Command. Harris, in cooperation with Portal, embarked upon a campaign of area and strategic bombing raids, ranging from massive 1,000-aircraft area raids to a small number of aircraft on strategic target raids to be discussed later in Chapter 7. Harris *was* Bomber Command; in 1942 he brought the war to the enemy with all the Command's might when the tide of war had turned from the defensive to the offensive. Educated at Allhallows School in Devon he emigrated to Rhodesia to seek his fortune. He joined the 1st Rhodesian regiment on the outbreak of war. In 1915 he returned to Britain and immediately joined the war effort again, this time by joining the Royal Flying Corps. He assumed command of No. 45 Squadron in France and returned to Britain in 1918 to command No. 44 Squadron on Home Defence duties. Staying in the RAF he was appointed station commander of Royal Air Force, Digby, and commander of No. 3 Flying Training School. Harris became involved in aerial bombing when he subsequently served in India, Mesopotamia, and specifically area bombing in Persia. Returning to Britain in 1924 he commanded No. 58 Squadron, the first post-war heavy bomber squadron. He developed, with Air Chief Marshal Salmond, night training for bomber operations. By 1927 he was a Wing Commander and attended the Army Staff College at Camberley, was Commander of a flying-boat squadron, Deputy Director of Plans at the Air Ministry, and Middle East Command in Egypt, and by 1938 he was commanding No. 4 (Bomber) Group. Posted to Palestine and Transjordan as Officer Commanding, he returned to Britain in 1939. He had pressured the decision makers during these years to consider strategic bombers that could attack Germany. In September 1939 he was in command of Royal Air Force No. 5 Group, by 1940 he was Deputy Chief of the Air Staff, and in June 1941 was promoted to the acting rank of Air Marshal. The Butt Report circulated in August 1941 commented on the inaccuracy of the bomber aircraft and Harris was part of the government response. Subsequent promotion was to acting Air Chief Marshal on March 1943.

The headquarters for Bomber Command, motto 'Strike hard, strike sure', was established by Air Chief Marshal Steel at Hillingdon House on Lord Bathurst's grounds at Richings Park, Buckinghamshire, on 13 July 1936. It remained there until 1940 when it was moved to a more secure and discreet location further away from London in the village of Walters Ash near High Wycombe in the Chiltern Hills, Buckinghamshire. The station was known as 'Southdown' to further preserve secrecy. The selected site was in a wooded area which provided some camouflage from the air. Buildings were disguised to represent other uses; the fire station had a tower to represent a church. A subterranean network of tunnels connected all the buildings to the Operations Block, which was fifty-five feet (seventeen metres) below ground, to maintain the impression of a quintessential sleepy English village in the woods.

Bomber Command was divided into Groups under an Air Vice-Marshal to make the Command more manageable and to allow for specialities and commonalities. The individual numbered Groups were comprised of squadrons, flights, and aircraft. Some also had flying wings, three or four squadrons functioning together, within the Group. These initial Groups in 1936 were designation as light, medium, or heavy. The Groups did vary as to number and content during the life of Bomber Command from 1936 to 1968. They were also separated, with designated bases and stations for the front-line squadrons on the eastern side of England and Moray, Scotland. The Operational Training Units were generally situated in the Midlands

In September 1939 Bomber Command was a mere embryo of what it would become, twenty-nine squadrons operated from grass airfields. No. 2 Group was in the Norfolk area, No. 3 Group in the Cambridge and Huntingdon area, No. 4 Group in the North and West Riding of Yorkshire, and No. 5 Group was in Lincolnshire and Nottinghamshire. No. 1 Group returned from France in 1940 and was assigned airfields in South Yorkshire and North Lincolnshire. By 1945 those twenty-nine squadrons had grown to ninety-plus, with a daily average of over 1,000 aircraft and crews available. That was the destructive power on hand for the commanders. Aircraft such as the Short Stirling, Handley Page Halifax, Avro Lancaster and the De Havilland Mosquito fighter/bomber had replaced the older, obsolete light bombers and now made up most of this force.

It is not the intention, and is indeed beyond the scope of this book, to provide a detailed breakdown of squadrons, stations, and aircraft for these Groups, but rather a general impression of the fluidity that was necessary during wartime with the resources that were available. Bomber Command 'rolled with the punches' and adapted to new aircraft, new technology, and new ideas on bomber strategy as the fortunes, or misfortunes, of war dictated. The following list is comprised of fighting, training, and specialty groups that were active in all or part of the years 1939 to 1945.

No. 1 Group

Motto: 'Swift to attack'
Formed: Abingdon, Berkshire 1 May 1936
Headquarters
Abingdon, Berkshire May 1936 – August 1939
Benson, Oxfordshire September 1939 – December 1939 (disbanded)
Hucknall, Nottinghamshire June 1940 (reformed) – July 1941
Bawtry Hall, Yorkshire July 1941 – September 1945

No. 1 Group was derived from the Central Area of the Air Defence of Great Britain. The three initial stations were Abingdon, Berkshire, Bircham Newton, Norfolk, and Upper Heyford, Oxfordshire. The ten squadrons were equipped with the Hawker Hind. Two years later it had expanded to eight stations with seventeen squadrons equipped with Bristol Blenheim or Fairey Battle aircraft. By August 1939 it was equipped with Fairey Battles only, designated the Advanced Air Striking Force, and sent to France. The No. 1 Group Headquarters now became the Headquarters Advanced Air Striking Force and the respective squadrons at Abingdon, Harwell, Oxfordshire, Benson, South Oxfordshire, Boscombe Down, Wiltshire, and Bicester, Oxfordshire, became Nos. 71, 72, 74, 75, and 76 Wings respectively.

There were plans to have the Second Echelon, formerly No. 2 Group, join No. 1 Group in France but the decision was made at the end of September to reverse that decision. By June 1940 the Advanced Air Striking Force, despite a gallant fight against overwhelming odds, had been recalled to England to preserve resources. It was once again reformed as No. 1 Group with headquarters at Hucknall, Nottinghamshire, and by the end of the year had started converting to the Vickers Wellington. In April 1941 there were eight squadrons operating from four stations: Binbrook, Lincolnshire; Newton, Nottinghamshire; Swinderby, Lincolnshire; and Syerston, Nottinghamshire. These airfields were attacked by the Luftwaffe in August with little damage. Three months later the headquarters were moved to Bawtry Hall, South Yorkshire. By the end of 1941 the Group was using airfields at Binbrook, Lincolnshire; Elsham, Lincolnshire; Snaith, Yorkshire; Holme-on-Spalding Moor, Yorkshire; Hemswell, Lincolnshire; and Lindholme, South Yorkshire. Breighton, East Riding of Yorkshire, was being used in the spring of 1942.

By August the Handley Page Halifax had joined the Group followed by the Avro Lancaster in November. In February 1943 the Group delivered over 1,000 tons of bombs in one month for the first time, in fact delivering 1,649 tons. In June the Group operated out of Ludford Magna, Lincolnshire. During the summer the Group switched from the Battle of the Ruhr to the Battle of Hamburg. Targets also included Milan, Turin, Genoa in Italy, and Nuremberg and Berlin in Germany. By the autumn the Group's first base station, No. 12 Binbrook, Lincolnshire, was operational with sub-stations close-by at Grimsby, Lincolnshire and Kelstern, Lincolnshire. By the end of 1943 two more base stations were added: No. 13 Elsham, Linconshire, with sub-stations Kirmington, Lincolnshire and North Killingholme, North Lincolnshire; and No. 14 Ludford Magna, Lincolnshire, with sub-stations Wickenby, Lincolnshire, and Faldingworth, Lincolnshire. The Group included Australian and Polish squadrons.

During February 1944 the Group's 139 Lancasters attacked the German capital in the heaviest attack so far. At Binbrook, Lincolnshire, in May the Australian Prime Minister was presented with Lancaster W4783 'G – George' which now can be seen in the War Museum at Canberra, Australia. It had logged ninety operational sorties. In June 1944 the Group broke all records by delivering 15,062 tons of bombs to the enemy. In preparation for the invasion of Europe. 101 Squadron played an historically important role through prolonged patrols electronically jamming the enemy's defences. The Group record was followed closely by another when No. 460 Squadron dropped 1,867 tons of bombs in August, a tally unsurpassed by the end of the war. In October the Group damaged the sea wall at Walcheren, Zeeland, Netherlands, and flooded the occupying enemy's defences. No. 15 base was established at Scampton, Lincolnshire, with sub-stations at Hemswell, Lincolnshire and Fiskerton, Lincolnshire

In January 1945 one of the Group's Lancasters, No. 103 Squadron's ED888 'M2', was withdrawn from service after having flown 140 sorties, ninety-eight to Germany including fifteen to Berlin. No other Lancaster in Bomber Command had achieved such longevity. The Group ceased fire in April but not before taking part in the last big attack on Berchtesgaden and taking part in the sinking of the pocket battleship *Admiral Scheer* at Kiel. The summer was filled with dropping food supplies in Holland and bringing home liberated prisoners of war.

Operational sorties: 57,900

No. 2 Group

Motto: 'We will conquer'
Formed: Abingdon, Berkshire 20 March 1936
Headquarters
Abingdon, Berkshire May 1936 – January 1937
Andover, Hampshire January 1937 – April 1938
Wyton, Huntingdonshire April 1938 – October 1939
Castlewood House, Huntingdonshire October 1939 – May 1943
(disbanded)

By the 1 August 1936 No. 2 Group had taken command of its first station at Abbotsinch, Renfrewshire, and its first squadrons, Nos. 21 and 34, of Hawker Hind aircraft. At the outbreak of war the headquarters had been moved to Wyton, Cambridgeshire, and the Group had been organised into five Wings with two squadrons each: No. 70 Wing at Upper Heyford, Oxfordshire, with Nos. 18 and 57 Squadrons; No. 79 Wing at Watton, Norfolk, with Nos. 21 and 82 Squadrons; No. 81 Wing at West Raynham, Norfolk, with Nos. 90 and 101 Squadrons; No. 82 Wing at Wyton, Cambridgeshire, with Nos. 114 and 139 Squadrons; and No. 83 Wing at Wattisham, Suffolk, with Nos. 107 and 110 Squadrons.

Four of the Wings, Nos. 79, 80, 81, and 82, had been earmarked for the 2nd Echelon of the Advanced Air Striking Force destined for France. No. 2 Group was immediately active and on 3 September 1939 a Bristol Blenheim made the first operational sortie to aggressively cross the German border in the Second World War. On 4 September 1939 some of the Group's Bristol Blenheims made the first bombing attack of the war. By the spring of 1940 the Group was bombing the advancing German army as they broke through into France. On 17 May 1940 No. 82 Squadron lost eleven out of twelve Bristol Blenheims attacking enemy columns at Gembloux, Belgium.

The Group bombed the invasion barges being prepared for the assault on England during the Battle of Britain; attempted to intercept the German Navy as they made their famous 'Channel Dash' from Brest, France, back to Germany with two Scharnhorst class battleships and a heavy cruiser; dropped Commandos in the ill-fated sortie in preparation for the Dieppe invasion; and made the first daylight attacks on Berlin. No. 2 Group had several different types of aircraft, among them the North American B-25 Mitchell and the only heavy bombing unit in the Group flying the Boeing Fortress IIs. In May 1943 No. 2 Group left Bomber Command and joined the new Tactical Air Force which better described its new role.

Operational sorties: 57,000

No. 3 Group

Motto: 'Nothing without labour'
Formed: Andover, Hampshire 01 May 1936
Headquarters
Andover, Hampshire May 1936 – January 1937
Mildenhall, Suffolk January 1937 – March 1940
Exning, Suffolk March 1940 – September 1945

No. 3 Group was responsible for the Western Area of the Air Defence of Great Britain. The Vickers Wellington replaced such aircraft as the Vickers Virginia and Handley Page Heyford in the Group. The first squadron to receive the Vickers Wellington into Royal Air Force service was No. 99 Squadron in October 1938. The second bombing operation of the war was carried out by No. 3 Group Wellingtons against German warships near Brunsbuttel.

Two squadrons were sent temporarily to Coastal Command in Northern Scotland and one of them, No. 115 Squadron, was the first to bomb a mainland target, Stavanger airfield in Norway. A raid was carried out on Italy from Salon-de-Provence in the south of France in early June 1940, but the squadrons were quickly withdrawn due to the imminent collapse of France. Later in the year the first four-engine bomber, the Shorts Stirling, joined the Group, followed by the Avro Lancaster in 1942.

The first 1,000 bomber raid was on the night of 30/31 May 1942 against Cologne. A new technique was also adopted in 1942: a flare force guided by radar lit up the target for the main bombing force. Aircraft were drawn from all squadrons and were located under the administrative control of airfields in No. 3 Group. On 3/4 November 1943 No. 3 Group led a blind bombing attack on Dusseldorf using the G-H radar bombing aid. The following year the Group attacked flying bomb sites during the summer. The build up to the D-Day invasion was preceded by attacks on railway junctions and marshalling yards.

During the final push for Berlin No. 3 Group bombed the town of Wesel in preparation for the crossing of the Rhine. Just prior to VE-Day the Group were involved in *Operation Manna,* dropping food to the citizens of the Netherlands.

Operational sorties: 66,600

No. 4 Group

No badge or motto authorised
Formed: Mildenhall, Suffolk 1 April 1937
Headquarters
Mildenhall, Suffolk April 1937 – June 1937
Linton-on-Ouse, Yorkshire June 1937 – April 1940
Heslington Hall, Yorkshire April 1940 – May 1945 (disbanded)

The headquarters were moved to Linton-on-Ouse, Yorkshire, when No. 4 Group took over the following Yorkshire stations and squadrons from No. 3 Group: Leconfield (Nos. 97 and 166 Squadrons), Driffield (Nos. 75 and 215 Squadrons), Dishforth (Nos. 10 and 78 Squadrons), Finningley (Nos. 7 and 76 Squadrons), and Linton-on-Ouse (Nos. 51 and 58 Squadrons). No. 4 Group was primarily located south and east of York, mostly flying the Handley Page Heyford biplane bomber.

On the night of the 3/04 September 1939 Armstrong Whitworth Whitleys of Nos. 51 and 58 Squadrons dropped leaflets over Hamburg, Bremen, and the Ruhr area. From this auspicious beginning No. 4 Group spawned two other groups – a training group and No. 6 Group. They trained many crews and continued to attack Germany and Italy. No. 4 Group also facilitated the establishment of two French Air Force heavy bomber squadrons, Nos. 346 and 347, at Elvington, Yorkshire. No. 4 Group opened seven new fields and assumed responsibility for the Fido (Fog Investigation and Dispersal Operation) equipped emergency landing field at Carnaby, Yorkshire. The Group initially took part in anti-shipping and reconnaissance roles together with nickelling, the dropping of leaflets. In the spring of 1941, the Group was involved in the daylight attacks on the *Scharnhorst* and *Gneisenau* of the German navy at Brest. This was followed by taking part in the Battle of the Ruhr using Vickers Wellington and Handley page Halifax bombers.

By 1944 the Group took on new roles with daylight bombing raids and as a semi-tactical force attacking French marshalling yards and coastal gun emplacements, troop choke points, and against the new V-weapon sites. By June it had a set a record by shooting down thirty-three fighters and for a short period assumed a new role transporting petrol to Brussels to assist the British Second Army in their Arnhem campaign.

Operational sorties: 61,570

No. 5 Group

Motto: 'Undaunted'
Formed: Mildenhall, Suffolk 1 September 1937
Headquarters
Mildenhall, Suffolk September 1937 – October 1937
Grantham, Lincolnshire October 1937 – November 1943
Swinderby, Lincolnshire November 1943 – September 1945

The initial allocation at Grantham was ten squadrons of Handley Page Hampdens on five stations. The future Air Officer Commanding in Chief of Bomber Command was at one time in command of No. 5 Group, Air Vice-Marshal A. T. Harris. The Hampdens lasted until the winter of 1940/41 when the Group started to convert to Avro Manchesters.

The Group was unique in that it pioneered the art of minelaying and in fact had been responsible for all minelaying from the air. The Group was involved in some of the more specialised and dramatic attacks of the war: for example, the breaches of the Dortmund-Ems Canal, the destruction of the Mohne and Eder dams, the sinking of the *Tirpitz*, and the shuttle raids flying between England and North Africa.

In the spring of 1941, the Group was involved in the daylight attacks on the *Scharnhorst* and *Gneisenau* at Brest. A year later the Group had started to re-equip with the Lancaster and the first operation was minelaying in the Heligoland Bight. The Augsburg MAN diesel engine factory was attacked in April at very low level and casualties were high.

Cologne was attacked by a 1,000-bomber raid of which No. 5 Group contributed 162 aircraft.

During October the Group made five significant raids. The Schneider armament works at Le Creusot, and Genoa and Milan were among them. The most famous of all raids took place in May 1943: The dams raid on the Mohne, Sorpe and Eder Dams by No. 617 Squadron led by Wing Commander Guy Gibson. The Group also played a full part in the Battle of Berlin. Spring 1944 was devoted to softening up targets in advance of the planned May invasion. In November the Bismarck class battleship *Tirpitz* was sunk in Tromso Fjord.

June saw the Group fly more than 5,000 sorties and the first 12,000-pound Tallboy dropped, which blocked the Saumur Tunnel. The Group also took part in the attack on Wesel to permit the crossing of the Rhine and in March dropped the heaviest bomb yet, the 22,400-pound Grand Slam. No. 5 Group was selected for the Tiger Force to be deployed against Japan, which fortunately did not take place as Japan surrendered in August 1945.

Operational sorties: 70,350

No. 6 (Royal Canadian Air Force) Group

Motto: 'Initiative and skill'
Formed: Allerton Park, Yorkshire 25 October 1942
Headquarters
Allerton Park, Yorkshire October 1942 – September 1945

No. 6 Group was unique in the history of Bomber Command because of its Canadian personnel. It grew to fourteen heavy bomber squadrons and established a battle record second to none. The entire cost of No. 6 Group was born by the Canadian Government except for RAF and local personnel attached to the Group. January 1943 saw the initial transfer of six stations to Royal Canadian Air Force squadrons: they were Leeming, Yorkshire (Nos. 408 and 424 Squadrons); Middleton St George, Durham (Nos. 419 and 420 Squadrons); Dishforth, Yorkshire (Nos. 425 and 426 Squadrons); Croft, Yorkshire (No. 427 Squadron); Dalton, Yorkshire (No. 428 Squadron); and Skipton-on-Swale, Yorkshire, which was still being built. The stations were all to the north of York. The Squadrons were flying the Handley Page Halifax, the Vickers Wellington or the Avro Lancaster.

The eventual seven operational stations were organised as bases and each had sub-stations with operational squadrons. The largest base was No. 62 (Beaver) Base at Linton-on-Louse with Nos. 408 and 426 as resident squadrons. The two sub-stations were East Moor (Nos. 415

and 432 Squadrons) and Tholthorpe (Nos. 420 and 425 Squadrons). The other two bases with their own sub-stations were No. 63 Base at Leeming and No. 64 Base at Middleton St George. No. 61 Base at Topcliffe, North Yorkshire, later renamed No. 76 and associated with the Royal Air Force, was established as the training organisation and supported several Heavy Conversion Units.

Many Royal Canadian Air Force Squadrons were formed and added to the Group later and there was constant movement of all squadrons from base to base. The only exception was No. 419 Squadron, which remained at Middleton St George until the end of the war. The first Canadian-built Avro Lancaster Mark X, KB700 *Ruhr Express*, was initially delivered to No. 405 Squadron and saw subsequent action with No. 419 Squadron. Worthy of mention are the two attacks on Duisburg, sixteen hours apart, when the Group put up over 500 aircraft. The previous week, the night of 6 October 1943, the Group bombed Dortmund with close to 300 aircraft. The Group overall had a great history of serviceability.

Eight squadrons were earmarked for the Tiger Force and Avro Lancasters were ferried back to Canada in preparation. Four squadrons remained active in Great Britain for a short time. By the end of August 1945, the Canadian Bomber Group came to an end. Canadian airmen both at home, in the British Commonwealth Air Training Plan and home defence, and abroad with the Royal Air Force and Royal Canadian Air Force, can be proud of their contribution to the war effort.

Operational sorties: 40,200

No. 8 (Pathfinder Force) Group

Motto: 'We guide to strike'
Formed: Wyton, Huntingdonshire 15 August 1942
Headquarters
Wyton, Huntingdonshire August 1942 – June 1943
Castle Hill House, Huntingdonshire June 1943 – September 1945

There was a confusing start to this famous Group with title changes and a time overlap. Initially founded in September 1941 with headquarters at Brampton, Cambridgeshire, as No 8 (Bomber) Group it was not until after No. 8 Pathfinder Force was formed in August 1942 that in January 1943 No. 8 (Bomber) Group was disbanded. No. 8 (Bomber) Group never became operational. The Pathfinder Force became the No. 8 (Pathfinder Force) Group in January 1943 with Headquarters at Wyton.

The Butt Report released on 18 August 1941 came as a total shock to many but was not surprising to those involved with the night navigation and target finding of Bomber Command. It revealed the widespread failure of the bombers to hit their targets. The reason that this situation was revealed was that night cameras had been installed in the aircraft to verify crews' claims whether or not the target had been hit. The summer of 1941 revealed that only about one-third of aircraft had actually bombed within 5 miles (8km) of the assigned target. The Pathfinder Force to guide the main bomber stream was one of the solutions.

The East Midlands of England became known as 'Pathfinder country'. It was comprised of five specially chosen squadrons, one squadron from each of the Groups.

No. 1 Group No 156 Squadron	Vickers Wellington
No. 2 Group No 109 Squadron	Vickers Wellington & De Havilland Mosquito
No. 3 Group No 7 Squadron	Shorts Stirling
No. 4 Group No 35 Squadron	Handley Page Halifax
No. 5 Group No 83 Squadron	Avro Lancaster

The idea was that these handpicked squadrons and crews from each Group would be under the direct command of Air Chief Marshal Harris, Air Officer Commanding-in-Chief, Bomber Command. By the end of 1941 Bomber Command wanted to have specialist squadrons, the idea first used by the Luftwaffe, to initiate the bombing stream. No 3 Group had been doing it in a limited way using the new Gee apparatus. The squadrons initially flew their original aircraft but eventually they all standardised by using the Avro Lancaster and De Havilland Mosquito.

The elite Pathfinder Group was not without its detractors; the elite connotation made sme feel uneasy. The crews were all volunteers who had agreed to do another additional tour. However, actions speak louder than words. The Pathfinder Force Group so improved the accuracy of the bombing raids by their navigational skills that it became the recognised method for pinpointing the target for the main force. Group Captain D. C. T. Bennett then assumed command in January 1943 for all of its existence.

The use of the blind bombing aids Oboe and H2S, as well as highly visible marker aids of different types, increased the efficiency of the Group. The Group continued to grow throughout the war and was comprised of nineteen squadrons just prior to VE-Day. Its contribution was immeasurable to the success of Bomber Command – but the Pathfinder Force squadrons paid a high price for their dangerous role.

Operational sorties: 51,000

No. 100 (Bomber Support) Group

Motto: 'Confound and destroy'
Formed
Radlett, Hertfordshire 23 November 1943
Headquarters
Radlett, Hertfordshire 23 November 1943
West Raynham, Norfolk December 1943
Bylaugh Hall, nr Swanton Morley, Norfolk
January 1944 – September 1945

This special, and very secret, group was formed to combat the sophisticated defence systems employed by the Luftwaffe fighters. Initially, the main German defence weapon were Flak batteries supplemented by radar-guided searchlights that the Bf109D fighters used to attack the Allied bombers. This system was weather dependent and of no use in inclement weather or even the industrial haze over the Ruhr valley. Germany then proceeded to develop a radar guided system for their night fighters to find the Allied bombers in the night sky.

No. 100 (Bomber Support) Group was tasked with protecting the bomber force by using electronic and radar countermeasures to confuse the German defence system. By using air and ground radar, homing and jamming equipment, and newly developed navigational and radio aids the Group's bomber aircraft confused the enemies defence systems. During the Group's lifetime it investigated and used thirty-two different electronic jamming devices with names such as Airborne Cigar, Mandrel, Serrate, Carpet, and Lucero.

In addition, the Group's intruder nightfighter aircraft roamed the night skies over Europe in a deadly cat and mouse sortie to find and destroy the Luftwaffe nightfighters. The De Havilland Mosquitos claimed over 250 Luftwaffe aircraft shot down using homing devices such as the Serrate.

The thirteen squadrons were equipped with the Handley Page Halifax, Boeing Fortress I (Royal Air Force designation), Short Stirling, Consolidated Liberator, and Vickers Wellington for countermeasure duties and the Bristol Beaufighter and De Havilland Mosquito for intruder missions. The Group operated from eight airfields in North Norfolk with over 250 aircraft, over half being the De Havilland Mosquito. By the end of the war the Group had significantly reduced the effectiveness of the German nightfighter network. Its electronic warfare concept would now take on another role during the Cold War.

The combination of the Pathfinder's operations, the activities of No. 100 Group, the British advantage in radar, jamming, and Window techniques, combined with the intelligent attacking tactics, as well as the discipline and bravery of the RAF crews, have been remarkable. We had our severe problems in trying to defend Germany in the air.

Generalleutnant Adolf Galland, Luftwaffe

Operational sorties: 16,800 (Electronic Counter Measures and Serrate)

No. 6 (Training) Group

Formed: Abingdon, Berkshire 03 September 1939

Headquarters

Abingdon, Berkshire September 1939

This Group controlled fourteen squadrons responsible for the operational training of newly trained aircrew. Some of the aircraft which had been used as front line bombers during the war were assigned to these squadrons; these were war weary examples which left a lot to be desired as training aircraft. The aircraft types seconded to the squadrons were the Armstrong Whitworth Whitley, Vickers Wellington, Bristol Blenheim, Fairey Battle, Handley Page Hampden and the Avro Anson.

Initially these squadrons were assigned stations and then the squadrons were later designated Operational Training Units and during their lifetime they could change stations many times. For example, in 1939 Nos. 97 and 166 Squadrons were flying Armstrong Whitworth Whitley aircraft at Abingdon, Berkshire. In 1941 the squadrons became No. 10 Operational Training Unit and subsequently by 11 May 1942 were incorporated in No. 91 (Operational Training Unit) Group. There had been up to nine operational training units in No. 6 (Training) Group and six in No. 91 (Operational Training Unit) Group.

No. 7 (Training) Group

Formed: Bicester, Oxfordshire 15 July 1940

Headquarters

Bicester, Oxfordshire July 1940

Winslow Hall, Buckinghamshire September 1941

Grantham, Lincolnshire September 1944

By 1940 it was becoming evident that additional facilities were needed to cope with the increased need for training operational crews. No. 92 (Training) Group started with five Operational Training Units: Bristol Blenheims at Bicester, Oxfordshire, and Upwood, Cambridgeshire; and Handley Page Hampdens at Cottesmore, Cambridgeshire, Upper Heyford, Oxfordshire, and Finningley, South Yorkshire. The Group changed to the Vickers Wellington and Avro Manchester as the war advanced. The Group reverted to No. 7 (Training) Group in 1944 to control the growing number of heavy Conversion Units that previously had been under the control of the individual Bomber Groups.

Nos. 91, 92 & 93 (Operational Training Unit) Groups

91 formed: Abingdon, Berkshire 11 May 1942
Renumbered from No. 6 (Training) Group
92 formed: Winslow Hall, Buckinghamshire 14 May 1942
Renumbered from No. 7 (Training) Group
93 formed: Egginton Hall, Derbyshire 15 June 1942

For two and a half years the No. 93 Group supplemented bomber aircrew operational training until absorbed into Nos. 91 and 92 (Training) Groups in January 1945. It utilised Vickers Wellington aircraft at Finningley, South Yorkshire; Lichfield, Staffordshire; Bramcote, Warwickshire; Wymeswold, Leicestershire; Hixon, Staffordshire; Ossington, Nottinghamshire; and Peplow, Shropshire, with one Armstrong Whitworth Whitley Operational Training Unit, No. 81, at Whitchurch Heath, Shropshire.

Royal Air Force Wings

In the early years of the RAF, a wing commander commanded a flying wing, typically a group of three or four aircraft squadrons. The following are examples of wings associated with Bomber Command.

WING	STATION	YEARS	SQUADRONS
70	RAF Upper Heyford	1939/40	Nos. 18, 57
71	France	1939/40	Nos. 105, 114, 139, 150
75	France	1939/40	Nos. 88, 103, 208
76	France	1939/40	Nos. 12, 142, 226
79	RAF Watton	1939	Nos. 21, 82
80	RAF Radlett	1939/45	Electronic Counter Measures
82	RAF Wyton	1939	Nos. 114, 139
83	RAF Wattisham	1939	Nos. 107, 110

3

BOMBER COMMAND SQUADRONS

The following are examples of front-line Squadrons of Bomber Command based in Britain at some time from September 1939 to September 1945. Some of the squadrons were created in the First World War and are extant, a long history of active service. Some of the squadrons were created during the Second World War and ceased to exist either before the end of the war or shortly thereafter. Some returned to their commonwealth roots, Canada for example, at the end of the war, having served 'Mother England' with great distinction. Some of the squadrons came with previous illustrious histories with the Royal Flying Corps and some were short-lived, either created towards the end of the war or were transferred to another command, Coastal Command as an example, to carry on the offensive with a different set of challenges. Flexibility was demanded of the squadrons, they had to adapt quickly to new tactics as technology changed. The squadrons also had to adapt rapidly to new equipment, as can be seen by the squadron 'Primary Aircraft' list of No. 12 Squadron that flew the Fairey Battle in 1939, then the Vickers Wellington for two years, and finally the Avro Lancaster in 1942, all in the space of three years.

This same squadron, No. 12, returned from France in 1940 and was stationed at six different Stations for varying lengths of time in five years. The exigencies of war took its toll on resources. The squadron had to cope with changing station, changing aircraft, and changing crews due to casualties, prisoners of war, injuries, sickness, leave, tour expired, promotions, and transfers. There was only one answer to all of these demands: leadership. And the squadrons fortunately had that.

A 'main force' bomber squadron had a Wing Commander and Squadron Leaders in charge of the squadron flights. Famous names such as Guy Gibson and Leonard Cheshire immediately come to mind, although there were many Wing Commanders who distinguished themselves over the course of the war. Until mid-1943 the squadrons usually consisted of three flights A, B, and C. Following the expansion in squadron numbers in the summer of 1943, they were reduced to two flights, A and B. The new squadrons would be formed around a B or C flight taken from an experienced established squadron.

The pilot, the 'skipper', who was the acknowledged leader during flight operations, responsible for the effectiveness of the aircraft, the flight, and the squadron. There was a lot of rivalry over having the best bombing statistics and the greatest number of Primary Aircraft available in the individual squadrons for bombing raids, especially with squadrons sharing the same station and flying a similar type of aircraft.

A natural corollary to pride in one's squadron life was the comradeship experienced by the crews. I certainly enjoyed it as part of No. 414 (Electronic Warfare) Squadron, Royal Canadian Air Force during the Cold War of the 1970s. I can only imagine what the intensity of comradeship was like first of all among the individual crews, then among the flights, and finally among the members of the squadron during 'the best of times, the worst of times'. War brought previously unconnected people into an extended family of crews, flights, and squadrons.

Every victory and every loss was personally felt by the members of the squadron and other squadron's losses were felt through the monthly reports. Friends, relatives, and strangers were all united throughout the Bomber Command Groups' struggles to bring the war to a victorious end.

The squadron was the glamour end of Bomber Command, full of action, heroics, and living life to the full, circumstances permitting, carousing around the piano in the Mess or local pub. The less glamorous part of Bomber Command, but essential, was the work done by the headquarters and various group staffs connected to the squadrons only by telephone wires, often buried to protect them against bombing and sabotage.

Once again statistics given below are for general squadron comparison purposes only, as some are difficult to verify. The statistics cannot describe the extreme highs and lows of squadron life. The high of the successful mission, and surviving it, and the low of lost aircraft and missing crew. The squadron in peacetime is a tight-knit group of comrades, but in wartime it could be just fleeting moments of crew solidarity interrupted by loss over enemy territory, injury or death, which inevitably took it its toll on squadron morale.

For those having a personal interest in a particular squadron it is hoped the information below will assist in the quest.

No. 7 Squadron

Motto: 'By day and by night'

Wing Commander Charles Portal, later to become Marshal of the Royal Air Force, was the bomb aimer of the winning crew of the Laurence Minot memorial bombing trophy of 1927. Initially, the squadron trained crews to operational standard in No. 5 Group before it reformed as a Hampden bombing squadron. In 1940 the squadron was the first in Bomber Command that flew a four-engine bomber, the Short Stirling. In February 1941 the squadron's first raid with the Stirling was on the oil tanks at Rotterdam followed shortly after by its first raid on Berlin. In 1942 minelaying was added to its duties and in the summer it took part in the 1,000 Primary Aircraft bomber raids on Cologne, Essen, and Bremen. In August 1943 its Lancasters took part in the famous raid on the Peenemunde Army Research Centre.

Sorties: 5,060. Aircraft lost: 165

WARTIME STATIONS	PRIMARY AIRCRAFT	DATES
Doncaster, Yorkshire	Handley Page Hampden	April 1939 – April 1943
Finningley, Yorkshire	Avro Anson	March 1939 – April 1940
Upper Heyford, Oxfordshire	Short Stirling	August 1940 – August 1943
Leeming, Yorkshire	Avro Lancaster	July 1943 – September 1945
Oakington, Cambridgeshire		
Mepal, Cambridgeshire		

No. 9 Squadron

Motto: 'Throughout the night we fly'
Victoria Cross: Flight Sergeant George Thompson

At the outbreak of the war the squadron immediately took part in the raid on the German battleships at Brunsbuttel; a third of the aircraft failed to return. In August 1943 its Lancasters took part in the famous raid on the Peenemunde Army Research Centre. In November 1944, along with No. 617 Squadron, it attacked and destroyed the battleship *Tirpitz* using 12,000lb (5,443kg) Tallboy bombs.

Sorties: 5,828. Aircraft lost: 177

WARTIME STATIONS	PRIMARY AIRCRAFT	DATES
Honington, Suffolk	Vickers Wellington	February 1939 – August 1942
Waddington, Lincolnshire	Avro Lancaster	August 1942 – September 1945
Bardney, Lincolnshire		
Waddington, Lincolnshire		

No. 10 Squadron

Motto: 'To hit the mark'

In October 1939 the squadron dropped leaflets over Berlin. It became the first squadron to fly over the city during wartime. In March 1940 the squadron attacked the seaplane minelaying base at Hornum on the island of Sylt. This was followed by a raid in June on the Fiat Works in Turin, Italy, staging through Guernsey, Channel Islands, in immediate response to Italy's declaration of war. In May 1945 it was transferred to Transport Command.

Sorties: 6,233. Aircraft lost: 156

WARTIME STATIONS	PRIMARY AIRCRAFT	DATES
Dishforth, Yorkshire	Armstrong Whitworth Whitley	Early 1937 – December 1941
Leeming, Yorkshire	Handley Page Halifax	December 1941 – May 1945
Melbourne, Yorkshire		

No. 12 Squadron

Motto: 'Leads the field'
Victoria Cross: Flying Officer Donald Garland and Sergeant Thomas Gray

The squadron was part of the No. 76 Wing of the Advanced Air Striking Force in France. After it withdrew to England it attacked the German-held Channel ports. In November 1941 it led all the squadrons in No. 1 Group by flying thirty-one sorties and dropping fifty-five tons of bombs. In May 1942 it sent twenty-eight aircraft on the 1,000-bomber raid.

Sorties: 5,160. Aircraft lost: 171

WARTIME STATIONS	PRIMARY AIRCRAFT	DATES
France	Fairey Battle	September 1939 – November 1940
Finningley, Yorkshire	Vickers Wellington	November 1940 – November 1942
Binbrook, Lincolnshire	Avro Lancaster	November 1942 – September 1945
Thorney Island, Hampshire		
Eastchurch, Kent		
Binbrook, Lincolnshire		
Wickenby, Lincolnshire		

No. 13 Squadron

Motto: 'We assist by watching'

While at Odiham the squadron participated in Army exercises, diversionary intruder operations, and in June 1942 it contributed Blenheims to the 1,000-bomber raid on Bremen. In August it helped lay the smoke screen for the Dieppe raid. By November it had moved its operations to North Africa as part of the Tactical Bombing Force supporting the First Army.

Sorties: Unknown. Aircraft lost: Unknown

WARTIME STATIONS	PRIMARY AIRCRAFT	DATES
France	Bristol Blenheim	July 1941 – May 1943
Odiham, Hampshire	Martin Baltimore	December 1943 – October 1944
Algeria, Egypt, Italy	Douglas Boston	October 1944 – September 1945

No. 15 Squadron

Motto: 'Aim sure'

The day before the outbreak of war the Fairey Battles departed for France as part of the Advanced Air Striking Force with No. 12 Squadron. In May 1940 it flew its first bombing mission over Waalhaven

Airport, near Rotterdam. By December it was flying Wellingtons and attacked the dockyards at Bremen. It was the second squadron to receive Stirlings and at the end of April 1941 attacked Berlin. By autumn 1944 it was a specialised squadron using G-H airborne radar for daylight bombing through cloud. In April 1945 it bombed Bremen and dropped food supplies over Holland.

Sorties: 5,787. Aircraft lost: 166

WARTIME STATIONS	PRIMARY AIRCRAFT	DATES
France	Fairey Battle	September 1939 – December 1939
Wyton, Huntingdonshire	Bristol Blenheim	December 1939 – November 1940
Alconbury, Huntingdonshire	Vickers Wellington	November 1940 – May 1941
Bourn, Cambridgeshire	Short Stirling	April 1941 – December 1943
Mildenhall, Suffolk	Avro Lancaster	December 1943 – September 1945

No. 18 (Burma) Squadron

Motto: 'With courage and faith'

Victoria Cross: Acting Wing Commander Hugh Malcolm

At the outbreak of war the squadron went to France as part of the Royal Air Force Component of the British Expeditionary Force. It suffered heavy losses and withdrew to England in May 1940. On a raid to France it dropped a right artificial leg at St. Omer for the famous fighter ace Wing Commander Douglas Bader, who had been shot down. In 1942 it operated against European targets before returning to North Africa.

Sorties: 1,242. Aircraft lost: 40

WARTIME STATIONS	PRIMARY AIRCRAFT	DATES
France	Bristol Blenheim	May 1939 – May 1943
Lympne, Kent	Douglas Boston	May 1943 – September1945
Watton, Suffolk		
Gatwick, Surrey		

WARTIME STATIONS	PRIMARY AIRCRAFT	DATES
West Raynham, Norfolk		
Great Massingham, Norfolk		
Oulton, Norfolk		
Horsham St. Faith, Norfolk		
Wattisham, Suffolk		
Algeria, Tunisia, Sicily, Italy		

No. 21 Squadron

Motto: 'By strength we conquer'

Early in the war the squadron played an important role with No. 2 Group; it bombed the shipping in the English Channel and North Sea. From Malta in 1942 it attacked shipping in the Mediterranean Sea and land targets in North Africa. In December it took part in the daring raid on the Phillips radio factory at Eindhoven using its Ventura aircraft. Mainly employed as a night bomber squadron, it did however take part in the precision daylight raids on the Gestapo Headquarters at Aarhus in Denmark on 31 October 1944 and on 21 March 1945 the Gestapo Headquarters at Copenhagen, Denmark. It finished the war based on the mainland Europe.

Sorties: 1,419. Aircraft lost: 39

WARTIME STATIONS	PRIMARY AIRCRAFT	DATES
Watton, Norfolk	Bristol Blenheim	August 1938 – July 1942
Lossiemouth, Morayshire	Lockheed Ventura	Mid 1942 – September 1943
Malta	De Havilland Mosquito	September 1943 – September 1945
Bodney, Norfolk		
Methwold, Norfolk		
Oulton, Norfolk		
Hartford Bridge, Hampshire		
Sculthorpe, Norfolk		

WARTIME STATIONS	PRIMARY AIRCRAFT	DATES
Hunsdon, Hertfordshire		
Gravesend, Kent		
Thorney Island, Hampshire		
France, Belgium		

No. 35 (Madras Presidency) Squadron

Motto: 'We act with one accord'

Initially the squadron was a training unit and then it was the first squadron to introduce the Halifax into operational service. In March 1941 it flew its first raid on Le Havre in France. Unfortunately, one aircraft was misidentified and shot down by a friendly fighter. In July the first aircraft bombed Berlin; one was under the command of then Flying Officer G. L. Cheshire. In February 1942 it was one of the squadrons which attempted to stop the warships *Scharnhorst* and *Gneisenau* breaking out of Brest, France, to dash up the Channel to Germany. Two months later the squadron attacked, unsuccessfully, the *Tirpitz* in Trondheim Fjord. In May 1942 there eighteen Halifaxes from the squadron were in the 1,000-bomber raid on Cologne. In August 1942 the squadron was chosen to be one of the founding members of the Pathfinder Force. The Force's first raid was on Flensburg and it proved the new technique's effectiveness for target accuracy. In March 1943 No. 35 Squadron Halifaxes backed up Mosquitos using the new target finding aid, Oboe; the raid on Essen caused a lot of damage. The following months saw participation in the major operations against Le Creusot and Peenemunde. By 1944 the squadron was equipped with Lancasters and bombed coastal batteries during the D-Day landings on 6 June followed by gun batteries on Walcheren Island, part of the defence of Antwerp.

Sorties: 4,709. Aircraft lost: 127

WARTIME STATIONS	PRIMARY AIRCRAFT	DATES
Cranfield, Bedfordshire	Fairey Battle	September 1939 – February 1940
Bassingbourn, Cambridgeshire	Bristol Blenheim Handley Page Halifax	November 1939 – April 1940 November 1940 – March 1944

WARTIME STATIONS	PRIMARY AIRCRAFT	DATES
Upwood, Huntingdonshire	Avro Lancaster	March 1944 – September 1945
Boscombe Down, Wiltshire		
Leeming, Yorkshire		
Linton-on-Ouse, Yorkshire		
Graveley, Huntingdonshire		

No. 37 Squadron

Motto: 'Wise without eyes'

Within hours of the start of the war the squadron sent their Wellingtons to attack warships in the Heligoland area. In December the squadron had a disastrous operation; five out of six aircraft were shot down by the Luftwaffe Messerschmitt Bf109 and Bf110 fighters making beam attacks on the Wellington. Because of its limited field of fire the aircraft had no response to such attacks. Wellingtons were subsequently removed from all daylight attacks and extra armour plating was added.

Sorties: 688. Aircraft lost: 15

WARTIME STATIONS	PRIMARY AIRCRAFT	DATES
Feltwell, Norfolk	Vickers Wellington	September 1939 – December 1944
Malta, Egypt, Libya, Tunisia, Italy	Consolidated Liberator	October 1944 – September 1945

No. 38 Squadron

Motto: 'Before the dawn'

In December 1939 it flew its first raids against the German warships in the Heligoland area. These were no great success, but a fighter was shot down by a rear gunner who became aware of its presence by a bullet lodged in his harness. Attacks followed on invasion ports and Berlin before shipping out.

Sorties: 659. Aircraft lost: 7

WARTIME STATIONS	PRIMARY AIRCRAFT	DATES
Marham, Norfolk	Vickers Wellington	September 1939 – early 1942
Egypt		

No. 40 Squadron

Motto: 'To drive the enemy from the sky'

The squadron bombed targets in France, the Low Countries, and Germany prior to heading to the Middle East. In May and June 1940 it suffered heavy casualties and within eight days it lost two Commanding Officers.

Sorties: 1,250. Aircraft lost: 53

WARTIME STATIONS	PRIMARY AIRCRAFT	DATES
France, Egypt, Libya,	Fairey Battle	September 1939 – December 1939
Tunisia	Bristol Blenheim	December 1939 – November 1940
Wyton, Huntingdonshire	Vickers Wellington	November 1940 – March 1945
Alconbury, Huntingdonshire	Consolidated Liberator	March 1945 – September 1945

No. 44 (Rhodesia) Squadron

Motto: 'The King's thunderbolts are righteous'
Victoria Cross: Acting Squadron Leader John Nettleton

Its commander at the outbreak of war was Wing Commander J. N. Boothman of 1931 Schneider Trophy fame. The trophy was awarded annually (and later, biennially) to the winner of a race for seaplanes and flying boats. If a country won it three times within a certain time, it got to keep the trophy. The Schneider Trophy is now held at the Science Museum, South Kensington, London. Initial targets were North Sea sweeps, security patrols, and minelaying followed by invasion barges. In September 1941 the squadron included 'Rhodesia' in its title in recognition of the country's generous support to the war effort. About a quarter of the squadron's personnel were Rhodesian. Early in 1942 No. 44 was the first squadron to convert completely to the Lancaster. In a memorable daylight raid on 17 April along with No. 97 Squadron, the Lancasters flew low-level and attacked the M. A. N. Diesel factory at Augsburg, Southern Bavaria. This was followed by raids on ports, U-Boat shelters, Peenemunde, and Northern Italy

Sorties: 6,405. Aircraft lost: 192

WARTIME STATIONS	PRIMARY AIRCRAFT	DATES
Waddington, Lincolnshire	Handley Page Hampden	September 1939 – December 1941
Dunholme Lodge, Lincolnshire	Avro Lancaster	December 1941 – September 1945
Spilsby, Lincolnshire		
Mepal, Cambridgeshire		
Mildenhall, Suffolk		

No. 49 Squadron

Motto: 'Beware of the dog'
Victoria Cross: Acting Flight Lieutenant Roderick Learoyd

In April 1940 the squadron helped initiate the sea-mining campaign. In May, Nelles Timmerman, later an Air Commodore, was returning from an abortive mine laying mission in the Frisian Islands in a Hampden when he made Bomber Command history by engaging an Arado 196 floatplane with his front gun and driving it into the sea. He was awarded the D.S.O. In October 1942 it led a No. 5 Group dusk attack on the Schneider armament and locomotive works at Le Creusot. In June 1943 it took part in the first 'shuttle-bombing' raid; this was a tactic where bombers flew from their home base to bomb a first target, in this case Friedrichshafen, and continued to a different location (Algeria) where they were refuelled and rearmed. They then bombed a second target, La Spezia, on the return leg to their home base. In December 1944 the squadron attacked the Baltic Fleet at Gdynia and in March 1945 softened up the defences prior to the Army crossing the Rhine.

Sorties: 6,501. Aircraft lost: 163

WARTIME STATIONS	PRIMARY AIRCRAFT	DATES
Scampton, Lincolnshire	Handley Page Hampden	September 1939 – April 1942
Fiskerton, Lincolnshire	Avro Manchester	April 1942 – June 1942
Fulbeck, Lincolnshire	Avro Lancaster	June 1942 – September 1945
Syerston, Nottinghamshire		

No. 50 Squadron

Motto: 'Thus we keep faith'
Victoria Cross: Flying Officer Leslie Manser

The squadron participated in the first attack on a land-based target at Hornum on the island of Sylt. The squadron attacked the industrial area of Mannheim in the first area bombing attack of the war. In December 1941 it took part in a combined operation against the German-held Norwegian island of Vaagso; it dropped smoke bombs and attacked a gun battery. In 1942 it flew with No. 49 Squadron and attacked Le Creusot and flew the same shuttle-bombing mission described above. In 1944 it attacked the V-1 storage caves in the Loire valley and the dykes on the German-held Dutch island of Walcheren. In April 1945 its last operation was against the oil refinery at Vallo in Norway.

Sorties: 7,135. Aircraft lost: 176

WARTIME STATIONS	PRIMARY AIRCRAFT	DATES
Waddington, Lincolnshire	Handley Page Hampden	September 1939 – April 1942
Lindholme, Yorkshire	Avro Manchester	April 1942 – June 1942
Swinderby, Lincolnshire	Avro Lancaster	May 1942 – September 1945
Skellingthorpe, Lincolnshire		
Sturgate, Lincolnshire		

No. 51 Squadron

Motto: 'Swift and sure'

On the very first night of the war, 3 September 1939, the squadron's Whitleys dropped leaflets, a 'nickel' raid over Germany. In 1940 it shared in several firsts for Bomber Command: first attack on a land target, Hornum mine-laying seaplane base; the first big attack on the German mainland, Munchen-Gladbach; first attack on Italy, Fiat works at Turin; and the first area bombing attack, Mannheim. The squadron later participated in two notable successful paratrooper missions, targeting an aqueduct in Southern Italy and a Wurzburg radar installation near Le Havre. In May 1942 it was attached to Coastal Command for a period of time and then subsequently was transferred to Transport Command.

Sorties: 5,959. Aircraft lost: 158

WARTIME STATIONS	PRIMARY AIRCRAFT	DATES
Linton-on-Ouse, Yorkshire Dishforth, Yorkshire	Armstrong Whitworth Whitley	September 1939 – October 1942
Snaith, Yorkshire	Handley Page Halifax	November 1942 – May 1945
Leconfield, Yorkshire		

No. 57 Squadron

Motto: 'I change my body, not my spirit'

In June 1940, after the retreat from France, the squadron went to Northern Scotland and conducted anti-shipping sweeps over the North Sea. In October 1942 it contributed to the low-level attack on the Schneider works at Le Creusot. In 1943 the King and Queen visited the squadron. Among the targets in 1944 were the V-1 storage sites at St. Leu d'Esserent, Mondeville steel works at Caen, and the German Baltic Fleet at Gdynia. 1945 saw the destruction of the defences around Wesel prior to the Army crossing the Rhine.

Sorties: 5,151. Aircraft lost: 172

WARTIME STATIONS	PRIMARY AIRCRAFT	DATES
France	Bristol Blenheim	September 1939 – November 1940

WARTIME STATIONS	PRIMARY AIRCRAFT	DATES
Wyton, Huntingdonshire	Vickers Wellington	November 1940 – September 1942
Lossiemouth, Morayshire	Avro Lancaster	September 1942 – September 1945
Feltwell, Norfolk		
Scampton, Lincolnshire		
East Kirkby, Lincolnshire		

No. 58 Squadron

Motto: 'On the wings of the night'

On the very first night of the war the squadron's Whitleys dropped leaflets in conjunction with No. 51 Squadron on Germany. From October 1939 to February 1940 it was attached to Coastal Command, then returned to the night bombing offensive. Targets included the usual variety, from roads and railways to Channel ports and oil and petrol facilities. These continued with the first big attack on the German mainland, Munchen-Gladbach; the first attack on Italy, Fiat works at Turin; and the first attack on Berlin on 26 August 1940. In April 1942 the squadron was transferred to Coastal Command. (It converted to the Handley Page Halifax in January 1943.)

Sorties: 1,757. Aircraft losses: 49

WARTIME STATIONS*	PRIMARY AIRCRAFT	DATES
Linton-on-Ouse, Yorkshire Boscombe Down, Wiltshire	Armstrong Whitworth Whitley	September 1939 – early 1940

No. 61 Squadron

Motto: 'Thundering through the clear air'
Victoria Cross: Acting Flight Lieutenant William Reid

Flying with No. 5 Group in 1940 it shared in several firsts for Bomber Command: first attack on a land target, Hornum mine-laying seaplane base; the first big attack on the German mainland, Munchen-Gladbach; first attack on Berlin; and the raids on Le Creusot and Peenemunde. It also was part of the successful draining of the Dortmund-Ems and

Mitteland Canals. Four of its Lancasters were notable as they survived more than 100 operations. In the summer of 1942, it was loaned to Coastal Command; Flight Lieutenant P. R. Casement became the first Bomber Command crew to be credited with sinking a submarine.

Sorties: 6,082. Aircraft lost: 156

WARTIME STATIONS*	PRIMARY AIRCRAFT	DATES
Hemswell, Lincolnshire	Handley Page Hampden	September 1939 – October 1941
North Luffenham, Rutland	Avro Manchester	June 1941 – June 1942
Woolfox Lodge, Rutland	Avro Lancaster	April 1942 – September 1945
Syerston, Nottinghamshire		
Skellingthorpe, Lincolnshire		
Coningsby, Lincolnshire		
Skellingthorpe, Lincolnshire		
Sturgate, Lincolnshire		

No. 75 (New Zealand) Squadron

Motto: 'For ever and ever be strong'
Victoria Cross: Sergeant James Ward

Equipped with Wellingtons No. 75 was the first Commonwealth squadron to be formed in Bomber Command and took part in raids on Germany, Italy, and enemy occupied countries. The Stirling aircraft in 1942 took part in the Battle of the Ruhr and the devastation of Hamburg. A squadron Lancaster was the first British heavy bomber to land on French soil, a beach-head landing strip after the D-Day invasion. Medical attention was needed for the wounded flight engineer.

Sorties: 8,017. Aircraft lost: 193

WARTIME STATIONS	PRIMARY AIRCRAFT	DATES
Harwell, Berkshire	Vickers Wellington	September 1939 – October 1942
Feltwell, Norfolk	Short Stirling	November 1942 – April 1944

WARTIME STATIONS	PRIMARY AIRCRAFT	DATES
Mildenhall, Suffolk	Avro Lancaster	March 1944 – September 1945
Newmarket, Suffolk		
Mepal, Cambridgeshire		
Spilsby, Lincolnshire		

No. 76 Squadron

Motto: 'Resolute'

Initially designated as a training unit and subsequently an Operational Training Unit, the squadron became the second operator of the Halifax as part of No. 4 Group. Targets included the usual variety from road and railways to Channel ports, oil facilities and gun batteries. It made history on 10/11 April 1942 when it dropped the first 8,000lb (3,600kg) H. C. (High Capacity) bomb during a raid on Essen. It also took part in three raids on the German battleship *Tirpitz* and the heavy raid in 1943 on Peenemunde. In May 1945 it was transferred to Transport Command. From August 1942 to April 1943 the squadron was under Wing Commander G. L. Cheshire who would go on to become a Group Captain and retire with the following awards: VC, OM, DSO & Two Bars, and DFC.

Sorties: 5,123. Aircraft lost: 139

WARTIME STATIONS	PRIMARY AIRCRAFT	DATES
Upper Heyford, Oxfordshire	Handley Page Hampden	September 1939 – mid 1940
West Raynham, Norfolk	Avro Anson	September 1939 – April 1940
Linton-on-Ouse, Yorkshire	Handley Page Halifax	May 1941 – May 1945
Middleton St. George, County Durham		
Holme-on-Spalding Moor, Yorkshire		

No. 77 Squadron

Motto: 'To be, rather than seem'

Early in the war the squadron used its Whitleys to drop propaganda leaflets on the Ruhr, Vienna, Prague, and Warsaw. In 1940 it shared in several firsts for Bomber Command: first attack on a land target, Hornum minelaying seaplane base; the first big attack on the German mainland, Munchen-Gladbach; and first attack on Italy, the Fiat works at Turin. In 1941 it was with Coastal Command when it sank a U-Boat, *U-705*, in the Sea of Biscay. Following this the squadron returned to No. 4 Group and took part in 'Gardening' operations, mine laying, and was part of the massive uplift of petrol to an airport near Brussels, Belgium, for the Second Army. In May 1945 it was transferred to Transport Command.

Sorties: 5,379. Aircraft lost: 131

WARTIME STATIONS	PRIMARY AIRCRAFT	DATES
Driffield, Yorkshire	Armstrong Whitworth Whitley	September 1939 – October 1942
Linton-on-Ouse, Yorkshire	Handley Page Halifax	December 1942 – May 1945
Topcliffe, Yorkshire		
Leeming, Yorkshire		
Chivenor, Devon		
Elvington, Yorkshire		
Full Sutton, Yorkshire		

No. 78 Squadron

Motto: 'Nobody unprepared'

In February 1941 the squadron supplied Whitleys, along with No. 51 Squadron, for the paratrooper attack on the large aqueduct at Tragino, Italy. It participated in the historic 1,000-bomber raid on Cologne in May 1942, Peenemunde in August 1943, and the coastal gun battery at Mont Fleury in June 1944. In May 1945 the squadron was transferred to Transport Command.

Sorties: 6,237. Aircraft lost: 192

WARTIME STATIONS	PRIMARY AIRCRAFT	DATES
Dishforth, Yorkshire	Armstrong Whitworth Whitley	September 1939 – March 1942
Linton-on-Ouse, Yorkshire		

WARTIME STATIONS	PRIMARY AIRCRAFT	DATES
Middleton St. George, County Durham	Handley Page Halifax	March 1942 – May 1945
Croft, County Durham		
Breighton, Yorkshire		

No. 82 (United Provinces) Squadron

Motto: 'Over all things everywhere'

In the early part of the war the squadron, with No.2 Group, took part in the offensive campaign against shipping in the English Channel and the North Sea. The squadron sank the German submarine, *U-31*, on 11 March 1940. On 17 May 1940 twelve Blenheims were sent to attack German forces near Gembloux, Belgium; one Blenheim was shot down by anti-aircraft flak and the remaining aircraft were intercepted by Messerschmitt Bf 109s; ten more aircraft were shot down. Without the determination of the Commanding Officer, Wing Commander the Earl of Bandon, the squadron would have ceased to operate. He reformed it again within forty-eight hours to resume operations. Early in 1942 it was transferred to the India campaign.

Sorties: 1,436. Aircraft lost: 62

WARTIME STATIONS	PRIMARY AIRCRAFT	DATES
Watton, Norfolk	Bristol Blenheim	September 1939 – early 1942
India	Vultee Vengeance	August 1942 – July 1944
	De Havilland Mosquito	July 1944 – September 1945

No. 83 Squadron

Motto: 'Strike to defend'
Victoria Cross: Sergeant John Hannah

April 1940 saw the squadron in 'Gardening' operations; more than half was spent on mine laying that month. Along with No. 49 Squadron it attacked the aqueduct forming part of the Dortmund-Ems-Canal in August and in that same month attacked the battleships *Scharnhorst, Tirpitz,* and *von Scheer.* It used its Manchesters to drop its first 4,000 lb (1,814 kg) bombs on Germany. In August 1942 it joined the newly formed Pathfinder Force and its first role was in the operation which targeted Flensburg. To finish off the year, missions were flown to Genoa and Turin, Northern Italy. The first 250 lb (113 kg) Target Indicator bombs were dropped on Berlin in early 1943. The Battle of the Ruhr, Battle of Hamburg, and the Peenemunde raids were prominent in the rest of the year. In spring 1944 the squadron transferred to lead Group No. 5 with pathfinding duties. In June No. 617 Squadron dropped the 12,000 lb (5,443 kg) D.P. (Deep Penetration) bomb to block the Saumur Tunnel.

Sorties: 5,521. Aircraft lost: 143

WARTIME STATIONS	PRIMARY AIRCRAFT	DATES
Scampton, Lincolnshire	Handley Page Hampden	September 1939 – January 1942
Wyton, Huntingdonshire	Avro Manchester	January 1942 – June 1942
Coningsby, Lincolnshire	Avro Lancaster	May 1942 – September 1945

No. 88 (Hong Kong) Squadron

Motto: 'Be on your guard'

The squadron immediately went to France as part of the Advanced Air Striking Force with its Battles. On 20 September 1939 the squadron recorded the first air combat 'kill' of the war when a Battle shot down a Messerschmidt Bf109. The squadron returned to England in 1940 after some very heavy losses and after a short time with Blenheims was re-equipped with Douglas Bostons. It attacked gun emplacements during the Dieppe raid of August 1942 and attacked the 'Noball' (flying bomb) sites for the next two years. On D-Day it laid a smoke screen for the attacking troops.

Sorties: 655. Aircraft lost: 11

WARTIME STATIONS	PRIMARY AIRCRAFT	DATES
France	Fairey Battle	September 1939 – July 1941
Driffield, Yorkshire	Bristol Blenheim	July 1941 – November 1941
Sydenham, N. Ireland	Douglas Boston	October 1941 – April 1945

WARTIME STATIONS	PRIMARY AIRCRAFT	DATES
Swanton Morley		
Attlebridge, Norfolk		
Oulton, Norfolk		
Hartford Bridge, Hampshire		

No. 90 Squadron

Motto: 'Swift'

Initially it was a training squadron but in May 1941 it was reformed and accepted delivery of the first Boeing B-17 Flying Fortress aircraft from America. Its role was high altitude bombing and in July it attacked Wilhelmshaven from 30,000 feet (9,144 m). Changing to Short Stirlings the squadron made a significant contribution to the Battle of the Ruhr, the Battle of Hamburg, and the Peenemunde raids.

Sorties: 4,613. Aircraft lost: 86

WARTIME STATIONS	PRIMARY AIRCRAFT	DATES
Upwood, Huntingdonshire	Bristol Blenheim	September 1939 – April 1940
Watton, Norfolk	Boeing Fortress	May 1941 – February 1942
West Raynham, Norfolk	Short Stirling	November 1942 – June 1944
Polebrook, Northhamptonshire	Avro Lancaster	May 1944 – September 1945
Bottesford, Leicestershire		
Ridgewell, Essex		
Wratting Common, Cambridgeshire		
Tuddenham, Suffolk		

No. 97 (Straits Settlements) Squadron

Motto: 'Achieve your aim'

The squadron started life as a training squadron but after a very short time with Whitleys reformed with Manchesters and began operations against Fortress Europe. With Lancasters it attacked the M. A. N. Diesel engine works in Augsburg. It took part in the 1,000-bomber raids on Cologne, Bremen, and Essen. In the autumn it was part of the dusk attack on the Schneider Locomotive and armament works at Le Creusot. In April 1943 the squadron joined No. 8 Pathfinder Group and became a marker squadron. In June 1943 it marked/illuminated Freidrichshafen and Spezia for the first 'shuttle-bombing' raid.

Sorties: 3,934. Aircraft lost: 109

WARTIME STATIONS	PRIMARY AIRCRAFT	DATES
Abingdon, Berkshire	Armstrong Whitworth Whitley	September 1939 – May 1940
Driffield, Yorkshire		
Waddington, Lincolnshire	Avro Anson	September 1939 – July 1940
Coningsby, Lincolnshire	Avro Manchester	February 1941 – February 1942
Woodhall Spa, Lincolnshire	Avro Lancaster	January 1942 – September 1945
Bourn, Cambridgeshire		

No. 98 Squadron

Motto: 'Never failing'

The early days of the war was spent as a reserve squadron based in France in the spring of 1940. A tragedy struck the squadron as in the evacuation of France nearly 100 personnel perished onboard the SS *Lancastrian* when it was sunk in the English Channel; the survivors took weeks to reach home base. Reforming with Coastal Command it saw service in Iceland and reforming a second time with Mitchells it attacked the oil plants at Ghent in Belgium. In August 1943 it became part of the 2nd Tactical Air Force.

Sorties: 70. Aircraft losses: 2

WARTIME STATIONS	PRIMARY AIRCRAFT	DATES
Hucknall, Nottinghamshire	Fairey Battle	September 1939 – July 1940
Scampton, Lincolnshire	North American Mitchell	September 1942 – late 1945

WARTIME STATIONS	PRIMARY AIRCRAFT	DATES
Finningley, Yorkshire		
France		
Gatwick, Surrey		
West Raynham, Norfolk		
Foulsham, Norfolk		
Dunsfold, Surrey		
Swanton Morley, Norfolk		
Belgium		

No. 99 Squadron

Motto: 'Each tenacious'

The squadron started the war with aerial survey of the North Sea looking for German naval targets and Nickel missions. This was followed by steady bombing of naval targets, the *Scharnhorst* and *Gneisenau* included. In early 1942 the squadron moved to India.

Sorties: 1,786. Aircraft lost: 43

WARTIME STATIONS	PRIMARY AIRCRAFT	DATES
Newmarket, Cambridge	Vickers Wellington	September 1939 – August 1944
Waterbeach, Cambridge	Consolidated Liberator	September 1944 – September 1945
India, Cocos Islands		

No. 100 Squadron

Motto: 'Don't let anyone attack the hornet's nest'

After service overseas in Singapore and Java the squadron was reformed in England and by March 1943 was flying Avro Lancasters in missions against Berlin and Peenemunde. Its last mission was against the SS Barracks at Berchtesgaden. It had four Avro Lancasters that passed the 100 mission mark with one, ND458 'A-Able', surviving more than 120.

Sorties: 3,984. Aircraft lost: 92

WARTIME STATIONS	PRIMARY AIRCRAFT	DATES
Waltham, Lincolnshire	Avro Lancaster	January 1943 – September 1945
Elsham Wolds, Lincolnshire		

No. 101 Squadron

Motto: 'Mind over matter'

In July 1940 it made its first daylight attack on Germany but soon changed to night attacks against invasion barges in the English Channel and North Sea ports. By April 1941 it operated with Fighter Command's No. 11 Group as escorts to close the Straits of Dover to enemy shipping during daylight. In summer its Wellingtons took part in the 1,000-bomber raid on Cologne, Essen, and Bremen. Its Lancasters attacked Spezia and Milan in 1943, in addition to Peenemunde. In October it used 'Airborne Cigar' or 'ABC' for the first time. This radio counter-measure apparatus tracked the enemy's radio frequencies and jammed them. On New Year's Day 1944 the squadron attacked Berlin. During the D-Day landings the squadron jammed enemy wireless communications to prevent night fighters being directed against the airborne invasion forces. In April it attacked Berchtesgaden.

Sorties: 6,766. Aircraft lost: 171

WARTIME STATIONS	PRIMARY AIRCRAFT	DATES
West Raynham, Norfolk	Bristol Blenheim	September 1939 – May 1941
Oakington, Cambridge	Vickers Wellington	Early 1941 – October 1942
Bourn, Cambridge	Avro Lancaster	October 1942 – September 1945
Stradishall, Suffolk		
Holme-on-Spalding Moor, Yorkshire		
Ludford Magna, Lincolnshire		

No. 102 (Ceylon) Squadron

Motto: 'Attempt and achieve'

On the second night of the war the squadron's Whitleys were dropping leaflets on the Ruhr. In December it attacked Sylt. The night after Italy declared war seven Whitleys set out to an advanced base in the Channel Islands but due to weather and icing only one aircraft got to bomb the primary target, Turin. Group Captain G. L. Cheshire is associated with the squadron because as a Pilot Officer he brought his crippled Whitley back to home base after more than eight hours in the air. It took part in the three 1,000-bomber raids, the Battles of the Ruhr and Hamburg, and transported fuel to the petrol-starved Second Army in Belgium. In May 1945 the squadron was transferred to Transport Command.

Sorties: 6,106. Aircraft lost: 192

WARTIME STATIONS	PRIMARY AIRCRAFT	DATES
Driffield, Yorkshire	Armstrong Whitworth Whitley	September 1939 – February 1942
Leeming, Yorkshire	Handley Page Halifax	December 1941 – May 1945
Linton-on-Ouse, Yorkshire		
Topcliffe, Yorkshire		
Dalton, Yorkshire		
Pocklington, Yorkshire		

No. 103 Squadron

Motto: 'Touch me not'

Deployed to France as part of the Advanced Air Striking Force, its first mission was reconnaissance of the border near Lauterbourg. Initially day, and later night, bombing attacks followed including the Meure bridges and invasion ports. In 1943 it contributed twenty-four Lancasters to the approximately 600 aircraft that attacked Peenemunde, the German V-weapons experimental station. No. 103 squadron had the most distinguished Lancaster of all, ED888 'M2', that on retirement had logged 140 trips flying with Nos 103 and 576 Squadrons. Unfortunately, it was not preserved.

Sorties: 5,840. Aircraft lost: 179

WARTIME STATIONS	PRIMARY AIRCRAFT	DATES
France	Fairey Battle	September 1939 – October 1940
Abingdon, Berkshire	Vickers Wellington	October 1940 – July 1942
Honington, Suffolk	Handley Page Halifax	July 1942 – October 1942
Newton, Nottinghamshire	Avro Lancaster	October 1942 – September 1945
Elsham Wolds, Lincolnshire		

No. 104 Squadron

Motto: 'Strike hard'

At the outbreak of war it was a training squadron until it reformed as a Wellington medium-bomber squadron in 1941 with No. 4 Group and took part in the night bombing offensive against Fortress Europe. Shortly after it moved to the Middle East.

Sorties: 373. Aircraft lost: 13

WARTIME STATIONS	PRIMARY AIRCRAFT	DATES
Bassingbourn, Cambridge	Bristol Blenheim	September 1939 – April 1940
Bicester, Oxfordshire	Avro Anson	May 1939 – April 1940
Driffield, Yorkshire	Vickers Wellington	April 1941 – February 1945
Malta, Egypt, Libya	Consolidated Liberator	February 1945 – September 1945
Tunisia, Italy		

No. 105 Squadron

Motto: 'Valiant in battles'

Victoria Cross: Acting Wing Commander Hughie Edwards DFC

The squadron was sent to France as part of the Advanced Air Striking Force and bombed the Meuse bridges to try and stop the advancing

German army. Rearmed with Blenheims in July 1940 it served with No. 2 Group and attacked targets on the edge of Germany, France, and the Low Countries. Things changed drastically for the squadron when they received the Mosquito aircraft and could make fast daring daylight raids to such targets as the Gestapo headquarters in Oslo, Burmeister and Wain Diesel engine works in Copenhagen, and the graphic attack on the radio broadcasting station in Berlin. Field Marshal Goering was unable to deliver a programmed propaganda speech for over an hour until alternative arrangements were made. In 1943 their Mosquitos were equipped with 'Oboe', a British aerial blind bombing system based on radio transponder technology, and the squadron joined the Pathfinder Force for the remainder of the war.

Sorties: 6,187. Aircraft lost: 58

WARTIME STATIONS	PRIMARY AIRCRAFT	DATES
France	Fairey Battle	September 1939 – May 1940
Honington, Suffolk	Bristol Blenheim	June 1940 – December 1941
Watton, Norfolk	De Havilland Mosquito	November 1941 – September 1945
Swanton Morley, Norfolk		
Horsham St. Faith, Norfolk		
Marham, Norfolk		
Bourn, Cambridge		
Upwood, Huntingdonshire		

No. 106 Squadron

Motto: 'For freedom'

Victoria Cross: Sergeant Norman Jackson

Until 1941 the squadron was in a training role flying Hampdens. The Manchester heralded a change to front line status with night bombing operations. Some of its Manchesters took part in the 1,000-bomber raids on Cologne, Essen, and Bremen. In October 1942 the squadron contributed ten Lancasters to the epic raid on Le Creusot and the subsidiary raid on Montchanin flown by Wing Commander Guy Gibson who was Commanding Officer at the time. In 1943 it was involved in the 'shuttle-bombing' of Freidrichshafen and Spezia. In 1944 operations were conducted against the V-1 storage caves at St. Leu d'Esserent and the German Baltic Fleet at Gdynia. In 1945 it attacked the oil refinery at Vallo, Norway.

Sorties: 5,745. Aircraft lost: 169

WARTIME STATIONS	PRIMARY AIRCRAFT	DATES
Cottesmore, Rutland	Handley Page Hampden	September 1939 – March 1942
Finningley, Yorkshire	Avro Manchester	February 1942 – June 1942
Coningsby, Lincolnshire	Avro Lancaster	May 1942 – September 1945
Syerston, Nottinghamshire		
Metheringham, Lincolnshire		

No.107 Squadron

Motto: 'We shall be there'

The squadron's first operation was against the German warships anchored at Wilhelmshaven. Subsequent raids were on the power stations at Knapsack and Quadrath power stations near Cologne, the combined raid on Dieppe in August 1942, and the low-level raid on the Philips radio and valve factory in December 1942. In the closing stages of the European war it operated from France and Belgium.

Sorties: 1,599. Aircraft lost: 84

WARTIME STATIONS	PRIMARY AIRCRAFT	DATES
Wattisham, Suffolk	Bristol Blenheim	September 1939 – January 1942
Leuchars, Fifeshire	Douglas Boston	January 1942 – January 1944
Great Massingham, Norfolk	De Havilland Mosquito	February 1944 – September 1945

WARTIME STATIONS	PRIMARY AIRCRAFT	DATES
Hartford Bridge, Hampshire		
Lasham, Hampshire		
France, Belgium		

No. 109 Squadron

Motto: 'The first of the legion'
Victoria Cross: Acting Squadron Leader Robert Palmer

In 1940 the squadron was formed from the Wireless Intelligence Development Unit and was involved with radio countermeasures and the blind bombing aid, Oboe, flying the Anson and Wellington. It moved to Royal Air Force Wyton to become one of the original units of the Pathfinder Force in 1942 and converted to Mosquitos. It made history on 20/21 December 1942 when it flew the first Oboe mission over enemy territory. It made history again when it marked Dusseldorf for a raid of heavy bombers. It was joined in mid-1943 by No. 105 Squadron in friendly rivalry on the Pathfinder Force. One of the squadron's most significant raids was when eight of its Mosquitos led the bomber force in a devastating assault on Essen, which was the start of the Battle of the Ruhr. One of its Mosquitos dropped the last bomb on Berlin on 21 April 1945.

Sorties: 5,421. Aircraft lost: 18

WARTIME STATIONS	PRIMARY AIRCRAFT	DATES
Wyton, Huntingdonshire	De Havilland Mosquito	December 1942 – September 1945
Marham, Norfolk		
Little Staughton, Huntingdonshire		

No. 110 (Hyderabad) Squadron

Motto: 'I neither fear nor despise'

On the 4 September 1939 the squadron led the first bombing raid of the war from the civilian airport at Ipswich, Suffolk, to attack the German warships at Wilhelmshaven. It departed for India in early 1942.

Sorties: 1,402. Aircraft lost: 38

WARTIME STATIONS	PRIMARY AIRCRAFT	DATES
Wattisham, Suffolk	Bristol Blenheim	September 1939 – June 1942
India	Vultee Vengeance	October 1942 – January 1945
	De Havilland Mosquito	November 1944 – September 1945

No. 114 (Hong Kong) Squadron

Motto: 'With speed I strike'

Formed at Wyton, the squadron was sent to France for reconnaissance missions initially, which changed quickly to bombing troop movements. Back in England in July 1940 it bombed Channel ports and targets in enemy-occupied Europe. In March 1941 it was loaned to Coastal Command. In August it attacked the power stations at Cologne and in December, operating from Scotland, it attacked the airport at Herdla, Norway. During the 1,000-bomber raid on Cologne it provided diversionary raids on airfields such as Bonn, Twente, and Leeuwarden. In November 1942 the squadron left for North Africa.

Sorties: 731. Aircraft lost: 39

WARTIME STATIONS	PRIMARY AIRCRAFT	DATES
Wyton, Huntingdonshire	Bristol Blenheim	September 1939 – March 1943
France	Douglas Bolton	March 1943 – September 1945
Wattisham, Suffolk		
Horsham St. Faith, Norfolk		
Oulton, Norfolk		
Thornaby-on-Tees, Yorkshire		
Leuchars, Fife		
West Raynham, Norfolk		
Algeria, Tunisia, Sicily		
Italy		

No. 115 Squadron

Motto: 'Despite the elements'

In April 1940 while on loan to Coastal Command at Leuchars, Fife, the squadron bombed the enemy-held Norwegian airport of Stavanger/Sola. It also was involved in extensive mine laying activities. In August 1941 it undertook the trials for 'Gee', the first radar navigational bombing aid. As a result of these trials Gee was put into full production for Bomber Command.

Sorties: 7,753. Aircraft lost: 208

WARTIME STATIONS	PRIMARY AIRCRAFT	DATES
Marham, Norfolk	Vickers Wellington	September 1939 – March 1943
Mildenhall, Suffolk	Avro Lancaster	March 1943 – September 1945
East Wretham, Norfolk		
Little Snoring, Norfolk		
Witchford, Cambridge		

No. 128 Squadron

Motto: 'Like a thunderbolt'

The squadron reformed as a light-bomber squadron of No. 8 (Pathfinder) Group in September 1944. It was part of the Fast Night Striking Force and carried out nuisance raids on important industrial and political centres. These included Berlin (on sixty-five nights), Frankfurt, Hamburg, and Cologne. On New Year's Day 1945 it 'skip-bombed' the tunnels in the Coblenz region of Germany.

Sorties: 1,531. Aircraft lost: 2

WARTIME STATIONS	PRIMARY AIRCRAFT	DATES
Wyton, Huntingdonshire	De Havilland Mosquito	September 1944 – September 1945
Warboys, Huntingdonshire		

No. 138 Squadron

Motto: 'For freedom'

Prior to joining Bomber Command in March 1945, the squadron was designated 'Special Operations Executive', whose operation was to promote sabotage against the enemy. The squadron, which started out as a flight but grew too big, did this by using Westland Lysander aircraft and dropping or collecting agents and important persons behind enemy lines. The squadron was equipped with Lancasters and managed to get in some pure bombing missions before war's end.

Sorties: 105 (Bomber); 2,578 (Special Operations). Aircraft lost: 70

WARTIME STATIONS*	PRIMARY AIRCRAFT	DATES
Tuddenham, Suffolk	Avro Lancaster	March 1945 – September 1945

No. 139 (Jamaica) Squadron

Motto: 'We destroy at will'

The squadron Blenheims flew the first mission that crossed the German frontier to reconnoitre and photograph the German Fleet on 3 September 1939. Pilot Flying Officer A. McPherson was awarded a Distinguished Flying Cross. Returning to England the squadron attacked fringe targets in North West Europe and invasion ports. A Jamaican newspaper started a fund to help Britain buy bombers; by 1941 it had donated enough money to buy twelve Blenheims. This was the start of the 'Bombers for Britain' Fund to which many other countries subsequently donated. Towards the end of 1942 it received Mosquitos and, along with No. 103 Squadron, made many daring lightning-fast daylight raids into the heart of Germany. By 1943 it had changed to night bombing when it joined the Pathfinder Force. It was involved with electronic countermeasures using strips of foil, 'window', to confuse the enemy's radar. By 1944 it had become equipped with 'H2S', a new ground reading radar system, and marked the well-known targets and others such as Duisberg and Lubeck. In early 1945 it made thirty-six attacks on Berlin in just over a month; the end was nigh.

Sorties: 5,544. Aircraft lost: 70

WARTIME STATIONS	PRIMARY AIRCRAFT	DATES
Wyton, Huntingdonshire	Bristol Blenheim	September 1939 – December 1941

WARTIME STATIONS	PRIMARY AIRCRAFT	DATES
France	De Havilland Mosquito	late 1942 – September 1945
West Raynham, Norfolk		
Horsham St. Faith, Norfolk		
Oulton, Norfolk		
Marham, Norfolk		
Upwood, Huntingdonshire		

No. 141 Squadron

Motto: 'We slay by night'

The squadron started the war as a day fighter squadron based in Scotland. In April 1943 it moved to Wittering and flew Beaufighter night intruder missions in support of Bomber Command. It later re-equipped with Mosquitos and joined No. 100 Group, Bomber Command's Support Group. The Beaufighter saw limited operations with the Support Group.

Sorties: 1,214. Aircraft lost: 11

WARTIME STATIONS	PRIMARY AIRCRAFT	DATES
Wittering, Cambridgeshire	De Havilland Mosquito	October 1943 – September 1945
West Raynham, Norfolk	Bristol Beaufighter	December 1943 – July 1945
Little Snoring, Norfolk		

No. 142 Squadron

Motto: 'Determination'

In the early months of the war it served with the Advanced Air Striking Force in France. It had the distinction of being the first squadron to bomb the enemy as the German army advanced into the Low Countries. On withdrawing to England it converted to Wellingtons and took part in the night bombing offensive. In December 1942 it relocated to North Africa. Disbanded in Italy in 1944, it returned to England to become a Mosquito light-bomber unit of the No. 8 Pathfinder Light Night Striking Force.

Sorties: 2,231. Aircraft lost: 53

WARTIME STATIONS*	PRIMARY AIRCRAFT	DATES
France	Fairey Battle	September 1939 – November 1940
Waddington, Lincolnshire	Vickers Wellington	November 1940 – October 1944
Eastchurch, Kent	De Havilland Mosquito	October 1944 – September 1945
Binbrook, Lincolnshire		
Waltham, Lincolnshire		
Kirmington, Lincolnshire		
Algeria, Tunisia, Italy		
Gransden Lodge, Bedfordshire		

No. 144 Squadron

Motto: "Who shall stop us'

Its first mission was to locate and attack enemy vessels in the North Sea. Unfortunately, a five-plane section led by the Commanding Officer in the area of the Heligoland disappeared and was never heard from again. Early in 1940 it dropped leaflets on Hamburg and took part in the first attack on a German land target, the seaplane base at Hornum. It continued night-bombing attacks, mine laying tasks, and night intruder operations against searchlight installations. In November 1941 it set on fire a large merchantman ship off the Frisian Islands. It transferred to Coastal Command in April 1942.

Sorties: 2,045. Aircraft lost: 62

WARTIME STATIONS	PRIMARY AIRCRAFT	DATES
Hemswell, Lincolnshire	Handley Page Hampden	September 1939 – April 1942
North Luffenham, Rutland		

No. 149 (East India) Squadron

Motto: 'Strong by night'

Victoria Cross: Flight Sergeant Rawdon Middleton

Along with No. 9 Squadron it shared in the second mission of the war with a raid on German warships at Brunsbuttel. It played a significant role in the early offensive against Germany, Italy, and enemy-held territories, the 1,000-bomber raids, the Battles of the Ruhr and Hamburg, Peenemunde, and in addition dropped supplies to the French Resistance.

Sorties: 5,905. Aircraft lost: 131

WARTIME STATIONS*	PRIMARY AIRCRAFT	DATES
Mildenhall, Suffolk	Vickers Wellington	September 1939 – December 1941
Lakenheath, Suffolk	Short Stirling	November 1941 – September 1944
Methwold, Norfolk	Avro Lancaster	August 1944 – September 1945

No. 150 Squadron

Motto: 'Always ahead'

The squadron served with the Advanced Air Striking Force in France and was one of the Battle squadrons which attacked the Meuse bridges to slow the advancing German army. It returned to England in 1940 and continued the strategic night-bombing campaign. In December 1942 it relocated to North Africa and disbanded in Italy. It reformed in England with Lancasters and continued the offensive.

Sorties: 2,557. Aircraft lost: 56

WARTIME STATIONS	PRIMARY AIRCRAFT	DATES
France	Fairey Battle	September 1939 – September 1940
Stradishall, Suffolk	Vickers Wellington	October 1940 – October 1944
Newton, Nottinghamshire	Avro Lancaster	November 1944 – September 1945
Snaith, Yorkshire		

WARTIME STATIONS	PRIMARY AIRCRAFT	DATES
Kirmington, Lincolnshire		
Algeria, Tunisia, Italy		
Fiskerton, Lincolnshire		
Hemswell, Lincolnshire		

No. 153 Squadron

Motto: 'Seeing by night'

After service with Beaufighters in Northern Ireland and Africa the squadron reformed in Bomber Command with Lancasters in October 1944. Its first raid with No. 1 Group was to Emmerich, Germany, escorted by Spitfires.

Sorties: 1,041, Aircraft lost: 22

WARTIME STATIONS*	PRIMARY AIRCRAFT	DATES
Kirmington, Lincolnshire	Avro Lancaster	October 1944 – September 1945
Scampton, Lincolnshire		

No. 156 Squadron

Motto: 'We light the way'

In February 1942 the squadron was re-founded as a medium-bomber squadron operating Wellingtons. In August it was one of the four squadrons to form the Pathfinder Force. It marked targets with incendiary and flares to provide more accurate bombing for the main bombing stream. It finished by marking the Drop Zones at Rotterdam and repatriating prisoners of war.

Sorties: 4,584. Aircraft lost: 143

WARTIME STATIONS	PRIMARY AIRCRAFT	DATES
Alconbury, Huntingdonshire	Vickers Wellington	February 1942 – January 1943
Warboys, Huntingdonshire	Avro Lancaster	January 1943 – September 1945
Upwood, Huntingdonshire		
Wyton, Huntingdonshire		

No. 158 Squadron

Motto: 'Strength in unity'

The squadron was listed in February 1942 as part of No. 4 Group. Initially it flew Wellingtons followed by Halifaxes. The squadron attacked major naval and industrial targets, was active in mine laying, and took part in the first 1,000-aircraft bombing raid. In May 1945 the squadron was transferred to Transport Command.

Sorties: 5,368. Aircraft lost: 159

WARTIME STATIONS	PRIMARY AIRCRAFT	DATES
Driffield, Yorkshire	Vickers Wellington	February 1942 – June 1942
East Moor, Yorkshire	Handley Page Halifax	June 1942 – May 1945
Rufforth, Yorkshire		
Lissett, Yorkshire		

No. 159 Squadron

Motto: 'Whither not? When not?'

The squadron was formed in January 1942 with the Liberator heavy bomber and was immediately transferred to the Middle East, to Palestine and then to India. The first operation against the Japanese was on 17 November 1942, and during the rest of the war, the squadron flew mine-laying, bombing, and reconnaissance missions

Sorties: 0 Aircraft lost: 0 (European Operations)

WARTIME STATIONS	PRIMARY AIRCRAFT	DATES
Molesworth, Huntingdonshire	Consolidated Liberator	Early 1942 – September 1945
Egypt, India		

No. 160 Squadron

Motto: 'We seek and strike'

Similar to No. 159 Squadron it was formed in January 1942 with the Liberator heavy bomber and was immediately transferred to India.

Sorties: 0 Aircraft Lost: 0 (European Operations)

WARTIME STATIONS	PRIMARY AIRCRAFT	DATES
Thurleigh, Bedfordshire	Consolidated Liberator	Early 1942 – January 1943
India		

No. 162 Squadron

Motto: 'One time, one purpose'

The squadron re-formed as a member of No. 8 Pathfinder Group in December 1944. It was classified initially as part of the Light Night Striking Force and was in the transition to becoming the second 'H2S' marking squadron, the first being No. 139 Squadron. It had done much of the marking for the thirty-six raids on Berlin.

Sorties: 913. Aircraft losses: 1

WARTIME STATIONS	PRIMARY AIRCRAFT	DATES
Bourn, Cambridgeshire	De Havilland Mosquito	December 1944 – July 1945

No. 163 Squadron

Motto: No badge authorised

The squadron re-formed in January 1945 in No. 8 (Pathfinder) Group's Light Night Striking Force. It was principally engaged in nuisance raids on industrial targets and Berlin; in March it visited the city twenty-four times and sometimes twice in one night.

Sorties: 636. Aircraft lost: 3

WARTIME STATIONS	PRIMARY AIRCRAFT	DATES
Wyton, Huntingdonshire	De Havilland Mosquito	January 1945 – August 1945

No. 166 Squadron

Motto: 'Tenacity'

Initially a training squadron, it merged with No. 97 Squadron to form No. 10 Operational Training Unit. It re-formed in January 1943 playing an active part in mine laying, 'Gardening', and participated in regular night sorties with No. 1 Group. Its first operation was to Lorient shortly after forming in January 1943.

Sorties: 5,068. Aircraft lost: 153

WARTIME STATIONS	PRIMARY AIRCRAFT	DATES
Abingdon, Berkshire	Armstrong Whitworth Whitley	September 1939 – April 1940
Kirmington, Lincolnshire	Vickers Wellington	January 1943 – September 1943
	Avro Lancaster	September 1943 – September 1945

No. 170 Squadron

Motto: 'To see (and) not be seen'

Originally an army co-operation squadron, it re-formed as a heavy-bomber squadron from 'C' Flight of No. 625 Squadron and took part in many major raids. On its first mission twelve Lancasters bombed Stuttgart and it ended its service by dropping food supplies to the Netherlands and transporting troops back home.

Sorties: 980. Aircraft lost: 13

WARTIME STATIONS	PRIMARY AIRCRAFT	DATES
Kelstern, Lincolnshire	Avro Lancaster	October 1944 – September 1945
Dunholme Lodge, Lincolnshire		
Hemswell, Licolnshire		

No. 180 Squadron

Motto: 'Agreeable in manner, forceful in act'

The squadron was formed as a light bomber squadron in September 1942 flying Mitchells. It flew its first operational mission in January 1943 attacking oil targets in the enemy-held Ghent in Belgium. In August 1943 it transferred to the 2nd Tactical Air Force.

Sorties: 151. Aircraft lost: 4

WARTIME STATIONS	PRIMARY AIRCRAFT	DATES
West Raynham, Norfolk	North American Mitchell	September 1942 – September 1945
Foulsham, Norfolk		
Dunsfold, Surrey		
Belgium, Germany		

No. 186 Squadron

Motto: No badge authorised

Initially an army support squadron, it re-formed from No. 90 Squadron's 'C' Flight as a heavy-bomber squadron flying Lancasters in October 1944 as part of No. 3 Group. The squadron's first raid was an attack on Bonn on 18 October.

Sorties: 1,254. Aircraft lost: 8

WARTIME STATIONS	PRIMARY AIRCRAFT	DATES
Tuddenham, Suffolk	Avro Lancaster	October 1944 – July 1945
Stradishall, Suffolk		

No. 189 Squadron

Motto: No badge authorised

The squadron was formed late in the war as a heavy-bomber squadron. It flew with No. 5 Group. Its first mission was to bomb Homberg, a coal deposits area in Central Germany.

Sorties: 1,254. Aircraft lost: 8

WARTIME STATIONS	PRIMARY AIRCRAFT	DATES
Bardney, Lincolnshire	Avro Lancaster	October 1944 – September 1945
Fulbeck, Lincolnshire		

No. 195 Squadron

Motto: 'Strong by speed'

Originally an army support squadron, it re-formed in 1944 as a heavy-bomber squadron. On its first mission ten Lancasters bombed Leverkusen, which is close to Cologne.

Sorties: 1,384 Aircraft Lost: 14

WARTIME STATIONS	PRIMARY AIRCRAFT	DATES
Witchford, Cambridgeshire	Avro Lancaster	October 1944 – August 1945
Wratting Common, Cambridgeshire		

No. 196 Squadron

Motto: 'Thus we keep faith'

The squadron was formed as a night bomber squadron and made many raids on enemy ports, took part in 'Gardening', and attacked industrial centres. Its first mission was to Lorient, a seaport in Brittany, France. In December 1943 it was transferred to the Allied Expeditionary Force, No. 38 Group, to serve as a glider-tug, to train for D-Day invasion and transport roles.

Sorties: 683. Aircraft lost: 24

WARTIME STATIONS	PRIMARY AIRCRAFT	DATES
Driffield, Yorkshire	Vickers Wellington	December 1942 – July 1943
Leconfield, Yorkshire	Short Stirling	July 1943 – November 1943
Witchford, Cambridgeshire		
Leicester East, Leicestershire		

No. 199 Squadron

Motto: 'Let tyrants tremble'

The squadron was formed as a bomber squadron in No. 3 Group and in December 1942 its first mission was to attack Mannheim on the Rhine

River. It was involved in regular bombing and mine laying missions until May 1944 when it joined No. 100 Group. It subsequently was employed on radio counter-measures operations, as 'Window' and 'Mandrel' patrols. Window is tin foil released to confuse radar and Mandrel is a radar site jammer.

Sorties: 2,863. Aircraft lost: 32

WARTIME STATIONS	PRIMARY AIRCRAFT	DATES
Blyton, Lincolnshire	Vickers Wellington	November 1942 – June 1943
Ingham, Lincolnshire	Short Stirling	July 1943 – March 1945
Lakenheath, Suffolk	Handley Page Halifax	February 1945 – July 1945
North Creake, Norfolk		

No. 207 Squadron

Motto: 'Always prepared'

Initially a training squadron, it was re-formed at Waddington especially to introduce the Manchester to operational service. In February 1941 the Manchesters attacked a cruiser at Brest and later attacked the warships *Scharnhorst* and *Gneisenau* when they dashed in daylight from Brest to Germany. The Rolls-Royce Vulture engines in the Manchester were not reliable and the Manchesters were exchanged for Lancasters. The squadron ranged far and wide for targets in Poland and Italy and raids were sometimes very costly in aircraft and personnel. In March 1944 the squadron lost two Commanding Officers in raids on Dusseldorf and Frankfurt.

Sorties: 4,563. Aircraft lost: 148

WARTIME STATIONS	PRIMARY AIRCRAFT	DATES
Cranfield, Bedfordshire	Fairey Battle	September 1939 – April 1940
Cottesmore, Rutland	Avro Anson	September 1939 – April 1940
Waddington, Lincolnshire	Avro Manchester	November 1940 – March 1942
Bottesford, Leicestershire	Handley Page Hampden	July 1941 – August 1941

WARTIME STATIONS	PRIMARY AIRCRAFT	DATES
Langar, Nottinghamshire	Avro Lancaster	March 1942 – September 1945
Spilsby, Lincolnshire		

No. 214 (Federated Malay States) Squadron

Motto: 'Avenging in the shadow'

The squadron flew Wellingtons and Stirlings in No. 3 Group against naval and industrial targets in Europe. In January 1944 it transferred to No. 100 Group flying the Boeing Fortress to detect and jam the enemy radio and radar equipment. In May 1945 the squadron was disbanded in England and its number transferred to a Liberator bomber squadron in Italy.

Sorties: 4,189. Aircraft lost: 112

WARTIME STATIONS	PRIMARY AIRCRAFT	DATES
Methwold, Norfolk	Vickers Wellington	September 1939 – April 1942
Stradishall, Suffolk	Short Stirling	April 1942 – January 1944
Honington, Suffolk	Boeing Fortress	January 1944 – July 1945
Chedburgh, Suffolk	Consolidated Liberator	July 1945 – September 1945
Downham Market, Norfolk		
Sculthorpe, Norfolk		
Oulton, Norfolk		
Italy, Palestine		

No. 215 Squadron

Motto: 'Arise, night is at hand'

The squadron flew Ansons and Wellingtons at the outbreak of war and in April 1940 merged with Station Headquarters to form No. 11 Operational Training Unit. In December 1941 it re-formed as a bomber unit and went to India.

WARTIME STATIONS	PRIMARY AIRCRAFT	DATES
Bassingbourn, Cambridge	Avro Anson	1940
Honington, Suffolk	Vickers Wellington	September 1939 – May 1940
Newmarket, Suffolk	Vickers Wellington	March 1942 – mid 1944
Stradishall, Suffolk	Consolidated Liberator	August 1944 – April 1945
India		

No. 218 (Gold Coast) Squadron

Motto: 'In time'

Victoria Cross: Flight Sergeant Arthur Aaron

In September 1939 the squadron flew Battles in France on reconnaissance and leaflet dropping missions. Up until June 1940 it was bombing the enemy's lines of communication and troop movements before retreating to Mildenhall where it was re-equipped with Blenheims. Five months later it was flying Wellingtons on long-range missions. The targets ranged from industrial centres to railways, V-weapon sites, Channel ports and gun batteries. On Its last mission eighteen Lancasters attacked the marshalling yards at Bad Oldesloe.

Sorties: 5,302. Aircraft lost: 130

WARTIME STATIONS	PRIMARY AIRCRAFT	DATES
France	Fairey Battle	September 1939 – May 1940
Mildenhall, Suffolk	Bristol Blenheim	June 1940 – November 1940
Oakington, Cambridge	Vickers Wellington	November 1940 – February 1942
Marham, Norfolk	Short Stirling	January 1942 – August 1944
Downham Market, Norfolk	Avro Lancaster	August 1944 – August 1945
Woolfox Lodge, Rutland		

WARTIME STATIONS	PRIMARY AIRCRAFT	DATES
Methwold, Norfolk		
Chedburgh, Norfolk		

No. 223 Squadron

Motto: 'Wings defend Africa'

After extensive service overseas in East and North Africa the squadron was repatriated to Oulton to fly bomber support missions with No. 100 Group. It flew specially modified Liberators and Fortresses in the counter-measures war. It disbanded in July 1945.

Sorties: 625. Aircraft lost: 3

WARTIME STATIONS	PRIMARY AIRCRAFT	DATES
Sudan, Egypt, Libya	Vickers Wellesley	September 1939 – April 1941
Tunisia, Italy	Martin Maryland	May 1941 – April 1942
Oulton, Norfolk	Douglas Boston	December 1942 – early 1943
	Martin Baltimore	January 1942 – August 1944
	Consolidated Liberator	August 1944 – June 1945
	Boeing Fortress	April 1945 – July 1945

No. 226 Squadron

Motto: 'For country not for self'

Its Fairey Battles operated out of Rheims as part of the Advanced Air Striking Force, bombing targets in an attempt to slow the enemy's advance through Belgium and France. After returning to Britain it deployed to Sydenham, Northern Ireland, to fly patrols along the coast to prevent enemy agents coming ashore. Returning to England it resumed anti-shipping operations. In the summer of 1942 at Swanton Morley, the squadron facilitated the first operational action of the United States Army Air Force as the spearhead of the Eighth Air Force. One of the squadron's Mitchells became the only Mitchell to achieve

100 operational sorties. From October 1944 the squadron was based on the continent in close support of the army.

Sorties: 740. Aircraft lost: 28

WARTIME STATIONS	PRIMARY AIRCRAFT	DATES
France	Fairey Battle	September 1939 – May 1941
Thirsk, Yorkshire	Bristol Blenheim	May 1941 – December 1941
Sydenham, N. Ireland	Douglas Boston	November 1941 – June 1943
Wattisham, Suffolk	North American Mitchell	May 1943 – September 1945
Swanton Morley, Norfolk		
Hartford Bridge, Hampshire		
Holland, France		

No. 227 Squadron

Motto: No badge authorised

Reformed as a heavy-bomber squadron, it took part in many heavy bomber raids with No. 5 Group. In May 1945 it repatriated prisoner of war troops to Britain.

Sorties: 815. Aircraft lost: 15

WARTIME STATIONS	PRIMARY AIRCRAFT	DATES
Balderton, Nottinghamshire	Avro Lancaster	October 1944 – September 1945
Strubby, Lincolnshire		
Graveley, Huntingdonshire		

No. 300 (Masovian) (Polish) Squadron

Motto: No badge authorised

This was the first Polish-manned bomber squadron in the Royal Air Force. Originally in No. 6 (Training) Group, it transferred to No.1 (Bomber) Group. It attacked cities, invasion harbours, Boulogne in

September 1940, concentrations of troops, and Panzer divisions. It was also involved in mine laying and its last mission was to bomb Berchtesgaden.

Sorties: 3,684. Aircraft lost: 77

WARTIME STATIONS	PRIMARY AIRCRAFT	DATES
Bramcote, Warwickshire	Fairey Battle	July 1940 – August 1940
Swinderby, Lincolnshire	Vickers Wellington	October 1940 – March 1944
Hemswell, Lincolnshire	Avro Lancaster	April 1944 – September 1945
Ingham, Lincolnshire		
Faldingworth, Lincolnshire		

No. 301 (Pomeranian) (Polish) Squadron

Motto: No badge authorised

This was the second Polish-manned bomber squadron. Originally in No. 6 (Training) Group it transferred to No.1 (Bomber) Group in August. Some of its original crews had previously served in Polish fighter units. It continued offensive bombing operations until the end of March 1943 when its last mission was to bomb Bochum, a centre of mining and steel production. The squadron disbanded and the personnel were posted to Nos 138 (Special Duties), 300, and 305 Squadrons. It reformed in November 1944 when its number was given to No. 1586 (Polish) (Special Duties) Squadron where it flew arms and supplies from Italy to the Polish Home Army and other resistance groups in enemy-occupied territory.

Sorties: 1,260. Aircraft lost: 29

WARTIME STATIONS	PRIMARY AIRCRAFT	DATES
Bramcote, Warwickshire	Fairey Battle	July 1940 – August 1940
Swinderby, Lincolnshire	Vickers Wellington	October 1940 – April 1943
Hemswell, Lincolnshire		

No. 304 (Silesian) (Polish) Squadron

Motto: No badge authorised

The squadron had previously served with No. 6 (Training) Group. The personnel were mainly Polish who had served with French Forces prior to the capitulation of that country. To facilitate their training, Polish personnel who had previously been trained in Britain were added to the squadron strength. In April 1941 its Wellingtons attacked the oil storage depot at Rotterdam. In May the squadron transferred to Coastal Command.

Sorties: 464. Aircraft lost: 18

WARTIME STATIONS	PRIMARY AIRCRAFT	DATES
Bramcote, Warwickshire	Fairey Battle	August 1940 – November 1940
Syerston, Nottinghamshire	Vickers Wellington	November 1940 – May 1942
Lindholme, Yorkshire		

No. 305 (Ziemia Wielkopolska) (Polish) Squadron

Motto: No badge authorised

No. 305 was the fourth, and last, Polish squadron to form at Bramcote. Originally with No. 6 (Training) Group it started operational flying with No. 1 Group. In April 1941 its Wellingtons also attacked the oil storage depot at Rotterdam. In September 1943 the squadron transferred to the Second Tactical Air Force.

Sorties: 1,063. Aircraft lost: 30

WARTIME STATIONS	PRIMARY AIRCRAFT	DATES
Bramcote, Warwickshire	Fairey Battle	September 1940 – November 1940
Syerston, Nottinghamshire	Vickers Wellington	November 1940 – August 1943
Lindholme, Yorkshire	North American Mitchell	September 1943 – December 1943
Hemswell, Lincolnshire	De Havilland Mosquito	December 1943 – September 1945
Ingham, Lincolnshire		

WARTIME STATIONS	PRIMARY AIRCRAFT	DATES
Swanton Morley, Norfolk		
Lasham, Hampshire		
Hartford Bridge, Hampshire		
France, Holland		

No. 311 (Czechoslovak) Squadron

Motto: 'Never regard their numbers'

The squadron was formed with Czech personnel who had served in France prior to its collapse. It was part of No. 3 Group and its first operational mission was to attack the airfield at Antwerp, Belgium, in September 1940. It attacked such targets as Kiel, Flushing, Brest, Paris, and Turin. In April 1942 it transferred to Coastal Command.

Sorties: 1,029. Aircraft lost: 19

WARTIME STATIONS	PRIMARY AIRCRAFT	DATES
Honington, Suffolk	Vickers Wellington	April 1940 – April 1942
East Wretham, Norfolk		

No. 320 (Dutch) Squadron

Motto: 'We are guided by the mind of liberty'

Formed in March 1943 the squadron converted to Mitchells with No. 2 Group Bomber Command. Two weeks later it was assigned to the Second Tactical Air Force. During the previous three years the personnel, Royal Dutch Naval Air Service, patrolled the Irish and North Sea in convoy patrols, air/sea rescues, and anti-submarine duties.

Sorties: 0 Aircraft lost: 0

WARTIME STATIONS*	PRIMARY AIRCRAFT	DATES
Methwold, Norfolk	North American Mitchell	March 1943 – August 1945
Attlebridge, Norfolk		

No. 342 (Lorraine) Squadron, Free French Air Force

Motto: No badge authorised

The Free French squadron, comprised of components of two Free French bomber units, had a long history in the Middle East prior to forming a squadron in Bomber Command with Boston aircraft. In June 1943 the squadron attacked the power station at Rouen. Shortly thereafter it transferred to the Second Tactical Air Force.

Sorties: Unknown. Aircraft lost: Unknown

WARTIME STATIONS	PRIMARY AIRCRAFT	DATES
West Raynham, Norfolk	Douglas Boston	April 1943 – April 1945
Sculthorpe, Norfolk	North American Mitchell	March 1945 – September 1945
Great Massingham, Norfolk		

No. 346 (Guyenne) Squadron, French Air Force

Motto: No badge authorised

The squadron was the first of the two French Air Force heavy-bomber squadrons that served in Britain. Many of the aircrew had served previously with the French Air Force in North Africa. In addition to its operational bombing missions it flew petrol to Brussels for the Second Army.

Sorties: 1,371. Aircraft lost: 15

WARTIME STATIONS	PRIMARY AIRCRAFT	DATES
Elvington, Yorkshire	Handley Page Halifax	May 1944 – September 1945

No. 347 ('Tunisie') Squadron, French Air Force

Motto: No badge authorised

The squadron was the second of the two French Air Force heavy bomber squadrons that served in Britain. Many of the aircrew had served previously with the French Air Force in North Africa. In addition to its operational bombing missions it flew petrol to Brussels for the Second Army.

Sorties: 1,355. Aircraft lost: 15

WARTIME STATIONS	PRIMARY AIRCRAFT	DATES
Elvington, Yorkshire	Handley Page Halifax	June 1944 – September 1945

No. 405 (Vancouver) Squadron, Royal Canadian Air Force

Motto: 'We lead'

This was the first Royal Canadian Air Force bomber squadron formed overseas. In April 1941 the squadron was formed at Driffield and flew its first Wellington mission to the marshalling yards at Schwerte in June. It converted to the Halifax and flew in the historic 1,000-bomber raid to Cologne. It was loaned to Coastal Command until March 1943 returning to No. 6 (Royal Canadian Air Force) Group for a short time before being picked to be a part of No. 8 (Pathfinder) Group. Converted to Lancasters in August 1943, it was the first unit to operate a Canadian-built Lancaster X overseas, number KB700. In June 1945 it flew its Lancasters back to Canada.

Sorties: 3,852. Aircraft lost: 112

WARTIME STATIONS	PRIMARY AIRCRAFT	DATES
Driffield, Yorkshire	Vickers Wellington	May 1941 – April 1942
Pocklington, Yorkshire	Handley Page Halifax	April 1942 – September 1943
Topcliffe, Yorkshire	Avro Lancaster	August 1943 – June 1945
Beaulieu, Hampshire		
Leeming, Yorkshire		
Gransden Lodge, Bedfordshire		
Linton-on-Ouse, Yorkshire		

No. 408 (Goose) Squadron, Royal Canadian Air Force

Motto; 'For freedom'

This was the second Royal Canadian Air Force bomber squadron formed overseas in June 1941. It began operations with Hampdens and its first mission was to Rotterdam in August 1941. It was active in bombing industrial and naval targets, and took part in mine laying operations. Equipped twice with the Halifax, it was re-equipped with Lancasters to fly back to Canada in preparation for the continuing war against Japan.

Sorties: 4,453. Aircraft lost: 129

WARTIME STATIONS	PRIMARY AIRCRAFT	DATES
Lindholme, Yorkshire	Handley Page Hampden	July 1941 – September 1942
Syerston, Nottinghamshire	Handley Page Halifax	October 1942 – August 1943
Balderton, Nottinghamshire	Avro Lancaster	August 1943 – August 1944
Leeming, Yorkshire	Handley Page Halifax	July 1944 – May 1945
Linton-on-Ouse, Yorkshire	Avro Lancaster	May 1945

No. 415 (Swordfish) Squadron, Royal Canadian Air Force

Motto: 'To the mark'

The squadron was formed originally at Thorney Island, Hampshire, in August 1941 as a torpedo-bomber squadron with Coastal Command. In July 1944 it was transferred to No. 6 (Royal Canadian Air Force) Group at Royal Canadian Air Force station East Moor. The same month it attacked Hamburg and subsequently attacked both strategic and tactical targets from the French coast to Chemnitz, Saxony, in Eastern Germany.

Sorties: 1,526. Aircraft lost: 13

WARTIME STATIONS	PRIMARY AIRCRAFT	DATES
East Moor, Yorkshire	Handley Page Halifax	July 1944 – May 1945

No. 419 (Moose) Squadron, Royal Canadian Air Force

Motto: 'Moosa aswayita'
Victoria Cross: Pilot Officer Andrew Mynarski

This was the third Royal Canadian Air Force squadron to form overseas at Mildenhall in December 1941. Originally in No. 3 Group Bomber

Command it joined No. 6 (Royal Canadian Air Force) Group in January 1943 at Mildenhall. It was a very active squadron flying three types of aircraft before it returned with its Lancasters to Canada in June 1945.

Sorties: 4,293. Aircraft lost: 129

WARTIME STATIONS	PRIMARY AIRCRAFT	DATES
Mildenhall, Suffolk	Vickers Wellington	January 1942 – November 1942
Leeming, Yorkshire	Handley Page Halifax	November 1942 – April 1944
Topcliffe, Yorkshire	Avro Lancaster	Early 1944 – June 1945
Croft, County Durham		
Middleton St. George, County Durham		

No. 420 (Snowy Owl) Squadron, Royal Canadian Air Force

Motto: 'We fight to a finish'

No. 420 was the fourth Royal Canadian Air Force bomber squadron formed overseas. It was located at Waddington with No. 5 Group in December 1941. After a short transfer to No. 4 Group the squadron transferred to No. 6 (Royal Canadian air Force) Group in January 1943. In May 1943 it was transferred to North Africa with No. 205 Group returning to England with No. 6 Group in November 1943 and converting to the Halifax. In June 1945 it flew its Lancasters back to Canada.

Sorties: 3,479. Aircraft lost 60

WARTIME STATIONS	PRIMARY AIRCRAFT	DATES
Waddington, Lincolnshire	Handley Page Hampden	December 1941 – August 1942
Skipton-on-Swale, Lincolnshire	Vickers Wellington	August 1942 – October 1943
Middleton St. George, County Durham	Handley Page Halifax	December 1943 – May 1945
Tunisia	Avro Lancaster	April 1945 – June 1945
Dalton, Yorkshire		
Tholthorpe, Yorkshire		

No. 424 (Tiger) Squadron, Royal Canadian Air Force

Motto: 'We chastise those that deserved to be chastised'

Originally formed at Topcliffe as a bomber squadron with No. 4 Group it was transferred in January 1943 to No. 6 (Royal Canadian Air Force) Group. In June 1943 it was transferred to North Africa with No. 205 Group. It returned to England with No. 6 (Royal Canadian Air Force) Group in November 1943 and converted to the Halifax. In August 1945 it joined No. 1 Group where it repatriated troops from Italy to England.

Sorties: 2,531. Aircraft lost: 33

WARTIME STATIONS	PRIMARY AIRCRAFT	DATES
Topcliffe, Yorkshire	Vickers Wellington	October 1942 – October 1943
Leeming, Yorkshire	Handley Page Halifax	December 1943 – January 1945
Dalton, Yorkshire	Avro Lancaster	January 1945 – September 1945
Tunisia		
Skipton-on-Swale		

No. 425 (Alouette) Squadron, Royal Canadian Air Force

Motto: 'I shall pluck you'

This was the fifth RCAF bomber squadron formed overseas. It was unique in that the organisational order stated 'French Canadian' in its title. It joined No. 4 Group in June 1942 and in October bombed Aachen close to the Belgium border. In June 1943 it was transferred to North Africa with No. 205 Group. It returned to England with No. 6 (Royal Canadian Air Force) Group in November 1943 and converted to the Halifax. In June 1945 it flew its Lancasters back to Canada.

Sorties: 2,927. Aircraft lost: 39

WARTIME STATIONS	PRIMARY AIRCRAFT	DATES
Dishforth, Yorkshire	Vickers Wellington	July 1942 – April 1943
Tunisia	Handley Page Halifax	December 1943 – May 1945
Tholthorpe, Yorkshire	Avro Lancaster	May 1945 – June 1945

No. 426 (Thunderbird) Squadron, Royal Canadian Air Force

Motto: 'On wings of fire'

The squadron was formed with No. 4 Group in October 1942 before it joined No. 6 (Royal Canadian Air Force) Group in January 1943 where it immediately bombed Lorient. Unlike the other Wellington-equipped squadrons it did not go to North Africa but continued the night bombing campaign in Europe. It flew the Bristol Hercules-powered Lancasters for a year before it converted to the Halifax. In May 1945 it transferred to Transport Command.

Sorties: 3,207. Aircraft lost: 68

WARTIME STATIONS	PRIMARY AIRCRAFT	DATES
Dishforth, Yorkshire	Vickers Wellington	October 1942 – June 1943
Linton-on-Ouse	Avro Lancaster	June 1943 – May 1944
	Handley Page Halifax	April 1944 – May 1945

No. 427 (Lion) Squadron, Royal Canadian Air Force

Motto: 'Strike sure'

The squadron was formed with No. 4 Group in November 1942. It laid mines in the Frisian Islands area in December before it joined No. 6 (Royal Canadian Air Force) Group in January 1943 where it attacked Lorient the same month. The squadron followed the normal progression of aircraft types.

Sorties: 3,309. Aircraft lost: 69

WARTIME STATIONS	PRIMARY AIRCRAFT	DATES
Croft, County Durham	Vickers Wellington	November 1942 – May 1943
Leeming, Yorkshire	Handley Page Halifax	May 1943 – March 1945
	Avro Lancaster	March 1945 – September 1945

No. 428 (Ghost) Squadron, Royal Canadian Air Force

Motto: 'To the very end'

The squadron was formed on 7 November 1942 at Dalton, one of three Canadian squadrons formed that day, No. 427 and No. 429 being the others. It joined No. 6 (Royal Canadian Air Force) Group in January 1943 where it bombed Lorient along with No. 426 (Royal Canadian Air Force) Squadron. In June 1945 it flew its Lancasters back to Canada.

Sorties: 3,433. Aircraft losses: 67

WARTIME STATIONS	PRIMARY AIRCRAFT	DATES
Dalton, Yorkshire	Vickers Wellington	November 1942 – June 1943
Middleton St. George, County Durham	Handley Page Halifax	June 1943 – June 1944
	Avro Lancaster	June 1944 – June 1945

No. 429 (Bison) Squadron, Royal Canadian Air Force

Motto: 'Nothing to chance'

The squadron was formed with No. 4 Group in November 1942 before it joined No. 6 (Royal Canadian Air Force) Group in January 1943 when it attacked Lorient the same month. The squadron continued its bombing and mine laying campaign when it moved to Leeming. In August 1945 it joined No. 1 Group where it repatriated troops from Italy to England.

Sorties: 3,175. Aircraft lost: 78

WARTIME STATIONS	PRIMARY AIRCRAFT	DATES
East Moor, Yorkshire	Vickers Wellington	November 1942 – August 1943
Leeming, Yorkshire	Handley Page Halifax	August 1943 – March 1945
	Avro Lancaster	March 1945 – September 1945

No. 431 (Iroquois) Squadron, Royal Canadian Air Force

Motto: 'Warriors of the air'

The squadron was formed with No. 4 Group in November 1942 before it joined No. 6 (Royal Canadian Air Force) Group in January 1943. Its first mission was to lay mines in the Frisian Islands area. It remained at Croft until June 1945 when the squadron flew its Lancasters back to Canada.

Sorties: 2,578. Aircraft lost: 75

WARTIME STATIONS	PRIMARY AIRCRAFT	DATES
Burn, Yorkshire	Vickers Wellington	December 1942 – August 1943
Tholthorpe, Yorkshire	Handley Page Halifax	July 1943 – October 1944
Croft, County Durham	Avro Lancaster	October 1944 – June 1945

No. 432 (Leaside) Squadron, Royal Canadian Air Force

Motto: 'Ferociously towards the light'

Formed in May 1943 as a bomber squadron with No. 6 (Royal Canadian Air Force) Group its first mission the same month was to bomb Dortmund. It continued its night bombing, which included attacks on the Ruhr and Berlin, and mine laying operations until it was disbanded in May 1945

Sorties: 3,100. Aircraft lost: 65

WARTIME STATIONS	PRIMARY AIRCRAFT	DATES
Skipton-on-Swale, Yorkshire	Vickers Wellington	May 1943 – November 1943
East Moor, Yorkshire	Avro Lancaster	October 1943 – February 1944
	Handley Page Halifax	February 1944 – May 1945

No. 433 (Porcupine) Squadron, Royal Canadian Air Force

Motto: 'Who opposes it gets hurt'

Formed in September 1943 as a heavy-bomber unit of No. 6 (Royal Canadian Air Force) Group it was based at Skipton-on-Swale for its entire wartime service. There were only a few other squadrons that remained at one location. Its first mission was to bomb Dortmund and it continued its night-time bombing and mine laying until disbanded in May 1945.

Sorties: 2,316. Aircraft lost: 31

WARTIME STATIONS	PRIMARY AIRCRAFT	DATES
Skipton-on-Swale	Handley Page Halifax	November 1943 – February 1945
	Avro Lancaster	January 1945 – September 1945

No. 434 (Bluenose) Squadron, Royal Canadian Air Force

Motto: 'We conquer in the heights'

The squadron was formed in June 1943 as a heavy-bomber unit of No. 6 (Royal Canadian Air Force) Group and was based at Tholthorpe. In August 1943 it initiated operations by bombing Turin, Italy. It continued its European operations until June 1945 when it flew its Lancasters back to Canada.

Sorties: 2,597. Aircraft lost: 58

WARTIME STATIONS	PRIMARY AIRCRAFT	DATES
Tholthorpe, Yorkshire	Handley Page Halifax	June 1943 – December 1944
Croft, County Durham	Avro Lancaster	December 1944 – June 1945

No. 455 Squadron, Royal Australian Air Force

Motto: 'Strike and strike again'

Originally formed in Australia, the squadron reformed at Swinderby in June 1941 as part of No. 5 Group. In February 1942 it took part in the *Scharnhorst* and *Gneisenau* raids. In April 1942 it transferred to Coastal Command in the torpedo bomber role.

Sorties: 424. Aircraft lost: 14

WARTIME STATIONS	PRIMARY AIRCRAFT	DATES
Australia	Handley Page Hampden	July 1941 – April 1942
Swinderby, Lincolnshire		
Wigsley, Nottinghamshire		

No. 458 Squadron, Royal Australian Air Force

Motto: 'We find and destroy'

Established in 1941 in Australia it formed in Britain in August at Holme-on-Spalding Moor as a medium-bomber unit in No. 1 Group. Its first operational sortie was in October when ten of its aircraft joined in night attacks against the ports of Emden, Antwerp, and Rotterdam. It was withdrawn from service with Bomber Command in preparation for embarkation to the Middle East in January 1942.

Sorties: 65. Aircraft lost: 3

WARTIME STATIONS	PRIMARY AIRCRAFT	DATES
Holme-on-Spalding Moor, Yorkshire	Vickers Wellington	August 1941 – January 1942

No. 460 Squadron, Royal Australian Air Force

Motto: 'Strike and return'

The squadron formed at Molesworth in November 1941 as part of No. 8 Group and transferred to No. 1 Group in January 1942. In September it stood down and prepared to convert to the Halifax but instead re-equipped with the Lancaster. It was involved in attacks on Berlin and Peenemunde. One of its Lancasters, a Mark I serial W4783, flew ninety sorties in forty-four days. It is presently in the Australian War Museum.

Sorties: 6,238. Aircraft lost: 169

WARTIME STATIONS	PRIMARY AIRCRAFT	DATES
Molesworth, Huntingdonshire	Vickers Wellington	November 1941 – September 1942
Breighton, Yorkshire	Handley Page Halifax	August 1942 – October 1942
Binbrook, Lincolnshire	Avro Lancaster	October 1942 – September 1945
East Kirkby, Lincolnshire		

No. 462 Squadron, Royal Australian Air Force

Motto: No badge authorised

After service in the Middle East the squadron reformed at Driffield in August 1943 as part of No. 4 Group. In December 1944 it joined

No.100 (Bomber Support) Group at Foulsham. It now acted as a 'Windows' carrier and carried a small bomb load to drop in feint attacks. By March 1945 it was flying jamming missions using 'Airborne Cigar' and 'Carpet'.

Sorties: 1,165. Aircraft lost: 13

WARTIME STATIONS	PRIMARY AIRCRAFT	DATES
Egypt, Libya, Italy	Handley Page Halifax	September 1942 – September 1945
Driffield, Yorkshire		
Foulsham, Norfolk		

No. 463 Squadron, Royal Australian Air Force

Motto: 'Press on regardless'

In November 1943 the squadron formed at Waddington as part of No. 5 Group. In order to give it wartime experienced crew 'C' Flight No. 467 Royal Australian Air Force formed the basis of the new squadron. Its first raid was on Berlin shortly after its formation. It took part in the preparations for the invasion of Europe. One of its Lancasters filmed the successful attack on the *Tirpitz* by Nos 617 and 9 Squadrons in November 1944.

Sorties: 2,525. Aircraft lost: 69

WARTIME STATIONS	PRIMARY AIRCRAFT	DATES
Waddington, Lincolnshire	Avro Lancaster	November 1943 – July 1945
Skellingthorpe, Lincolnshire		

No. 464 Squadron, Royal Australian Air Force

Motto: 'Equanimity'

The squadron was formed at Feltwell in September 1942 as part of No. 2 Group with the Ventura light bomber. Its first operation was the historic raid on the Philips radio factory at Eindhoven, Holland. The summer of 1943 it transferred to the Second Tactical Air Force and converted to Mosquitos.

Sorties: 226. Aircraft lost: 6

WARTIME STATIONS	PRIMARY AIRCRAFT	DATES
Feltwell, Norfolk	Lockheed Ventura	September 1942 – August 1943
Methwold, Norfolk	De Havilland Mosquito	August 1943 – September 1945
Sculthorpe, Norfolk		

No. 466 Squadron, Royal Australian Air Force

Motto: 'Brave and true'

The squadron was formed as a medium-bomber squadron in No. 4 Group with Wellingtons in October 1942. Its first mission was mine laying in the Frisian Islands. Converted to the Halifax it continued its attacks on such targets as Berlin, Cologne, Duisberg, Stuttgart, and Essen. In May 1945 it transferred to Transport Command.

Sorties: 3,328. Aircraft lost: 65

WARTIME STATIONS	PRIMARY AIRCRAFT	DATES
Driffield, Yorkshire	Vickers Wellington	October 1942 – September 1943
Leconfield, Yorkshire	Handley Page Halifax	September 1943 – May 1945

No. 467 Squadron, Royal Australian Air Force

Motto: 'Your opponents will retreat because of your courageous attack'

The heavy-bomber squadron was formed in November 1942 as part of No. 5 Group. In January it laid mines in the Furze area and it contributed to the war in Europe by taking part in all major battles, Battles of the Ruhr, Berlin, and Hamburg. It also was one of the inauguration squadrons in the 'shuttle bomb' attacks on Freidrichshafen and Spezia, Italy. It flew the second most active Lancaster with 137 operational sorties to its credit. It has been preserved and stands at Royal Air Force Museum Hendon.

Sorties: 3,833. Aircraft lost: 104

WARTIME STATIONS	PRIMARY AIRCRAFT	DATES
Scampton, Lincolnshire	Avro Lancaster	November 1942 – September 1945
Bottesford, Leicestershire		
Waddington, Lincolnshire		
Metheringham, Lincolnshire		

No. 487 Squadron, Royal New Zealand Air Force

Motto: 'Through to the end'

Victoria Cross: Squadron Leader Leonard Trent

The squadron was formed with Venturas as a light-bomber squadron. In December 1942 it took part in the low-level raid on the Philips radio works at Eindhoven. In May 1943 during a raid on Amsterdam eleven out of twelve Venturas were shot down. In June it was transferred to the Second Tactical Air Force.

Sorties: 273. Aircraft lost: 15

WARTIME STATIONS	PRIMARY AIRCRAFT	DATES
Feltwell, Norfolk	Lockheed Ventura	September 1942 – September 1943
Methwold, Norfolk	De Havilland Mosquito	August 1943 – September 1945

No. 514 Squadron

Motto: 'Nothing can withstand'

The squadron formed as a heavy-bomber squadron in September 1943 as a member of No. 3 Group. Its first missions were operations to Dusseldorf and mine laying in the Frisian Islands on the same day in November. It dropped food supplies to Holland just before the end of the war.

Sorties: 3,675. Aircraft lost: 66

WARTIME STATIONS	PRIMARY AIRCRAFT	DATES
Foulsham, Norfolk	Avro Lancaster	September 1943 – August 1945
Waterbeach, Cambridgeshire		

No. 550 Squadron

Motto: 'Through fire we conquer'

The squadron was a heavy-bomber squadron in No. 1 Group at Waltham. It was formed from 'C' Flight of No. 100 (Bomber) Squadron. Its first mission was to attack Berlin and its last operation was to attack Berchtesgaden. The squadron had three Lancaster IIIs that passed the 100 sorties mark, EE139 'Phantom of the Ruhr', ED905, and PA995.

Sorties: 3,582. Aircraft lost: 59

WARTIME STATIONS	PRIMARY AIRCRAFT	DATES
Grimsby/Waltham, Lincolnshire	Avro Lancaster	November 1943 – September 1945
North Killingholme, Lincolnshire		

No. 571 Squadron

Motto: no badge authorised

The squadron was formed late in the war, in April 1944, as a light-bomber unit of No. 8 (Pathfinder Force) Group's Light Night Striking Force. It struck at industrial centres, focusing on Berlin. It hit the city twenty-two times in March 1945. It also laid mines in the Dortmund-Ems Canal.

Sorties: 2,681. Aircraft lost: 8

WARTIME STATIONS	PRIMARY AIRCRAFT	DATES
Downham Market, Norfolk	De Havilland Mosquito	April 1944 – September 1945
Oakington, Cambridgeshire		
Warboys, Huntingdonshire		

No. 576 Squadron

Motto: 'Seize the opportunity'

The squadron was formed with 'C' Flight No. 103 Squadron as its nucleus. It was part of No. 1 Group. Its first mission was to attack Berlin and its last operation was to attack Berchtesgaden.

Sorties: 2,788. Aircraft lost: 66

WARTIME STATIONS	PRIMARY AIRCRAFT	DATES
Elsham Wolds, Lincolnshire	Avro Lancaster	November 1943 – September 1945
Fiskerton, Lincolnshire		

No. 578 Squadron

Motto: 'Accuracy'
Victoria Cross: Pilot Officer Cyril Barton

The squadron was formed as a heavy-bomber squadron with Halifaxes in January 1944 as part of No. 4 Group. First operational sortie was to Berlin and the last was to Wuppertal in the North Rhine region. Two of its Halifaxes, LW587 and MZ527, survived over 100 operations.

Sorties: 2,721. Aircraft lost: 40

WARTIME STATIONS	PRIMARY AIRCRAFT	DATES
Snaith, Yorkshire	Handley Page Halifax	January 1944 – March 1945
Burn, Yorkshire		

No. 582 Squadron

Motto: 'We fly before marking'
Victoria Cross: Captain Edwin Swales D.F.C.

The squadron was formed in April 1944 with personnel from Nos. 7 and 156 Squadrons. It was part of No. 8 (Pathfinder Force) Group.

Sorties: 2,157. Aircraft lost: 28

WARTIME STATIONS	PRIMARY AIRCRAFT	DATES
Little Staughton, Huntingdonshire	Avro Lancaster	April 1944 – September 1945

Right: Marshal of the Royal Air Force Sir Arthur (Bomber) Harris. (Courtesy of Imperial War Museum. With thanks to Gary Vincent for the supply and collation of images.)

Below: Bylaugh Hall, HQ No. 100 (Bomber Support) Group. (Courtesy of Ben Budworth)

No. 75 Royal New Zealand Air Force, RAF Newmarket. (Courtesy of No. 75 Squadron R.N.Z.A.F.)

Marsham Arms, near RAF Swannington, Norfolk. (Courtesy of Marsham Arms, Jenna)

RAF Station Strubby, Lincolnshire. (Courtesy of Barb Petticrew)

RAF Station Snaith Watch Tower, Yorkshire. (Courtesy of Imperial War Museum)

Rolls-Royce Hillington, Glasgow July 1940. (Courtesy of the Rolls-Royce Heritage Trust)

Avro factory, Woodford, Cheshire. (Courtesy of Imperial War Museum)

Armstrong Whitworth Whitley. (Courtesy of RCAF Archives)

Avro Manchester. (Courtesy of Imperial War Museum)

Avro Lancaster with replica Dr Barnes Wallis bouncing bomb. (Courtesy of Douglas Bowman, Archer Photo Works)

Boeing Fortress. (Courtesy of RCAF Archives)

Bristol Blenheim. (Courtesy of RCAF Archives)

Douglas Boston. (Courtesy of RCAF Archives)

Fairey Battle. (Courtesy of RCAF Archives)

Handley Page Halifax. (Courtesy of RCAF Archives)

Handley Page Hampden. (Courtesy of RCAF Archives)

North American Mitchell. (Courtesy of RCAF Archives)

Vickers Wellington. (Courtesy of RCAF Archives)

Above: De Havilland Mosquito. (Courtesy of Malcolm Nason)

Below right: Flying Officer Bruce A. Grant. (Courtesy of M. Hogg/D. Harkin)

Below left: No. 420 (Snowy Owl) RCAF Squadron 'missing' letter to Grant's father. (Courtesy of M. Hogg/D. Harkin)

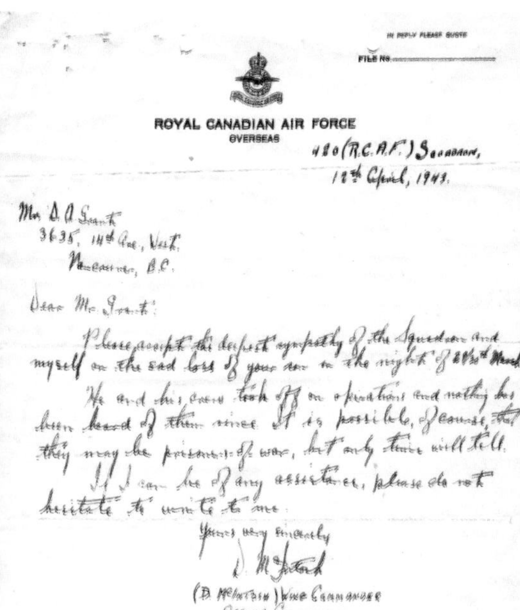

IN REPLY PLEASE QUOTE

FILE No. ....

ROYAL CANADIAN AIR FORCE
OVERSEAS

420 (R.C.A.F.) Squadron,
12th April, 1943.

Mr. D. A. Grant
3635, 14th Ave., West,
Vancouver, B.C.

Dear Mr. Grant:

Please accept the deepest sympathy of the Squadron and myself on the sad loss of your son on the night of 29/30th March.

He and his crew took off on operations and nothing has been heard of them since. It is possible, of course, that they may be prisoners of war, but only time will tell.

If I can be of any assistance, please do not hesitate to write to me.

Yours very sincerely

D. McIntosh

(D. McIntosh) Wing Commander
Officer Commanding
420 (RCAF) Squadron

Rolls-Royce Merlin at Vintage V12s, California. (Courtesy of Atsushi 'Fred' Fujimori)

Luftwaffe Messerschmitt Bf110 Night Interceptor. (Courtesy of Malcolm Nason)

Church Service No. 428 (Ghost) RCAF Squadron. (Courtesy of Canadian Museum of Flight, Langley, British Columbia)

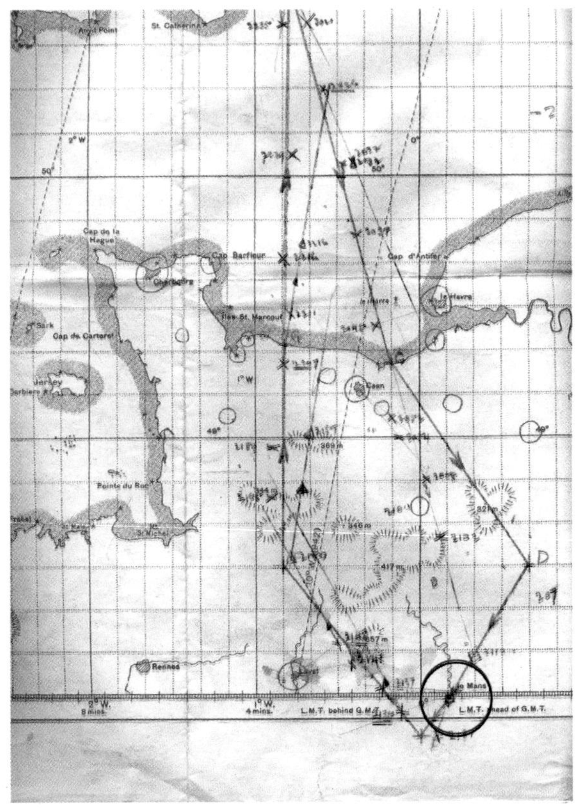

'Target for tonight', Le Mans, France. (Courtesy of Jerry Vernon Collection)

De Havilland Mosquitos attacking shipping. (Courtesy of RCAF Archives)

By.............................. MESSAGE SLIP. R.A.F. Form 228
(For use in the air only.)
Date..........................

To.. From..
Text:—

S/C TARGET AREA
167
CROSS COAST IN 4 MINUTES

PTO

T.O.O.............................
T.O.R.............................

Target route pilot Message Slip, Sgt David Vandervord. (Courtesy of Richard Vandervord)

Above: Krupp Works, Essen, Germany. (Courtesy of Bomber Command Museum of Canada, Nanton, Alberta)

Right: Avro Lancasters on perimeter track. (Courtesy of Canadian Museum of Flight, Langley, British Columbia)

Personal message from No. 419 (Moose) RCAF Squadron. (Courtesy of Bomber Command Museum of Canada, Nanton, Alberta)

Avro Lincoln. (Courtesy of Malcolm Nason)

Boeing Washington. (Courtesy of Adrian Balch Collection)

English Electric Canberra. (Courtesy of Patrick Martin Collection)

Avro Vulcan. (Courtesy of Bill Powderly)

Vickers Valiant. (Courtesy of Patrick Martin Collection)

Handley Page Victor. (Courtesy of Imperial War Museum)

No. 608 (North Riding) Squadron

Motto: 'With all talons'

After it returned from Italy the squadron reformed with No. 8 (Pathfinder Force) Group's Light Night Striking Force. Its first mission was to attack Wanne Eickel, the largest marshalling yard in the central Ruhr area. It continued to attack such targets as Nuremberg, Hanover, and Kiel.

Sorties: 1,726. Aircraft lost: 9

WARTIME STATIONS	PRIMARY AIRCRAFT	DATES
Downham Market, Norfolk	De Havilland Mosquito	August 1944 – August 1945

No. 617 Squadron

Motto: 'After me, the flood'

Victoria Crosses: Acting Wing Commander Guy Gibson D.S.O., D.F.C. Wing Commander Geoffrey Cheshire D.S.O., D.F.C.

This is the only squadron in wartime Royal Air Force Bomber Command to be formed specifically for an operation, the breaching of dams in Germany. It was formed under the command of Wing Commander Guy Gibson, an already distinguished pilot and leader, who was given the authority to select his own crews for the secret operation from all the crews in Bomber Command. The raid on the dams the Mohne, Eder, and Sorpe on the night of 16 May 1943 was called 'Operation Chastise'. It is beyond the scope of this book to fully describe this event. Many books have been devoted to the 'Dam Busters' and their historic mission. The squadron continued as a precision bombing unit when it attacked power stations in Northern Italy, landed in North Africa, and on the return trip attacked Livorno. In September it attacked the Dortmund-Ems canal and then performed pin-point attacks on factories in France to ensure minimum loss of life to French citizens. This was possibly due to a low-level target marking technique devised by Wing Commander Geoffrey Cheshire. In June 1944 the squadron dropped 'Tallboy' bombs, 12,000lb (5,433kg), on the Saumur railway tunnel in Northern France. The squadron also dropped the first 'Grand Slam' bomb, 22,000lb (9,979kg), on the Bielefeld railway viaduct in Germany.

Sorties: 1,599. Aircraft lost: 32

WARTIME STATIONS	PRIMARY AIRCRAFT	DATES
Scampton, Lincolnshire	Avro Lancaster	March 1943 – September 1945
Coningsby, Lincolnshire		
Woodhall Spa, Lincolnshire		
Waddington, Lincolnshire		

No. 619 Squadron

Motto: 'To higher things'

The squadron was formed in No. 5 Group with elements of No. 97 Squadron at Woodhall Spa as a heavy-bomber squadron flying Lancasters against targets in mainland Europe. Its first mission was to bomb Dusseldorf in June 1943. One of its Lancasters destroyed a V-1 in flight on the night of the 3 March 1945. In May it flew prisoners-of-war home from France and Belgium and was disbanded in July.

Sorties: 3,011. Aircraft lost: 32

WARTIME STATIONS	PRIMARY AIRCRAFT	DATES
Woodhall Spa, Lincolnshire	Airspeed Oxford	April 1943 – September 1943
Coningsby, Lincolnshire	Avro Lancaster	April 1943 – July 1945
Dunholme Lodge, Lincolnshire		
Strubby, Lincolnshire		
Skellingthorpe, Lincolnshire		

No. 620 Squadron

Motto: 'We are coming bringing gifts'

The squadron was formed at Chedburgh in June 1943 as a heavy-bomber squadron in No. 3 Group. In November it was transferred to No. 38 Group and operated as Air Combat Service Support.

Sorties: 339. Aircraft lost: 17

WARTIME STATION	PRIMARY AIRCRAFT	DATES
Chedburgh, Suffolk	Short Stirling	June 1943 – November 1943

No. 622 Squadron

Motto: 'We wage war at night'

The squadron-initiated service as a heavy-bomber squadron at Mildenhall in August 1943 with Stirling aircraft. Its first mission was an attack on Nuremberg the same month. It shortly re-equipped with Lancasters in its night-time campaign in Europe. One of its Lancasters, LL885, flew 113 operational sorties in thirteen months. The squadron dropped food to Holland and ferried troops home from Italy. It disbanded in August 1945.

Sorties: 3,000. Aircraft lost: 51

WARTIME STATIONS	PRIMARY AIRCRAFT	DATES
Mildenhall, Suffolk	Short Stirling	August 1943 – December 1943
	Avro Lancaster	December 1943 – August 1945

No. 623 Squadron

Motto: No badge authorised

A short-lived squadron, it was formed in August 1943 from 'C' Flight No. 218 Squadron and crews from No. 3 Lancaster Finishing School and No. 1653 Conversion Unit. In August five Stirlings bombed Nuremberg and in the next four months attacked Hanover, Frankfurt, Kassel, and other targets.

Sorties: 150. Aircraft lost: 10

WARTIME STATIONS	PRIMARY AIRCRAFT	DATES
Downham Market, Norfolk	Short Stirling	August 1943 – December 1943

No. 625 Squadron

Motto: 'We avenge'

The squadron was formed at Kelstern in October 1943 with an element, 'C' Flight, from No. 100 Squadron. It flew Lancasters and shared the load in the attacks against Fortress Europe. Its first sortie was to Hanover in October 1943.

Sorties: 3,385. Aircraft lost: 66

WARTIME STATIONS	PRIMARY AIRCRAFT	DATES
Kelstern, Lincolnshire	Avro Lancaster	October 1943 – September 1945
Scampton, Lincolnshire		

No. 626 Squadron

Motto: 'To strive and not to yield'

The squadron was formed at Wickenby as part of No. 1 Group. In November 1943 it started operations by bombing Modane. It supported the night bombing campaign until April 1945 when it dropped food to liberated Holland.

Sorties: 2,728. Aircraft lost: 49

WARTIME STATION	PRIMARY AIRCRAFT	DATES
Wickenby, Lincolnshire	Avro Lancaster	November 1943 – September 1945

No. 627 Squadron

Motto: 'At first sight'

Formed in November 1943 as a light-bomber squadron it took part in many major raids. It started with No. 8 (Pathfinder Force) Group and after the Battle of Berlin ended, it transferred to No. 5 Group. The squadron took part in the attack on Munich in April 1944, the Gestapo Headquarters in Oslo on 31 December, and Wesel in March 1945. The squadron also took part in target marking, dropping 'Window', and photographic reconnaissance. On the night of 19 September 1944 Wing Commander Guy Gibson VC crashed and was killed on the return journey from a bombing mission to Rheydt.

Sorties: 1,535. Aircraft lost: 19

WARTIME STATIONS	PRIMARY AIRCRAFT	DATES
Oakington, Cambridge	De Havilland Mosquito	November 1943 – September 1945
Woodhall Spa, Lincolnshire		

No. 630 Squadron

Motto: 'Death by night'

The Lancaster squadron was formed at East Kirkby in November 1943 from 'B' Flight No. 57 Squadron. It took part in many major raids including the sixteen raids associated with the Battle of Berlin. It ferried troops back to Britain in April and disbanded in July 1945.

Sorties: 2,453. Aircraft lost: 59

WARTIME STATIONS	PRIMARY AIRCRAFT	DATES
East Kirkby, Lincolnshire	Avro Lancaster	November 1943 – July 1945

No. 635 Squadron

Motto: 'We lead, others follow'
Victoria Cross: Acting Squadron Leader Ian Bazalgette

'B' Flight of No. 35 Squadron and 'C' Flight of No. 97 Squadron were the basis of the squadron formed at Downham Market in March 1944. It joined No. 8 (Pathfinder Force) Group and attacked Frankfurt that same month. It dropped food for Holland and repatriated troops prior to war end.

Sorties: 2,225. Aircraft lost: 34

WARTIME STATION	PRIMARY AIRCRAFT	DATES
Downham Market, Norfolk	Avro Lancaster	March 1944 – August 1945

No. 640 Squadron

Motto: No badge authorised

The Halifax squadron was formed at Leconfield as a heavy-bomber unit with crews from 'C' Flight No. 158 Squadron. In January 1944 it bombed Berlin and it won the monthly No. 4 Group Bombing Cup five times, a record. It was disbanded in May 1945.

Sorties: 2,423. Aircraft lost: 40

WARTIME STATIONS	PRIMARY AIRCRAFT	DATES
Leconfield, Yorkshire	Handley Page Halifax	January 1944 – May 1945

No. 692 (Fellowship of the Bellows) Squadron

Motto: 'So long as the sky shall feed the stars'

The name of the squadron comes from the effort to purchase aircraft for the Royal Air Force by a group in Buenos Aires. The Mosquito light-bomber squadron was part of the No. 8 (Pathfinder Force) Group Light Night Striking Force. The Force made a name for itself by repeatedly attacking Berlin with the 'cookie' 4,000lb (1,814kg) bomb. On New Year's Day 1945 the squadron attempted a 'tunnel-busting' offensive by flying extremely low and lobbing the bombs at the open mouth of the railway tunnels.

Sorties: 3,237. Aircraft lost: 17

WARTIME STATIONS	PRIMARY AIRCRAFT	DATES
Graveley, Huntingdonshire	De Havilland Mosquito	January 1944 – September 1945
Gransden Lodge, Bedfordshire		

For all squadron wartime station dates see Chapter 4, 'Bomber Command Stations'.

Royal Air Force Pathfinder Force Squadrons, 15 August 1942

GROUP	SQUADRON	AIRCRAFT	WARTIME STATION
1	156	Wellington	RAF Warboys
2	109	Wellington/Mosquito	RAF Wyton
3	7	Stirling	RAF Oakington
4	35	Halifax	RAF Graveley
5	83	Lancasters	RAF Wyton

Royal Air Force No. 8 (Pathfinder Force) Group Squadrons, 8 January 1943

Avro Lancaster

SQUADRON	WARTIME STATION (APRIL 1945)
7	RAF Oakington, Cambridgeshire
35	RAF Graveley, Huntingdonshire
83*	RAF Coningsby, Lincolnshire
97*	RAF Bourn, Cambridgeshire
156	RAF Upwood, Huntingdonshire
405	RAF Linton-on-Ouse, Yorkshire
582	RAF Little Staughton, Huntingdonshire
635	RAF Downham Market, Norfolk

* Squadrons returned to lead No. 5 Group in April 1944

Sorties: 51,053. Aircraft lost: 675 and 3,700+ aircrew

De Havilland Mosquito

SQUADRON	WARTIME STATION (APRIL 1945)
105	RAF Upwood, Huntingdonshire
109	RAF Little Staughton, Huntingdonshire
128	RAF Warboys, Huntingdonshire
139	RAF Upwood, Huntingdonshire
142	RAF Gransden Lodge, Bedfordshire
162	RAF Bourn, Cambridgeshire
163	RAF Wyton, Huntingdonshire
571	RAF Warboys, Huntingdonshire
608	RAF Downham Market, Norfolk
627*	RAF Woodhall Spa, Lincolnshire
692	RAF Gransden Lodge, Bedfordshire

* Squadrons returned to lead No. 5 Group in April 1944

Sorties: 51,053. Aircraft lost: 675 and 3,700+ aircrew

No. 1409 (Meteorological) Flight, No. 8 (Pathfinder) Group

A very important part of the planning of any operation was the weather conditions that would exist over the target area, the departure airfield area, and the en route portion of the flight. These would include such factors as cloud cover, phases of the moon, icing conditions, winds, fog, turbulence, and thunderstorms, which all would have a major effect on the success of the mission.

The Flight was formed on 1 April 1943 to provide meteorological information for Royal Air Force Bomber Command and the United States Army Air Force. It was equipped with unarmed De Havilland Mosquito aircraft. The Flight would undertake long-range meteorological reconnaissance flights to the target area and report back to Bomber Command. These flights continued until the end of hostilities.

It formed at RAF Oakington, Cambridgeshire, in April 1943 as part of No. 8 (Pathfinder Force) Group from the disbandment of No. 521 Squadron. The weather missions were called Photo-recce And Meteorological Photography Aircraft flights (PAMPA).

Sorties: 1,364. Aircraft lost: 3

WARTIME STATIONS	PRIMARY AIRCRAFT	DATES
Oakington, Cambridgeshire	De Havilland Mosquito	April 1943 – September 1945
Wyton, Huntingdonshire		
Upwood, Huntingdonshire		

No. 100 (Special Duties/Bomber Support) Group

Motto: 'Confound and Destroy'

The squadrons in this specialised Group started operations in 1943 and 1944 except for No. 462 (Royal Australian Air Force) which started operations in 1945. The Bomber Support Development Unit used a wide range of aircraft flown by the Group and investigated and developed electronic countermeasures and radar technologies for these aircraft. This electronic warfare component developed rapidly as each side, Allied and Axis, brought out new devices to electronically 'see' and 'not be seen' and 'see the other side seeing you' which continued into the post war Cold War and the developing sophistication of twenty-first century equipment.

SQUADRON	AIRCRAFT	WARTIME STATION
23	De Havilland Mosquito	RAF Little Snoring
85	De Havilland Mosquito	RAF Swannington
141	Bristol Beaufighter, De Havilland Mosquito	RAF West Raynham

SQUADRON	AIRCRAFT	WARTIME STATION
157	De Havilland Mosquito	RAF Swannington
169	De Havilland Mosquito	RAF Little Snoring
171	Short Stirling, Handley Page Halifax	RAF North Creake
192	De Havilland Mosquito, Vickers Wellington, Handley Page Halifax	RAF Foulsham
199	Short Stirling, Handley Page Halifax	RAF North Creake
214	Boeing Fortress	RAF Sculthorpe, RAF Oulton
223	Consolidated Liberator, Boeing Fortress	RAF Oulton
239	De Havilland Mosquito	RAF West Raynham
462 (RAAF)	Handley Page Halifax	RAF Foulsham
515	De Havilland Mosquito	RAF Little Snoring
B.S.D.U.*	De Havilland Mosquito	RAF Swanton Morley

* Bomber Support Development Unit

The squadrons that had started life earlier in the First World War One in Britain but in the Second World War had served overseas, the squadrons that had served a very short time in Britain before they served overseas, and those that were formed overseas and served there, are listed below. Some squadrons served in one country, such No. 8 Squadron, some in many countries, such as No. 11 Squadron. Bomber Command fought on many fronts and countries alongside Fighter Command, Coastal Command, and the Tactical Air Force.

SQUADRON	COUNTRY
4	Holland
6	Palestine
8	Aden
11	Aden, Ceylon, Egypt, Greece, India, Libya, Palestine, Singapore
14	Egypt, Iraq, Libya, Palestine, Sudan, Transjordan
27	India

SQUADRON	COUNTRY
30	Egypt, Greece,
34	India, Java, Singapore, Sumatra
39	Aden, Egypt, Italy, Singapore
42	India
45	Egypt, India, Iraq, Libya, Palestine, Sicily, Tunisia
47	Burma, Eritrea India Sudan
52	Iraq
55	Egypt, Italy, Libya, Palestine, Sicily, Tunisia
60	Burma, India
62	Malaya, Singapore
69	France
70	Egypt, Italy, Libya, Tunisia,
84	Ceylon, Crete, Iraq, Libya, Palestine, Sumatra
113	Burma, Egypt, Greece, India, Libya, Palestine
148	Egypt, Italy, Libya, Malta
178	Egypt, Italy, Libya, Palestine
211	Crete, Egypt, Greece, Java, Palestine, Sudan, Sumatra
216	Egypt
355	India
356	Cocos Islands, India
358	India
454 RAAF	Iraq, Italy, Libya, Palestine

4

BOMBER COMMAND STATIONS

Scattered throughout the length and breadth of the British Isles are the physical remnants of the Second World War. They range from large naval shipyards to small concrete pillboxes. Some pillboxes have been removed; some are overgrown with vegetation and hardly noticeable; and some on the coast have tumbled from the cliff above and lie broken on the beach. These remnants, seventy-five years later, are indicative of a massive struggle involving all the citizens of this island nation.

The Royal Air Force Bomber Command's stations are part of that legacy. Some are still active airfields; some are now civilian airports; some have been ploughed up and reclaimed; some have had some of their buildings restored and preserved as living history; and some are no more than crumbling weed-infested runways with derelict buildings.

Just east of the city of Lincoln is a small village in the parish of West Lindsey. It is situated just north of the River Witham and is named Fiskerton. Driving north from the village on Reepham Road you pass a double gate on a weed-covered asphalt strip in the middle of farmland. This is one of the few visible remnants of Royal Air Force Fiskerton that was home to 49 and 576 Squadrons. Fiskerton was one of the few stations equipped with the Fog Investigation and Dispersal Operation (FIDO) landing system. Fiskerton is surrounded by the now nearly invisible remnants and ghosts of Royal Air Force stations Faldingworth to the north, Bardney to the east, and Metheringham to the south.

The best known part of the story of Bomber Command is about the raids, the aircraft, and the crews. This was the 'pointy end of the stick', the sensational tales of heroics, injuries, casualties, and the successes and failures of missions. But, behind them all was this vast infrastructure of support services which culminated at the station to support the operations of Bomber Command. The groups, squadrons, and flights all were dependent on having serviceable aircraft to perform their duties.

'A chain is as good as its weakest link', so all these supporting industries and personnel were equally important to the success of the mission. The hydraulic filter made in Manchester had an aircraft part journey of its own before it was finally fitted, perhaps on a freezing cold November night, to the aircraft. It was the station that had the organisation and resources to fit that part correctly, test it, and dispatch the aircraft and crew on their mission. It was the stations, with all their sections, that allowed Bomber Command to mount the famous 1,000-bomber raids. It was the stations that would provide safe home landing areas and, if necessary, safe alternative landing areas for the returning crews.

A few of the First World War airfields were updated for Bomber Command use but the vast majority were created from open farmland with suitable surroundings. The following stations were constructed at First World War locations: Bicester, Doncaster, Driffield, Finningley, Upper Heyford, and Upwood. The rest of the stations in England were roughly located east of a line from Middlesborough to Leeds to London in the counties of Bedfordshire, Cambridgeshire, Durham, Essex, Huntingdonshire, Lincolnshire, Norfolk, Northamptonshire, Nottinghamshire, Oxfordshire, Rutland, Suffolk, Warwickshire, and Yorkshire.

The reason for these chosen locations was of course to be closer to the targets in mainland Europe, to use the full range of the bomber aircraft and to allow more bomb payload and less weight used for fuel. Except for the hills of North York Moors, highest point 1,490ft (454m), and Lincolnshire Wolds, highest point 551ft (168m), the land is relatively flat with no mountain ranges to be crossed close to the stations. The higher elevations were to the west of the Bomber Command station areas. Lossiemouth in Scotland is situated within half a mile of the North Sea.

The selected area would have flat land for the runways with no major obstructions for taking off or landing. In later years the domestic buildings were removed from the airfield and scattered for safety in event of bombing of the airfield. A station had to avoid disruption to major thoroughfares, and be away from populated areas. Local weather was also considered.

A hand-coloured Ordinance Survey map would be prepared showing the different owners, occupiers, renters of the selected land and the district valuer would visit each to calculate a fair market value for releasing the land under the 1939 Compensation (Defence) Act. Initially the stations averaged 400 acres (162ha) but by 1945 this had nearly doubled because of the hard-surfaced runways.

The infrastructure of water and power had to be available along with accessibility to rail and road transport. The 'hydraulic pump from

Manchester' had to be able to reach the station within a reasonable time. Local villages and towns provided some labour. They would also provide local produce to the station. Although if you believed all the wartime stories, the only thing that really counted were the local pubs and village hall dances to keep the spirits up!

The station took its name from the closest railway halt. In the event of possible duplicate name confusion, the station would take its name from the local post office. This gave rise to great names such as Holme-on-Spalding Moor, Wratting Common, Little Staunton, Warboys, Ludford Magna, Strubby, and Skipton-on-Swale. All these names were familiar during the war and have remained so with historians seventy-five years later.

In 1939 the Air Ministry, as part of its defensive plans, implemented Colonel John Turner's station decoy programme to help protect the real stations from Luftwaffe attacks. The 'Q' sites were designed to attract night attacks and the 'K' sites to attract daytime raids. The 'Q' sites would be constructed fairly close to the real station but in an open area. From the air at night these sites would look like the real station with similar lighting. The idea was the Luftwaffe bombers would think they were dropping their bombs on the station, but they in fact would be bombing lights in open countryside. The 'K' sites would be set up with dummy aircraft, parking areas, and hangars similar to the real station. Large-scale night-time decoys, created during the Blitz to simulate burning British cities, were called 'Starfish' sites.

With over 100 stations used by Bomber Command, the next station was not too far away, and that did not count all the fighter, coastal command, and training airfields. As an example, Fiskerton, mentioned above, had at least six airfields within approximately 6 miles (10km) and Bardney, one of the closest, was only 3.6 miles (6km) to the east. To identify the stations from the air they were each given a unique two-letter Pundit code. For example, Fiskerton was FN and Bardney was BA, visible during the day and night to aircraft overhead the station. The Landmark, or Pundit, Beacon was an airfield identification and navigational beacon. Ten-foot (3m) high letters were displayed in the Signals Square near the Watch Office on the station. The letters were painted on the apron for expediency, or the more permanent airfields had the letters set in concrete rectangles. They could be seen clearly from 2,000ft (610m) altitude in good weather. The Pundit Beacon would flash the two-letter identifier in Morse Code using high-powered flashing red neon tubes. The Pundit Light was mobile and was positioned at briefed locations 2 miles (3.3km) to 5 miles (8.4km) from the airfield. It could also be used to indicate a dummy airfield in the countryside or divert returning aircraft to another station by putting the identifier in a red triangle.

At the outbreak of the Second World War, Bomber Command was operating from twenty-seven permanent grass airfields in England and Scotland. There also was a number of airfields nearing completion as a product of the Royal Air Force's pre-war Expansion Scheme. With the change in Air Ministry policy, due to the Emergency Powers (Defence) Act of 1939, it was able to requisition suitable land for new airfield construction and undertake major extensions at the stations. This consisted of additional barrack blocks, bomb stores, and ancillary buildings.

Bomber Command designated and constructed special airfields for handling damaged aircraft returning from operations. They were Carnaby, Yorkshire, Manston, Kent and Woodbridge, Suffolk. The airfields had a triple runway to accommodate the aircraft.

The Expansion Scheme stations were characterised by distinctive neo-classical red brick buildings in a centralised location, a generic example below, close to the C-type hangars.

Royal Air Force Coltishall (1938) Layout

TAKEOFF/LANDING AREA

WATCH TOWER
HANGARS SIX 'C' TYPE
FIRE TENDER GARAGE PETROL TANKER SHEDS
LUBRICANT & INFLAMMABLE STORE PARACHUTE STORE
WORKSHOPS MAIN STORES
BULK PETROL INSTALLATION ARMOURY CENTRAL HEATING STATION
ENGINE TEST BED FUEL STORE
MOTOR TRANSPORT SHEDS DECONTAMINATION CENTRE
SICK QUARTERS WORKS SERVICES BUILDING CHURCH
INCENDIARY BOMB STORES MACHINE GUN STORES & RANGE
PARADE GROUND FLAG STAFF STATION HQ OFFICES
LIVING QUARTERS MESSES DINING ROOM & INSTITUTE
GYMNASIUM SPORTS FACILITIES
RATION STORE FAMILY STORE

The grass runways were proving inadequate for the heavier bombers, so the runway requirements changed to facilitate all-weather operation. The advantages of tarmac and concrete resulted in a standard 'A' pattern of three runways, a perimeter track, and concrete dispersal hardstands. The dispersal system offered better protection in the event of an attack. Hangars were reserved for major engineering or repair work; day-to-day servicing took part on the hardstands.

From the end of 1940 all new bomber stations had one 4,200ft (1,280m) paved main runway and two 3,330ft (1,006m) sixty degree intersecting subsidiary runways. By October 1941 the main runway had been increased in length to 6,000ft (1,829m) and the subsidiaries were now 4,200ft (1,280m). The runways were 150ft (46m) wide.

The stations were being built rapidly, and in 1941 at its peak it is estimated that one station started construction every three days. The stations were being built as temporary structures that could be built quickly to address the urgent need. If the war was lost of course, a long-lasting permanent structure would have been a waste of time and effort. This rapid construction led to the development of prefabricated Nissen and Romney huts, and the T-Type hangars which were cost effective. The buildings were now dispersed against bombing attack.

Royal Air Force Station Fiskerton, previously mentioned, is a typical example of this Class 'A' type of station built in 1940 to accommodate 2,300 people. It had the standard concrete three intersecting runways with perimeter track, thirty-five concrete dispersal points (hardstands), and three hangars, two T2 and one B1.

There were five main hangar types used on the Bomber Command stations. The bomber aircraft required a larger, more accessible hangar that the fighter aircraft. The hangars were only used for major maintenance and overhaul purposes with regular maintenance being done in the open air at the hardstands connected to the perimeter track. The 'C' Type was the largest most permanent structure, then the B1, the T2, the J and the Blister. The Air Ministry in collaboration with Teesside Bridge & Engineering Ltd, developed a series of end-opening hangars known as Type 'T'. The first design was the T2 built with standard steel-fabricated lattice walls and roof units of welded-and-bolted construction. The complete framework was clad with galvanised corrugated iron.

The Beam Approach Beacon System helped aircraft to land at the station during low visibility and cloudy conditions. A transmitter, mounted on a van placed at the end of the runway, transmitted signals to allow the pilot to line up with the runway and other beacons gave the distance to the runway. When the aircraft was on track there was a steady signal. When the aircraft deviated from that track the signal would change to dots or dashes depending on which side of the track the aircraft had deviated. This would give the pilot the information to correct back to the track. An Outer and Inner Marker were positioned on the track so that the pilot could adjust his rate of descent to cross these beacons at a known height to position the aircraft to land visually on the 'Touch Down' zone. These landing systems required technicians to install and maintain them, both in the aircraft and on the airfield.

One of those technicians was Malcolm Dewar who, because of his amateur radio hobby in his youth, was posted to the

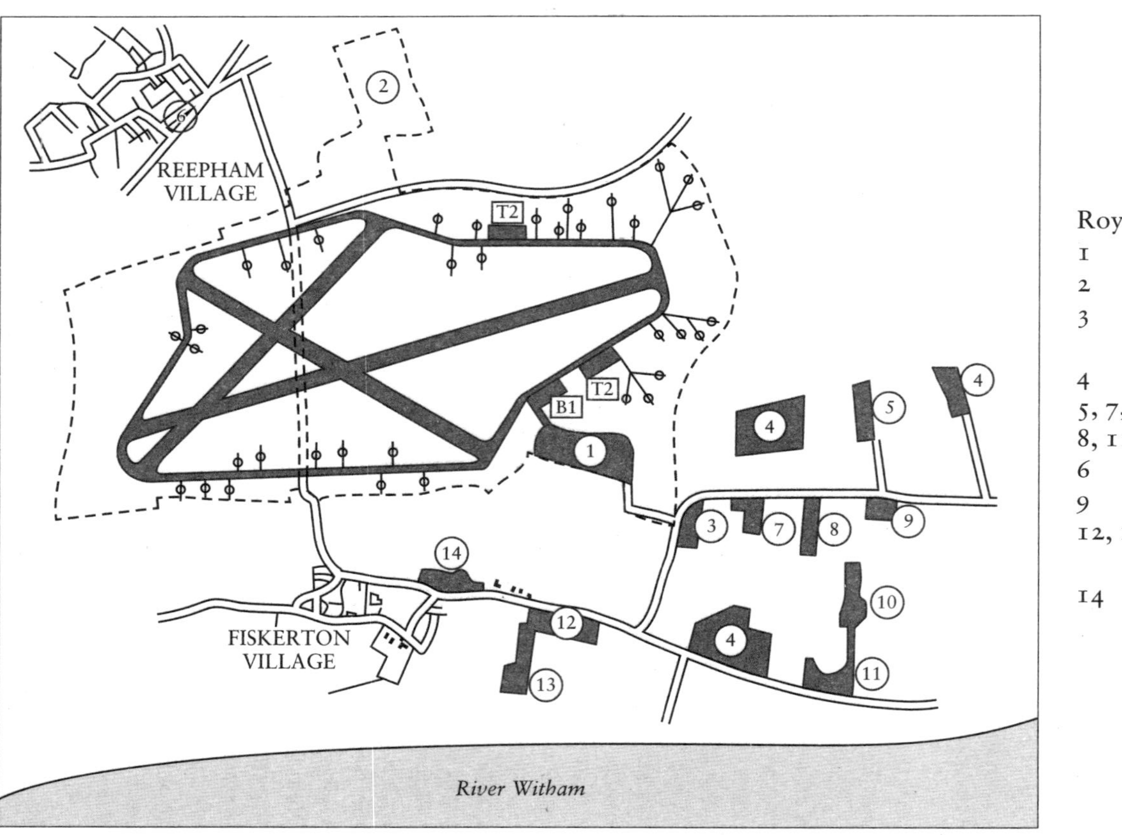

Royal Air Force Station Fiskerton

1	Technical Section
2	Bomb Stores
3	Main Gate & Operations Building
4	Communal Buildings
5, 7, 8, 11	Aircrew Quarters
6	The Fox and Hounds!
9	Sick Quarters
12, 13	Sewage Treatment Plant
14	Women's Auxiliary Air Force Quarters

Telecommunications Section of the RAF during the 1940s. He was later assigned to the famous Telecommunications Research Establishment (TRE) in Malvern, Worcestershire, to learn the top-secret intricacies of 'the landing beam' navigational aid. Returning to his squadron, Royal Air Force No. 12 Squadron based at Wickenby, Lincolnshire, he set up the runway landing system there. Dewar explained the setting up of the landing system:

> It consisted of driving a vehicle up on a ramp to project the beam down the length of the runway and beyond. Calibration to ensure perfect alignment of the beam was carried out mechanically. The entire transmitting apparatus was mounted in the back of the vehicle with the antennae unfolded in two arms. The basic principle was that there were two sectors, left or right of the beam, relayed to the pilot and it was necessary to follow the instrument indications to line up with the runway.

One night while setting up the landing system Dewar was listening to the Watch Office talking to an aircraft, Easy 2, that had aborted its mission as the bomb bay doors would not open. It was instructed to hold at 3,000ft (914m) while clearance was received for the aircraft to proceed to a special designated crash airfield. These special stations had better facilities for taking care of disabled aircraft, especially if a fiery crash was feared.

> Just then I heard the aircraft pass low overhead and was about to call the Watch Office to tell them of its position when the aircraft crashed close by into the bomb storage site. There were no survivors and I was lucky that the aircraft missed me and that the bomb site did not explode.

To further help the pilots see the runway in bad visibility conditions sixteen special airfields were equipped with the Fog Investigation and Dispersal Operation (FIDO) landing system. Fiskerton was one of these special airfields. Damaged aircraft and other aircraft experiencing weather problems would be diverted to FIDO-equipped stations to land safely.

The FIDO system consisted of pipelines alongside the runway which pumped petrol out of burner jets along both sides of the runway. Typically, the rate was 90,000 gallons (340,700 litres) of petrol burnt per hour. The vapours from these burners were lit by a vehicle with a flaming brand on it – driving fast! – down both sides of the runway. The heat from the flames evaporated suspended fog droplets so that there would be a clearing in the fog directly over the runway that would allow the pilot to see the landing area.

By 1939 two parallel sets of lights had been installed in the landing area but helpful as they were to the returning aircraft they were also highly visible to enemy aircraft. Airfield Lighting, usually referred to as 'Drem' lighting after the first airfield it was installed in, had hooded lights that could only be seen by the landing aircraft. In addition, it had approach lighting to guide the aircraft to the runway and a 12-mile (19-km) holding circle of lights, or orbiting lights, used while the aircraft waited its turn to land.

The Watch Tower was the controlling and communications heart of the station. Not only did it provide the air and ground traffic control and operations room, it was also the teleprinter communications centre. In some instances, it had the crew briefing area attached. It was fully equipped with a kitchen and rest area for twenty-four operations.

Local airfield defences were not included in Group-wide planning. Some were moderately defended, some heavily. The rationing after the hasty evacuation of Dunkirk led to the airfields receiving limited Anti-Aircraft assets. Locally, the airfields coordinated their defences from a battle headquarters. Mostly underground, it did have an observation post affording a slit view of the surrounding area.

Perimeter fences, foot and vehicle patrols, pillboxes, and a Guard House were part of the defences. Some airfields had Pickett-Hamilton Forts. This was a hydraulically controlled two-man concrete cylinder that was flush with the ground. When needed it was accessed by a small hatch and rung ladder and raised about 30in (0.76m) above ground level revealing three openings to be used similarly to a fixed pillbox as gunnery positions.

The runways could be completed in seven months with a 1,000-person work force completing a Class 'A' Heavy Bomber airfield in eighteen months. The average cost in 1942 for this type of airfield was one million pounds. In 1943, Lakenheath, Marham, and Sculthorpe were identified as suitable for improvements to Very Heavy Bomber status that required a 9,000ft (2,743m) runway and were closed to operations in 1944-1945.

I interviewed Barbara Petticrew, née Stovin, who lived on a farm during the war in Aby, just 2.4 miles (4km) west of Strubby, Lincolnshire, a Lancaster station. She was surrounded by seven active stations within approximately 10 miles (17km): Spilsby, East Kirkby, Woodhall Spa, Bardney, Wickenby, Ludford Magna, Kelstern, and North Coates. She was 'in the thick of it'.

She was ten years old at the start of the war and took her bike and train to go to school in Louth. I asked her what happened when the air raid sirens went off. She said 'I slept underneath a table. The noise you could not do much about, day or night.' During the blackout she said that everyone was afraid that they would be bombed, 'there were fighters and bombers everywhere.' There were air raid shelters at her school, and she mentioned that 'We dug one in the garden; everyone dug their own.' A bomb did explode on one of the family's fields and 'Everyone came to look at the hole in the ground. Very dangerous, it really was. The (Luftwaffe) bombers would drop their bombs, get out quick, and drop bombs on their way out.'

Air Raid Wardens would look for incendiary bombs; her brother volunteered. Everything was rationed but living on the farm they had their own butter, milk, and eggs, although

> I do remember that there was a lack of food, and clothing was rationed. I was sent away to boarding school in Bury St. Edmunds because my parents thought it would be safer because everything was flying over the top of us but, in fact, it was more dangerous with the V bombs. I remember going to Lincoln having to buy this terrible dress because I needed a dress for Sundays at boarding school. Still remember that dress; it was absolutely awful, but it was the only thing that would fit. It was bright green with red French frills.

After talking about the war and rekindling old memories, some not so pleasant, it was good to end the interview laughing together. Such was the indomitable spirit of the British people who were living the struggle daily.

The following is a list of the stations used by Bomber Command during the Second World War noting their location, some basic information, resident squadrons, and aircraft types.

Bedfordshire

CRANFIELD

PUNDIT CODE: CX

Location: 8.1 miles (13km) southwest of Bedford and 6.3 miles (10.5km) east of Milton Keynes.

Elevation: 358ft (109m) Construction Started: 1935

Paved Runway: Winter 1939

SQUADRON	DATES	STATION AIRCRAFT
35	September 1939 – December 1939	Fairey Battle
207	September 1939 – December 1939	Bristol Blenheim
207	April 1940	Avro Anson

Cambridgeshire

ALCONBURY

PUNDIT CODE: AY
Location: 1.8 miles (3km) north of Huntingdon and 1.2 miles (2km) west of Alconbury
Elevation: 151ft (46m) Construction Started: 1938
Used by United States Army Air Force from 1942

SQUADRON	DATES	STATION AIRCRAFT
40	February 1941 – February 1942	Vickers Wellington
156	February 1942 – August 1942	

BASSINGBOURN

PUNDIT CODE: BS
Location: 3 miles (5km) north of Royston and 11 miles (18km) south west of Cambridge
Elevation: 79ft (24m) Construction Started: March 1938
Paved Runways: Winter of 1941-1942
United States Army Air Force from October 1942
The station was attacked in April 1940; the wireless transmitter and direction-finding equipment were damaged, and in August a barrack block was bombed, which caused eleven fatalities.

SQUADRON	DATES	STATION AIRCRAFT
35	December 1939 – February 1940	Fairey Battle
104	September 1939	Bristol Blenheim
215	September 1939 – April 1940	Avro Anson
		Vickers Wellington

BOURN

PUNDIT CODE: AU
Location: 2 miles (3.2km) north of Bourn and 6.9 miles (11.1km) west of Cambridge
Elevation: 236ft (72m) Construction Started: 1940
Attacked in April 1941 with little damage and no fatalities
Damaged aircraft were repaired and test-flown 1941-1945
No. 8 (Pathfinder Force) Group station (April 1945)

SQUADRON	DATES	STATION AIRCRAFT
15	April 1942 – April 1943	Short Stirling
97	April 1943 – April 1944	Vickers Wellington
101	February 1942 – August 1942	Avro Lancaster

SQUADRON	DATES	STATION AIRCRAFT
105	March 1944 – June 1945	De Havilland Mosquito
162	December 1944 – July 1945	

GRANSDEN LODGE

PUNDIT CODE: GD

Location: 10.1 miles (16.3km) west of Cambridge

Elevation: 230ft (70m) Construction Started: April 1941

No. 8 (Pathfinder Force) Group station (April 1945)

SQUADRON	DATES	STATION AIRCRAFT
142	October 1944 – September 1945	De Havilland Mosquito
405	April 1943 – May 1945	Handley Page Halifax
692	June 1945 – September 1945	Avro Lancaster

MEPAL

PUNDIT CODE: MP

Location: 0.7 miles (1.1km) south of Mepal and 5.9 miles (9.5km) west of Ely

Elevation: 80ft (24m) Construction Started: June 1942

SQUADRON	DATES	STATION AIRCRAFT
7	July 1945 – September 1945	Short Stirling
44	July 1945 – August 1945	Avro Lancaster
75	June 1943 – July 1945	

OAKINGTON

PUNDIT CODE: OA

Location: 0.5 miles (0.8km) north of Oakington and 5.1 miles (8.2km) northwest of Cambridge

Elevation: 22ft (6.7m) Construction Started: 1939

No. 3 Photograph Reconnaissance Unit

No. 8 (Pathfinder Force) Group station (April 1945)

SQUADRON	DATES	STATION AIRCRAFT
7	October 1940 – July 1945	Bristol Blenheim
101	June 1940 – February 1942	Vickers Wellington
218	July 1940 – November 1940	Short Stirling
571	April 1944 – July 1945	Avro Lancaster
627	November 1943 – April 1944	De Havilland Mosquito

WATERBEACH

PUNDIT CODE: WJ

Location: 5.5 miles (8.9km) north of Cambridge

Elevation: 33ft (10m) Construction Started: 1940

SQUADRON	DATES	STATION AIRCRAFT
514	November 1943 – August 1945	Avro Lancaster

WITCHFORD

PUNDIT CODE: EL

Location: 2 miles (3km) southwest of Ely and 13 miles (21km) north of Cambridge

Elevation: 46ft (14m) Construction Started: 1942

SQUADRON	DATES	STATION AIRCRAFT
115	November 1943 – September 1945	Short Stirling
195	October 1944 – November 1944	Avro Lancaster
196	July 1943 – November 1943	

WRATTING COMMON

PUNDIT CODE: WW

Location: 1.2 miles (2km) west of West Wickham

Officially named West Wickham, changed name in August 1943

Elevation: 33ft (10m) Construction Started: 1942

SQUADRON	DATES	STATION AIRCRAFT
90	May 1943 – October 1943	Short Stirling
195	November 1944 – August 1945	Avro Lancaster

Durham

CROFT

PUNDIT CODE: CR

Location: 4.6 miles (7.4km) south of Darlington

Elevation:180ft (55m) Construction Started: 1941

Post-1942 a Royal Canadian Air Force station

SQUADRON	DATES	STATION AIRCRAFT
78	October 1941 – June 1942	Armstrong Whitworth Whitley
419	September 1942 – November 1942	Vickers Wellington
427	November 1942 – May 1943	Avro Lancaster

SQUADRON	DATES	STATION AIRCRAFT
431	December 1943 – June 1945	
434	December 1943 – June 1945	

MIDDLETON St. GEORGE
PUNDIT CODE: MG
Location: 5 miles (8.3km) east of Darlington
Elevation: 120ft (37m) Construction Started: 1940
Formerly Royal Air Force Station Goosepool, changed name in 1941

SQUADRON	DATES	STATION AIRCRAFT
76	June 1941 – September 1942	Armstrong Whitworth Whitley
78	April 1941 – October 1941	Handley Page Halifax
78	June 1942 – September 1942	Avro Lancaster
419	November 1942 – June 1945	
420	October 1942 – May 1943	
428	June 1943 – June 1945	

Essex

RIDGEWELL
PUNDIT CODE: RD
Location: 7.5 miles (12.1km) northwest of Halstead
Elevation: 151ft (46m) Construction Started: 1942

SQUADRON	DATES	STATION AIRCRAFT
90	December 1942 – May 1943	Short Stirling

Huntingdonshire

GRAVELEY
PUNDIT CODE: GR
Location: 5 miles (8.0km) south of Huntingdon
Elevation: 16ft (5m) Construction Started: 1941
No. 8 (Pathfinder Force) Group station (April 1945)

SQUADRON	DATES	STATION AIRCRAFT
35	August 1942 – September 1945	Handley Page Halifax
227	June 1945 – September 1945	Avro Lancaster
692	January 1944 – June 1945	

LITTLE STAUGHTON

PUNDIT CODE: LX
Location: 1.7m (2.7km) south of Great Staughton
Elevation: 207ft (63m) Construction Started: 1941
No. 8 (Pathfinder Force) Group station (April 1945)

SQUADRON	DATES	STATION AIRCRAFT
109	April 1944 – September 1945	De Havilland Mosquito
582	April 1944 – September 1945	Avro Lancaster

MOLESWORTH

Location: 10.6 miles (17km) northwest of Huntingdon
Elevation: 253ft (77m) Construction Started: 1940
1941 Royal Australian Air Force, 1942 United States Army Air Force

SQUADRON	DATES	STATION AIRCRAFT
159	January 1942 – mid 1942	Vickers Wellington
460	November 1941 – January 1942	Consolidated Liberator

UPWOOD

PUNDIT CODE: UD
Location: 0.9 miles (1.5km) southwest of Ramsey
Elevation: 72ft (22m) Construction Started: 1936 Paved Runways October 1943
The German spy Josef Jakobs was captured in the local area with information on Upwood
No. 8 (Pathfinder Force) Group station (April 1945)

SQUADRON	DATES	STATION AIRCRAFT
35	February 1940 – April 1940	Bristol Blenheim
90	September 1939 – April 1940	De Havilland Mosquito
105	June 1945 – September 1945	Avro Lancaster
139	February 1944 – September 1945	
156	March 1944 – June 1945	

WARBOYS

PUNDIT CODE: WB
Location: South of Warboys village
Elevation: 98ft (30m) Construction Started:1940
It had one exceptionally long runway measuring 6,290ft (1,917m)
No. 8 (Pathfinder Force) Group station (April 1945)

SQUADRON	DATES	STATION AIRCRAFT
128	June 1945 – September 1945	De Havilland Mosquito
156	August 1942 – March 1944	Vickers Wellington
571	July 1945 – September 1945	Avro Lancaster

WYTON

Location: 5 miles (8.3km) east of Huntingdon and 12 miles (20km) northwest of Cambridge

Elevation: 132ft (40.2m) Construction Started: 1915

Wyton was a merger of two separate bases, Brampton and Henlow

No. 8 (Pathfinder Force) Group station (April 1945)

SQUADRON	DATES	STATION AIRCRAFT
15	December 1939 – April 1940	Bristol Blenheim
40	December 1939 – February 1941	Vickers Wellington
57	May 1940 – June 1940	Avro Lancaster
83	August 1942 – April 1944	De Havilland Mosquito
109	December 1942 – July 1943	
114	September 1939 – December 1939	
128	September 1944 – June 1945	
139	September 1939 – December 1939	
139	July 1943 – February 1944	
156	June 1945 – September 1945	
163	January 1945 – August 1945	

Lincolnshire

BARDNEY

PUNDIT CODE: BA

Location: 1.7 miles (2.7km) north of Bardney, 10.2 miles (16.4km) east of Lincoln

Elevation: 39ft (12m) Construction Started: 1942

Satellite to Waddington

SQUADRON	DATES	STATION AIRCRAFT
9	April 1943 – July 1945	Avro Lancaster
189	October 1944 – November 1944	

BINBROOK

PUNDIT CODE: BK

Location: near village of Binbrook, domestic site now called Brookenby
Elevation: 328ft (100m) Construction Started: 1939 Paved Runways: 1943
Home to Royal Australian Air Force post 1943

SQUADRON	DATES	STATION AIRCRAFT
12	July 1940 – August 1940	Fairey Battle
12	September 1940 – September 1942	Vickers Wellington
142	July 1940 – August 1940	Avro Lancaster
460	May 1943 – July 1945	

BLYTON

PUNDIT CODE: AL

Location: 4.8 miles (7.7km) northeast of Gainsborough and 9.6 miles (15.4km) south of Scunthorpe
Elevation: 79ft (24m) Construction Started: 1941

SQUADRON	DATES	STATION AIRCRAFT
199	November 1942 – February 1943	Vickers Wellington

BOTTESFORD

PUNDIT CODE: AQ

Location: 6.8 miles (10.9km) northwest of Grantham and 7.6 miles (12.2km) south of Newark-on-Trent
Elevation: 108ft (33m) Construction Started: 1940
Home to Royal Australian Air Force post November 1942

SQUADRON	DATES	STATION AIRCRAFT
90	November 1942 – December 1942	Short Stirling
207	November 1941 – September 1942	Avro Manchester
467	November 1942 – June 1945	Avro Lancaster

CONINGSBY

Location: 8.5 miles (13.7km) southwest of Horncastle and 9.8 miles (15.8km) northwest of Boston
Elevation: 24ft (7m) Construction Started: 1940 Paved Runway: August 1943
No. 8 (Pathfinder Force) Group station (April 1945)
1976: home of Battle of Britain Memorial Flight

SQUADRON	DATES	STATION AIRCRAFT
61	February 1944 – April 1944	Handley Page Hampden
83	April 1944 – September 1945	Avro Manchester
97	March 1941 – March 1942	Avro Lancaster
106	February 1941 – September 1942	
617	August 1943 – January 1944	
619	January 1944 – April 1944	

DUNHOLME LODGE

PUNDIT CODE: DL

Location: 0.9 miles (1.5km) west of Dunholme

Elevation: 125ft (38m) Construction Started: 1941

1944 flying operations ceased due to proximity of other stations

SQUADRON	DATES	STATION AIRCRAFT
44	May 1943 – September 1944	Avro Lancaster
170	October 1944 – November 1944	
619	April 1944 – September 1944	

EAST KIRKBY

PUNDIT CODE: EK

Location: close to the village of East Kirkby 4.8 miles (8km) southeast of Horncastle

Elevation: 46ft (14m) Construction Started: 1943

SQUADRON	DATES	STATION AIRCRAFT
57	August 1943 – September 1945	Avro Lancaster
460	July 1945 – September 1945	
630	November 1943 – July 1945	

ELSHAM WOLDS

PUNDIT CODE: ES

Location: 2.4 miles (4km) northwest of Humberside airport, north side of Elsham

Elevation: 249ft (76m) Construction Started: 1939

SQUADRON	DATES	STATION AIRCRAFT
100	April 1945 – September 1945	Vickers Wellington
103	July 1941 – September 1945	Handley Page Halifax
576	November 1943 – October 1944	Avro Lancaster

FALDINGWORTH

PUNDIT CODE: FH

Location: 1.2 miles (2km) west of the village of Faldingworth

Elevation: 49ft (15m) Construction Started: 1943

Satellite of Lindholme and later of Ludford Magna

SQUADRON	DATES	STATION AIRCRAFT
300	March 1944 – September 1945	Avro Lancaster

FISKERTON

PUNDIT CODE: FN

Location: 5 miles (8km) east of Lincoln

Elevation: 56ft (17m) Construction Started: 1942

One of only fifteen Royal Air Force airfields equipped with the FIDO landing system

SQUADRON	DATES	STATION AIRCRAFT
49	January 1943 – October 1944	Avro Lancaster
150	November 1944	
576	October 1944 – September 1945	

FULBECK

PUNDIT CODE: FK

Location: 6.3 miles (10.1km) east of Newark-on-Trent and 10.9 miles (17.5km) west of Sleaford

Elevation: 39ft (12m) Construction Started: 1940

Used by the United States Army Air force post October 1943

SQUADRON	DATES	STATION AIRCRAFT
49	October 1944 – April 1945	Avro Lancaster
189	November 1944 – September 1945	

GRIMSBY/WALTHAM

PUNDIT CODE: GY

Location: 3.6 miles (6km) south of Grimsby close to the village of Waltham

Elevation: 72ft (22m) Construction Started: 1941

SQUADRON	DATES	STATION AIRCRAFT
100	December 1942 – April 1945	Vickers Wellington
142	November 1941 – December 1942	Avro Lancaster
550	November 1943 – January 1945	

HEMSWELL

PUNDIT CODE: HL

Location: 7.8 miles (12.6km) east of Gainsborough

Elevation: 177ft (54m) Construction Started: 1935

Paved Runways: 1943

SQUADRON	DATES	STATION AIRCRAFT
61	September 1939 – July 1941	Handley Page Hampden
150	November 1944 – September 1945	Vickers Wellington
170	November 1944 – September 1945	Avro Lancaster
300	July 1941 – May 1942	
300	January 1943 – June 1943	
301	July 1941 – April 1943	
305	July 1942 – June 1943	

INGHAM

Location: 10.3 miles (16.6km) north of Lincoln

Elevation: 200ft (61m) Construction Started: 1940

In November 1944 renamed Cammeringham to avoid confusion with two other Inghams

SQUADRON	DATES	STATION AIRCRAFT
199	February 1943 – June 1943	Vickers Wellington
300	May 1942 – January 1943	
300	June 1943 – March 1944	
305	June 1943 – September 1943	

KELSTERN

PUNDIT CODE: KS

Location: 3.6 miles (5.8km) southeast of Binbrook and 4.9 miles (7.9km) northwest of Louth

Elevation: 420ft (128m) Construction Started: 1943

SQUADRON	DATES	STATION AIRCRAFT
170	October 1944	Avro Lancaster
625	October 1943 – April 1945	

KIRMINGTON

PUNDIT CODE: KG

Location: 6.2 miles (10km) northeast of Brigg and 11 miles (18km) south of Grimsby

Elevation: 72ft (22m)   Construction Started: 1942

SQUADRON	DATES	STATION AIRCRAFT
142	December 1942 – January 1943	Vickers Wellington
150	October 1942 – January 1943	Avro Lancaster
153	October 1944	
166	January 1943 – September 1945	

LUDFORD MAGNA

PUNDIT CODE: LM

Location: South of Ludford and 21.4 miles (34.4km) northeast of Lincoln

Elevation: 430ft (131m) Construction Started: 1943

First airfield in No. 1 Group to be equipped with the FIDO landing system

SQUADRON	DATES	STATION AIRCRAFT
101	June 1943 – September 1945	Avro Lancaster

METHERINGHAM

PUNDIT CODE: MN

Location: Near the villages of Metheringham and Martin 12.1 miles (19.5km) southeast of Lincoln

Elevation: 200ft (61m)   Construction Started: 1942

It was equipped with an early experimental FIDO landing system

SQUADRON	DATES	STATION AIRCRAFT
106	November 1943 – September 1945	Avro Lancster
467	June 1945 – September 1945	

NORTH KILLINGHOLME

PUNDIT CODE: NK

Location: 3.6 miles (6km) northeast of Kirmington, west of the village of North Killingholme

Elevation: 26ft (8m)   Construction Started: 1943

SQUADRON	DATES	STATION AIRCRAFT
550	January 1945 – September 1945	Avro Lancaster

SCAMPTON

Location: 6 miles (9.7km) northwest of Lincoln
Elevation: 203ft (62m) Construction Started: 1936 Paved Runways: October 1944
Home of 617 (Dambusters) Squadron with 'Upkeep' bouncing bomb

SQUADRON	DATES	STATION AIRCRAFT
49	September 1939 – January 1943	Fairey Battle
57	September 1942 – August 1943	Handley Page Hampden
83	September 1939-August 1942	Avro Manchester
98	March 1940	Avro Lancaster
153	October 1944 – September 1945	
467	November 1942	
617	May 1943 – August 1943	
625	April 1945 – September 1945	

SKELLINGTHORPE

PUNDIT CODE: FG
Location: 2 miles (3.3km) southwest of the city of Lincoln
Elevation: 118ft (36m) Construction Started: 1940

SQUADRON	DATES	STATION AIRCRAFT
50	November 1941 – June 1942	Handley Page Hampden
61	November 1943 – February 1944	Avro Manchester
61	April 1944 – June 1945	Avro Lancaster
463	July 1945 – September 1945	
619	June 1945 – July 1945	

SPILSBY

PUNDIT CODE: SL
Location: Village of Great Steeping 2 miles (3.2km) southwest of Gunby
Elevation: 33ft (10m) Construction Started: 1942

SQUADRON	DATES	STATION AIRCRAFT
44	September 1944 – July 1945	Avro Lancaster
75	July 1945 – September 1945	
207	October 1943 – September 1945	

STRUBBY

PUNDIT CODE: NY

Location: 2.9 miles (4.7km) north of Alford and 8.6 miles (13.8km) southeast of Louth

Elevation: 39ft (12m) Construction Started: 1942

SQUADRON	DATES	STATION AIRCRAFT
227	April 1945 – June 1945	Avro Lancaster
619	September 1944 – June 1945	

STURGATE

Location: 10 miles (16km) north of Lincoln

Elevation: 52ft (16m) Construction Started: 1944

SQUADRON	DATES	STATION AIRCRAFT
50	June 1945 – September 1945	Avro Lancaster
61	June 1945 – September 1945	

SWINDERBY

PUNDIT CODE: SN

Location: 7.2 miles (12km) southwest of Lincoln

Elevation: 62ft (19m) Construction Started: 1940

Polish Air Force Colour presented to No. 300 Bomber Squadron

SQUADRON	DATES	STATION AIRCRAFT
50	July 1941 – November 1941	Handley Page Hampden
300	August 1940 – July 1941	Fairey Battle
301	August 1940 – July 1941	Vickers Wellington
455	June 1941 – February 1942	

WADDINGTON

Location: 4.2 miles (6.8km) south of Lincoln

Elevation: 230ft (70.1m) Construction Started: 1937

In November 1940 it was the first station to receive the Avro Manchester

No. 44 Squadron was the first to fly the Avro Lancaster in operations

SQUADRON	DATES	STATION AIRCRAFT
9	April 1942 – April 1943	Fairey Battle
9	July 1945 – September 1945	Handley Page Hampden

SQUADRON	DATES	STATION AIRCRAFT
44	September 1939 – May 1943	Vickers Wellington
50	September 1939 – July 1940	Avro Manchester
97	February 1941 – March 1941	Avro Lancaster
142	June 1940 – July 1940	
207	November 1940 – November 1941	
420	December 1941 – August 1942	
463	November 1943 – July 1945	
467	November 1943 – June 1945	
617	June 1945 – September 1945	

WICKENBY

PUNDIT CODE: UI

Location: 9.2 miles (15km) northeast of Lincoln between Wickenby and Holton cum Beckering

Elevation: 82ft (25m) Construction Started: 1942

SQUADRON	DATES	STATION AIRCRAFT
12	September 1942 – September 1945	Vickers Wellington
626	November 1943 – September 1945	Avro Lancaster

WOODHALL SPA

PUNDIT CODE: WS

Location: 2 miles (3.2km) north of Coningsby and 16 miles (26km) southeast of Lincoln

Elevation: 33ft (10m) Construction Started: 1941

The 12,000lb (5,443kg) 'Tallboy' bomb was first dropped by aircraft from this station

Tirpitz sank by aircraft from this station and Bardney

Petwood Hotel was the Officer's Mess for the station

No. 8 (Pathfinder Force) Group station (April 1945)

SQUADRON	DATES	STATION AIRCRAFT
97	March 1942 – April 1943	Airspeed Oxford
617	January 1944 – June 1945	Avro Lancaster
619	April 1943 – January 1944	De Havilland Mosquito
627	April 1944 – September 1945	

MORAY

LOSSIEMOUTH

Location: Western edge of the town of Lossiemouth, northeast Scotland

Elevation: 41ft (12.5m) Construction Started: 1939

SQUADRON	DATES	STATION AIRCRAFT
21	June 1940 – October 1940	Bristol Blenheim
57	June 1940 – August 1940	Vickers Wellington
		Avro Lancaster

Norfolk

ATTLEBRIDGE

PUNDIT CODE: AT

Location: 8 miles (13km) northwest of Norwich

Elevation: 197ft (60m) Construction Started: 1941

United States Army Air Force from September 1942

SQUADRON	DATES	STATION AIRCRAFT
88	August 1941 – September 1942	Bristol Blenheim
320	March 1943 – August 1943	Douglas Boston
		North American Mitchell

BODNEY

PUNDIT CODE: BO

Location: 4.5 miles (7.2km) west of Walton

Elevation: 131ft (40m) Construction Started: 1939

United States Army Air Force from May 1943

SQUADRON	DATES	STATION AIRCRAFT
21	March 1942 – October 1942	Bristol Blenheim
		Lockheed Ventura

DOWNHAM MARKET

PUNDIT CODE: DO

Location: 7.2 miles (12km) south of King's Lynn

Elevation: 121ft (37m) Construction Started: 1942

Satellite station for Marham. October 1943 equipped with FIDO

No. 8 (Pathfinder Force) Group station (April 1945)

SQUADRON	DATES	STATION AIRCRAFT
214	December 1943 – January 1944	Short Stirling

SQUADRON	DATES	STATION AIRCRAFT
218	July 1942 – March 1944	De Havilland Mosquito
571	April 1944	Avro Lancaster
608	August 1944 – August 1945	
623	August 1943 – December 1943	
635	March 1944 – September 1945	

EAST WRETHAM

PUNDIT CODE: UT

Location: 6 miles (9.7km) northeast of Thetford

Elevation: 131ft (40m) Construction Started: 1940

United States Army Air Force from October 1943

SQUADRON	DATES	STATION AIRCRAFT
115	November 1942 – August 1943	Vickers Wellington
311	September 1940 – April 1942	Avro Lancaster

FELTWELL

Location: 10 miles (16.5km) west of Thetford

Elevation: 52ft (16m) Construction Started: 1936

SQUADRON	DATES	STATION AIRCRAFT
37	September 1939 – November 1940	Lockheed Ventura
57	November 1940 – September 1942	Vickers Wellington
75	April 1940 – August 1942	
464	September 1942 – April 1943	
487	August 1942 – April 1943	

FOULSHAM

PUNDIT CODE: FU

Location: 15 miles (25km) northwest of Norwich

Elevation: 148ft (45m) Construction Started: 1941

No. 100 (Bomber Support) Group station

SQUADRON	DATES	STATION AIRCRAFT
98	October 1942 – August 1943	North American Mitchell
180	October 1942 – August 1943	Handley Page Halifax
192	December 1943 – September 1945	Avro Lancaster

SQUADRON	DATES	STATION AIRCRAFT
462	December 1944 – September 1945	De Havilland Mosquito
514	September 1943 – November 1943	

GREAT MASSINGHAM
Location: 8.1 miles (13.0km) southwest of Fakenham
Elevation: 279ft (85m) Construction Started: 1940
Satellite field for West Raynham

SQUADRON	DATES	STATION AIRCRAFT
18	September 1940 – April 1941	Bristol Blenheim
107	May 1941 – August 1943	Douglas Boston
342	July 1943 – September 1943	

HORSHAM St FAITH
PUNDIT CODE: HF
Location: Northern suburbs of Norwich
Elevation: 117ft (36m) Construction Started: 1939
Used by United States Army Air Force from September 1942

SQUADRON	DATES	STATION AIRCRAFT
18	July 1941 – December 1941	Bristol Blenheim
105	December 1941 – September 1942	De Havilland Mosquito
114	June 1940 – August 1940	
139	June 1940 – July 1941	
139	June 1942 – September 1942	

LITTLE SNORING
PUNDIT CODE: LS
Location: 1.8 miles (3km) northeast of Fakenham adjacent to Little Snoring village
Elevation: 157ft (48m) Construction Started: 1943
Satellite for Foulsham
No. 100 (Bomber Support) Group station

SQUADRON	DATES	STATION AIRCRAFT
23	June 1944 – September 1945	Avro Lancaster
115	August 1943 – November 1943	De Havilland Mosquito

SQUADRON	DATES	STATION AIRCRAFT
141	July 1945 – September 1945	
169	December 1943 – September 1945	
515	December 1943 – June 1945	

MARHAM

Location: 1.2 miles (2km) southeast of Marham, 7.2 miles (12km) southeast of King's Lynn

Elevation: 77ft (23.5m) Construction Started: 1935

Closed for wartime operations in March 1944 for paved runway construction

SQUADRON	DATES	STATION AIRCRAFT
38	September 1939 – November 1940	Vickers Wellington
105	September 1942 – March 1944	De Havilland Mosquito
109	April 1944 – September 1945	Short Stirling
115	September 1939 – September 1942	
139	June 1942 – September 1942	
218	November 1940 – July 1942	

METHWOLD

PUNDIT CODE: ML

Location: 2.1 miles (3.4km) northeast of Feltwell and 10.9 miles (17.5km) northwest of Thetford

Elevation: 49ft (15m) Construction Started: 1938 Paved Runways started: August 1943

SQUADRON	DATES	STATION AIRCRAFT
21	October 1942 – April 1943	Lockheed Ventura
149	May 1944 – September 1945	
214	September 1939 – February 1940	Short Stirling
218	August 1944 – December 1944	Vickers Wellington
320	March 1943	Avro Lancaster
464	April 1943 – July 1943	North American Mitchell
487	April 1943 – July 1943	

NORTH CREAKE

PUNDIT CODE: NO

Location: 3.3 miles (5.3km) southwest of Wells-next-the-Sea, 5.7 miles (9.2km) northwest of Fakenham

Elevation: 240ft (73m) Construction Started: 1942

No. 100 (Bomber Support) Group station

SQUADRON	DATES	STATION AIRCRAFT
171	December 1944 – July 1945	Short Stirling
199	May 1944 – July 1945	Handley Page Halifax

OULTON

PUNDIT CODE: OU

Location: 3 miles (4.8km) west of Aylsham, 12.5 miles (20.1km) northwest of Norwich

Elevation: 154ft (47km) Construction Started: 1939

No. 100 (Bomber Support) Group station

SQUADRON	DATES	STATION AIRCRAFT
18	April 1941 – July 1941	Bristol Blenheim
18	November 1941 – December 1941	Lockheed Ventura
21	April 1943 – August 1943	Douglas Boston
88	September 1942 – March 1943	Boeing Fortress
114	August 1940 – March 1941	Consolidated Liberator
139	July 1941 – October 1941	
214	May 1944 – July 1945	
223	August 1944 – July 1945	

SCULTHORPE

PUNDIT CODE: SP

Location: 3 miles (4.8km) west of Fakenham

Elevation: 154ft (47m) Construction Started: 1943

Satellite airport for West Raynham. Main runway 9,000ft (2,743m)

First squadron was the No. 342 (Lorraine) Free French Squadron

No. 100 (Bomber Support) Group station

SQUADRON	DATES	STATION AIRCRAFT
21	September 1943 – December 1943	De Havilland Mosquito
214	January 1944 – May 1944	Boeing Fortress

SQUADRON	DATES	STATION AIRCRAFT
342	May 1943 – July 1943	Douglas Boston
464	July 1943 – December 1943	
487	July 1943 – December 1943	

SWANNINGTON

Location: 1.9 miles (3.1km) south of Cawston, 9.3 miles (15km) northwest of Norwich

Elevation: 131ft (40m) Construction Started: 1942

No. 100 (Bomber Support) Group station. The local pub was the Marsham Arms

SQUADRON	DATES	STATION AIRCRAFT
85	June 1944 – September 1945	De Havilland Mosquito
157	May 1944 – August 1945	

SWANTON MORLEY

PUNDIT CODE: NG

Location: 1.2 miles (2km) northwest of Swanton Morley, 18 miles (30km) northwest of Norwich

Elevation: 148ft (45m) Construction Started: 1940

04 July 1942 first combined bombing raid, Royal Air Force and United States Army Air Force, of the war. Prime Minister Churchill and General Eisenhower attended the briefing at Bylaugh Hall, Headquarters of No.100 (Bomber Support) Group

SQUADRON	DATES	STATION AIRCRAFT
88	July 1941 – August 1941	Bristol Blenheim
88	March 1943 – August 1943	Douglas Boston
98	March 1943 – October 1944	North American Mitchell
105	October 1940 – December 1941	De Havilland Mosquito
226	December 1941 – February 1944	
305	September 1943 – November 1943	
B.S.D.U.	December 1944 – September 1945	

WATTON

PUNDIT CODE: WN

Location: 9 miles (14km) southwest of East Dereham

Elevation: 187ft (57m) Construction Started: 1937

United States Army Air Force from July 1943

SQUADRON	DATES	STATION AIRCRAFT
18	May 1940	Bristol Blenheim
21	September 1939 – June 1940	
21	October 1940 – December 1941	
82	August 1939 – March 1942	
90	May 1941	
105	July 1940 – October 1940	

WEST RAYNHAM

PUNDIT CODE: WR

Location: 2 miles (3.2km) west of West Raynham, 5.5 miles (8.9km) southwest of Fakenham.

Elevation: 253ft (77m) Construction Started: 1939

No. 100 (Bomber Support) Group station

SQUADRON	DATES	STATION AIRCRAFT
18	June 1940 – September 1940	Bristol Blenheim
75	April 1940 – May 1940	Handley Page Hampden
90	May 1941 – June 1941	Avro Anson
98	September 1942 – October 1942	Boeing Fortress
101	September 1939 – June 1940	North American Mitchell
114	July 1941 – November 1942	De Havilland Mosquito
139	May 1940 – June 1940	Douglas Boston
141	December 1943 – July 1945	Bristol Beaufighter
180	September 1942 – October 1942	
239	January 1944 – September 1945	
342	April 1943 – May 1943	

NORTHAMPTONSHIRE
POLEBROOK

PUNDIT CODE: PK

Location: 3.5 miles (5.6km) southeast of Oundle at Polebrook

Elevation: 230ft (70m) Construction Started: 1940

United States Army Air Force from June 1942

SQUADRON	DATES	STATION AIRCRAFT
90	June 1941 – February 1942	Boeing Fortress

Nottinghamshire

BALDERTON

PUNDIT CODE: BN

Location: 2 miles (3.2km) south of Newark-on-Trent

Elevation: 62ft (19m) Construction Started: 1941

Test flight location for Whittle's prototype jet engine in 1943

United States Army Air Force from January 1944

SQUADRON	DATES	STATION AIRCRAFT
227	October 1944 – April 1945	Handley Page Hampden
408	December 1941 – September 1942	Avro Lancaster

LANGAR

PUNDIT CODE: LA

Location: 6 miles (9.7km) southeast of Radcliffe-on-Trent

Elevation: 121ft (37m) Construction Started: 1942

United States Army Air Force from November 1943

SQUADRON	DATES	STATION AIRCRAFT
207	September 1942 – October 1943	Avro Lancaster

NEWTON

PUNDIT CODE: NA

Location: 7 miles (11km) east of Nottingham, 10.7 miles (17.2km) southwest of Newark-on-Trent

Elevation: 180ft (55m) Construction Started: 1939

Polish air training base

SQUADRON	DATES	STATION AIRCRAFT
103	July 1940 – July 1941	Fairey Battle
150	July 1940 – July 1941	Vickers Wellington

SYERSTON

Location: 4.8 miles (8km) southwest of Newark-on-Trent, northwest of Syerston

Elevation: 226ft (69m) Construction Started: 1939

SQUADRON	DATES	STATION AIRCRAFT
49	April 1945 – September 1945	Handley Page Hampden
61	May 1942 – November 1943	Vickers Wellington
106	September 1942 – November 1943	Avro Manchester
304	December 1940 – July 1941	Avro Lancaster
305	December 1940 – July 1941	
408	July 1941 – December 1941	

WIGSLEY

PUNDIT CODE: UG

Location: 7.3 miles (11.7km) east of Tuxford, 7.6 miles (12.2km) west of Lincoln

Elevation: 26ft (8m) Construction Started: 1941

Satellite for Swinderby

SQUADRON	DATES	STATION AIRCRAFT
455	February 1942 – April 1942	Handley Page Hampden

Oxfordshire

ABINGDON

PUNDIT CODE: AB

Location: 5 miles south of Oxford and 1 mile west of Abingdon

Elevation: 226ft (69m) Construction Started: September 1932

Bomber Command training station

SQUADRON	DATES	STATION AIRCRAFT
97	September 1939 – April 1940	Armstrong Whitworth Whitley
103	June 1940	Fairey Battle
166	September 1939 – April 1940	

BICESTER

PUNDIT CODE: BC

Location: Adjacent (northeast) to Bicester 10.8 miles (18km) northeast of Oxford

Elevation: 259ft (79m) Construction Started: 1925

First flight of the Handley Page Halifax in October 1939

Grass surface aerodrome

SQUADRON	DATES	STATION AIRCRAFT
104	September 1939 – April 1940	Bristol Blenheim

HARWELL

PUNDIT CODE: HW

Location: 4.8 miles (7.7km) east of Wantage, 17m (27km) north of Reading

Elevation: 282ft (86m) Construction Started: 1935 Paved Runways: November 1941

SQUADRON	DATES	STATION AIRCRAFT
75	September 1939 – April 1940	Vickers Wellington
148	September 1939 – April 1940	

UPPER HEYFORD

PUNDIT CODE: UH

Location: 5 miles (8.8km) northwest of Bicester

Elevation: 433ft (132m) Construction Started: 1918

Trained crews to fly, navigate and bomb at night

SQUADRON	DATES	STATION AIRCRAFT
7	September 1939 – September 1940	Handley Page Hampden
76	September 1939 – April 1940	Avro Anson
		Short Stirling

Rutland

COTTESMORE

PUNDIT CODE: CT

Location:13.2 miles (22km) east of Leicester, northwest of Cottesmore

Elevation: 463ft (141m) Construction Started: 1936

United States Army Air Force from September 1943

SQUADRON	DATES	STATION AIRCRAFT
106	September 1939 – October 1939	Handley Page Hampden
185	September 1939 – May 1940	Handley Page Hereford
207	December 1939 – April 1940	Fairey Battle
		Avro Anson

NORTH LUFFENHAM
PUNDIT CODE: NL
Location: 5 miles (8km) east of Uppingham, 7 miles (11km) west of Stamford
Elevation: 312ft (95m) Construction Started: 1940

SQUADRON	DATES	STATION AIRCRAFT
61	July 1941 – October 1941	Handley Page Hampden
144	July 1941 – April 1942	Avro Manchester

WOOLFOX LODGE
PUNDIT CODE: WL
Location: 4.2 miles (7km) east of Oakham, 2.4 miles (4km) north of Empingham
Elevation: 33ft (10m) Construction Started: 1940
Satellite for North Luffenham

SQUADRON	DATES	STATION AIRCRAFT
61	October 1941 – May 1942	Handley Page Hampden
218	March 1944 – August 1944	Short Stirling
		Avro Manchester

Suffolk

CHEDBURGH
PUNDIT CODE: CU
Location: 3.6 miles (6km) southwest of Bury St. Edmunds
Elevation: 33ft (10m) Construction Started: 1942

SQUADRON	DATES	STATION AIRCRAFT
214	October 1942 – December 1943	Short Stirling
218	December 1944 – August 1945	Avro Lancaster
620	June 1943 – November 1943	

HONINGTON

Location: 6 miles (9.7km) south of Thetford near Ixworth village
Elevation: 174ft (53m) Construction Started: 1935
9 Squadron flew one of the first Royal Air Force bombing raids on 04 September 1939
United States Army Air Force from June 1942

SQUADRON	DATES	STATION AIRCRAFT
9	July 1939 – August 1942	Fairey Battle
103	June – July 1940	Bristol Blenheim
105	June 1940 – July 1940	Avro Anson
214	January 1942	Vickers Wellington
215	April 1940 – May 1940	
311	July 1940 – September 1940	

LAKENHEATH

Location: 4.7 miles (7.6km) northeast of Mildenhall, 8.3 miles (13.4km) west of Thetford
Elevation: 33ft (10m) Construction Started: 1940 Paved Runways: 1941
1944 construction started to improve runways for Very Heavy bomber operations

SQUADRON	DATES	STATION AIRCRAFT
149	April 1942 – May 1944	Vickers Wellington
199	June 1943 – May 1944	Short Stirling

MILDENHALL

Location: Northwest suburbs of Mildenhall
Elevation: 33ft (10m) Construction Started: 1934
Start of the October 1934 MacRobertson Air Race to Australia
Site of the Crown Film Unit 1941 film *Target for Tonight*

SQUADRON	DATES	STATION AIRCRAFT
15	April 1943 – September 1945	Bristol Blenheim
44	August 1945 – September 1945	Short Stirling
75	August 1942 – November 1942	Vickers Wellington
115	September 1942 – November 1942	Avro Lancaster
149	September 1939 – April 1942	
218	June 1940 – July 1940	
419	December 1941 – August 1942	
622	August 1943 – August 1945	

NEWMARKET
PUNDIT CODE: NM
Location: Rowley Mile Racecourse, Newmarket
Elevation: 102ft (31m) Construction Started: 1941
1942 Gloster Meteor taxi tests

SQUADRON	DATES	STATION AIRCRAFT
75	November 1942 – June 1943	Short Stirling
215	December 1941 – January 1942	

STRADISHALL
PUNDIT CODE: NX
Location: 4.7 miles (7.6km) northeast of Haverhill, 9 miles (14km) southwest of Bury St. Edmunds
Elevation: 381ft (116m) Construction Started: 1937

SQUADRON	DATES	STATION AIRCRAFT
101	August 1942 – September 1942	Fairey Battle
148	April 1940 – May 1940	Vickers Wellington
150	June 1940 – July 1940	Short Stirling
186	December 1944 – July 1945	Avro Lancaster
214	February 1940 – October 1942	
215	January 1942	

TUDDENHAM
PUNDIT CODE: TD
Location: 3.2 miles (5.1km) southeast of Mildenhall, 7.8 miles (12.6) northwest of Bury St. Edmunds
Elevation: 62ft (19m) Construction Started: 1941

SQUADRON	DATES	STATION AIRCRAFT
90	October 1943 – September 1945	Short Stirling
138	March 1945 – September 1945	Avro Lancaster
186	October 1944 – December 1944	

WATTISHAM
PUNDIT CODE: WT
Location: 4.8 miles (8km) northwest of Ipswich
Elevation: 292ft (89m) Construction Started: 1938

Station aircraft flew one of the first Royal Air Force bombing raids on 04 September 1939
United States Army Air Force from September 1942

SQUADRON	DATES	STATION AIRCRAFT
18	December 1941 – August 1942	Bristol Blenheim
107	September 1939 – March 1941	
110	September 1939 – March 1942	
114	May 1940 – June 1940	
226	May 1941 – December 1941	

Warwickshire

BRAMCOTE

PUNDIT CODE: RT
Location: 4 miles (6.4km) southeast of Nuneaton
Elevation: 354ft (113m) Construction Started: 1939

SQUADRON	DATES	STATION AIRCRAFT
300	July 1940 – August 1940	Fairey Battle
301	July 1940 – August 1940	Vickers Wellington
304	August 1940 – December 1940	
305	August 1940 – December 1940	

Yorkshire

BREIGHTON

PUNDIT CODE: AC
Location: 9.6 miles (16km) south of York, 3 miles (5km) east of South Duffield
Elevation: 20ft (6m) Construction Started: 1940
Royal Australian Air Force first residence

SQUADRON	DATES	STATION AIRCRAFT
78	June 1943 – May 1945	Vickers Wellington
460	January 1942 – May 1943	Handley Page Halifax
		Avro Manchester
		Avro Lancaster

BURN
PUNDIT CODE: AZ
Location: 5 miles (8km) south of Selby
Elevation: 20ft (6m) Construction Started: 1941

SQUADRON	DATES	STATION AIRCRAFT
431	November 1942 – July 1943	Vickers Wellington
578	February 1944 – April 1945	Handley Page Halifax

DALTON
PUNDIT CODE: DA
Location: 0.6 miles (1km) east of Topcliffe, 0.6 miles (1km) southwest of Dalton
Elevation: 226ft (69m) Construction Started: 1940

SQUADRON	DATES	STATION AIRCRAFT
102	November 1941 – June 1942	Armstrong Whitworth Whitley
420	November 1943 – December 1943	Vickers Wellington
424	May 1943	Handley Page Halifax
428	November 1942 – June 1943	

DISHFORTH
PUNDIT CODE: DH
Location: 4.4 miles (7.1km) east of Ripon, 11.5 miles (18.5km) northeast of Harrogate
Elevation: 118ft (36m) Construction Started: 1936

SQUADRON	DATES	STATION AIRCRAFT
10	September 1939 – July 1940	Armstrong Whitworth Whitley
51	December 1939 – May 1942	Vickers Wellington
78	September 1939 – December 1939	Handley Page Halifax
78	July 1940 – April 1941	Avro Lancaster
425	June 1942 – May 1943	
425	December 1943 – June 1945	
426	October 1942 – June 1943	

DONCASTER

Location: 3.6 miles (6km) southeast of Doncaster
Elevation: 26ft (8m) Construction Started: 1926

SQUADRON	DATES	STATION AIRCRAFT
7	April 1939 – April 1943	Handley Page Hampden

DRIFFIELD

PUNDIT CODE: DR
Location: 2 miles (3km) southwest of Driffield, 11 miles (18km) northwest of Beverley
Elevation: 82ft (25m) Construction Started: 1935
First fatality of Women's Royal Air Force during Luftwaffe air raid

SQUADRON	DATES	STATION AIRCRAFT
88	June 1940	Armstrong Whitworth Whitley
97	May 1940	Fairey Battle
102	September 1939 – August 1940	Avro Anson
104	April 1941 – February 1942	Vickers Wellington
158	February 1942 – June 1942	Handley Page Halifax
196	November 1942 – December 1942	
405	April 1941 – June 1941	
462	August 1944 – December 1944	
466	October 1942 – December 1942	
466	June 1944 – May 1945	

EAST MOOR

PUNDIT CODE: EM
Location: 7.4 miles (11.9km) north of York, 5.5 miles (8.9km) southeast of Easingwold
Elevation: 92ft (28m) Construction Started: 1941
Royal Canadian Air Force from November 1942

SQUADRON	DATES	STATION AIRCRAFT
158	June 1942 – November 1942	Vickers Wellington
415	July 1944 – May 1945	Handley Page Halifax
429	November 1942 – August 1943	Avro Lancaster
432	September 1943 – May 1945	

ELVINGTON

PUNDIT CODE: EV

Location: 3.6 miles (6km) southeast of York

Elevation: 39ft (12m) Construction Started: 1939 Paved Runways: October 1942

SQUADRON	DATES	STATION AIRCRAFT
77	October 1942 – May 1944	Handley Page Halifax
346	May 1994 – September 1945	
347	June 1944 – September 1945	

FINNINGLEY

PUNDIT CODE: FB

Location: 3 miles (5.5km) southeast of Doncaster, 19 miles (31km) east of Sheffield

Elevation: 33ft (10m) Construction Started: 1915 Paved Runways: 1943

SQUADRON	DATES	STATION AIRCRAFT
7	September 1939	Handley Page Hampden
7	April 1940 – May 1940	Fairey Battle
12	June 1940 – July 1940	Avro Anson
97	March 1940 – April 1940	
106	October 1939 – February 1941	

FULL SUTTON

PUNDIT CODE: FS

Location: 2 miles (3.2km) southeast of Stamford Bridge

Elevation: 86ft (26m) Construction Started: 1943

SQUADRON	DATES	STATION AIRCRAFT
77	May 1944 – May 1945	Handley Page Halifax

HOLME-ON-SPALDING-MOOR

PUNDIT CODE: HM

Location: 9 miles (15km) southeast of York, 2.4 miles (4km) northwest of Holme-on-Spalding-Moor

Elevation: 16ft (5m) Construction Started: 1940

SQUADRON	DATES	STATION AIRCRAFT
76	June 1943 – May 1945	Vickers Wellington
101	September 1942 – June 1943	Handley Page Halifax
458	August 1941 – March 1942	Avro Lancaster

LECONFIELD

PUNDIT CODE: LC

Location: 1.8 miles (3km) north of Beverley

Elevation: 23ft (7m) Construction Started: 1936

SQUADRON	DATES	STATION AIRCRAFT
51	April 1945 – May 1945	Handley Page Halifax
196	December 1942 – July 1943	Vickers Wellington
466	December 1942 – June 1944	Avro Lancaster
640	January 1944 – May 1945	

LEEMING

Location: adjacent to Leeming

Elevation: 133ft (40.5m) Construction Started: 1939

1943 assigned to No. 6 Group Royal Canadian Air Force

SQUADRON	DATES	STATION AIRCRAFT
7	August 1940 – October 1940	Armstrong Whitworth Whitley
10	July 1940 – August 1942	Vickers Wellington
35	November 1940 – December 1940	Handley Page Halifax
7	September 1941 – May 1942	Avro Lancaster
102	August 1940 – September 1940	
405	March 1943 – April 1943	
408	September 1942 – August 1943	
419	August 1942	
424	April 1943 – May 1943	
427	May 1943 – September 1945	
428	August 1943 – March 1945	

LINDHOLME

PUNDIT CODE: LB

Location: 3.9 miles (6.3km) south of Thorne, 6.9 miles (11.1km) northeast of Doncaster

Elevation: 23ft (7m) Construction Started: 1937

Originally called Hatfield Woodhouse

SQUADRON	DATES	STATION AIRCRAFT
50	July 1940 – July 1941	Handley Page Hampden
304	July 1941 – May 1942	Vickers Wellington

SQUADRON	DATES	STATION AIRCRAFT
305	July 1941 – July 1942	
408	June 1941 – July 1941	

LINTON-ON-OUSE

Location: 10 miles (16km) northwest of York
Elevation: 53ft (16m) Construction Started: 1936
May 1941 a Luftwaffe bombing raid killed thirteen airmen including the station commander
No. 8 (Pathfinder Force) Group station (April 1945)

SQUADRON	DATES	STATION AIRCRAFT
35	December 1940 – August 1942	Armstrong Whitworth Whitley
51	September 1939 – December 1939	Handley Page Halifax
58	September 1939 – October 1939	Avro Lancaster
58	February 1940 – April 1942	
76	May 1941 – June 1941	
77	August 1940 – October 1940	
78	December 1939 – July 1940	
78	September 1942 – June 1943	
102	October 1940 – November 1940	
405	May 1945 – June 1945	
408	August 1943 – June 1945	
426	June 1943 – May 1945	

LISSETT

Location: 6 miles (9.8km) southwest of Bridlington
Elevation: 16ft (5m) Construction Started: 1940

SQUADRON	DATES	STATION AIRCRAFT
158	February 1943 – May 1945	Handley Page Halifax

MELBOURNE

PUNDIT CODE: ME
Location: 5 miles (8.2km) southwest of Pocklington
Elevation: Unknown Construction Started: 1940
Paved Runway: 1942
Equipped with FIDO landing system

SQUADRON	DATES	STATION AIRCRAFT
10	August 1942 – May 1945	Handley Page Halifax

POCKLINGTON

PUNDIT CODE: OC

Location: 9.6 miles (16km) east of York, adjacent to Pocklington

Elevation: 98ft (30m) Construction Started:1940 Paved Runways: 1941

SQUADRON	DATES	STATION AIRCRAFT
102	August 1942 – May 1945	Vickers Wellington
405	June 1941 – August 1941	Handley Page Halifax

RUFFORTH

PUNDIT CODE: RU

Location: 3.6 miles (6km) west of York, adjacent to Rufforth

Elevation: 52ft (16m) Construction Started: 1941

SQUADRON	DATES	STATION AIRCRAFT
158	November 1942 – February 1943	Handley Page Halifax

SKIPTON-ON-SWALE

PUNDIT CODE: SK

Location: 4 miles (6.4km) west of Thirsk

Elevation: 82ft (25m) Construction Started: 1942

Hosted four Royal Canadian Air Force squadrons

SQUADRON	DATES	STATION AIRCRAFT
420	August 1942 – October 1942	Vickers Wellington
424	November 1943 – September 1945	Handley Page Halifax
432	May 1943 – September 1943	Avro Lancaster
433	September 1943 – September 1945	

SNAITH

PUNDIT CODE: SX

Location: 7 miles (11km) southwest of Goole, close to Pollington village

Elevation: 43ft (13m) Construction Started: 1940

SQUADRON	DATES	STATION AIRCRAFT
51	October 1942 – April 1945	Handley Page Halifax
150	July 1941 – October 1942	Vickers Wellington
578	January 1944 – February 1944	

THIRSK

Location: Adjacent to the A61 road, and 0.5 miles (0.8km) west of Thirsk
Elevation: 131ft (40m) Construction Started: Racecourse opened 1923
The 'chute' of the present-day racecourse is 3960ft (1208m)
Used occasionally as emergency landing ground for Topcliffe and Skipton
No. 226 Squadron used Thirsk for nine days in transition from France to Northern Ireland

SQUADRON	DATES	STATION AIRCRAFT
226	18-27 June 1940	Fairey Battle

THOLTHORPE

PUNDIT CODE: TH
Location: 2.4 miles (4km) west of Easingwold, 0.6 miles (1km) northeast of Tholthorpe
Elevation: 66ft (20m) Construction Started: 1941
Paved Runway: 1943
Hosted four Royal Canadian Air Force squadrons

SQUADRON	DATES	STATION AIRCRAFT
420	December 1943 – June 1945	Handley Page Halifax
425	December 1943 – June 1945	Avro Lancaster
431	July 1943 – December 1943	
434	June 1943 – December 1943	

TOPCLIFFE

Location: 15 miles (25km) north of York, 1.2 miles (2km) north of Topcliffe
Elevation: 92ft (28m) Construction Started: 1939

SQUADRON	DATES	STATION AIRCRAFT
77	October 1940 – September 1941	Armstrong Whitworth Whitley
102	November 1940 – November 1941	Vickers Wellington
405	August 1941 – October 1942	Handley Page Halifax
405	March 1943 – April 1943	
419	August 1942 – September 1942	
424	October 1942 – April 1943	

No. 100 (Bomber Support) Group

Sorties: 16,746 Aircraft Lost: 122; Aircrew: 550+

BASE	SQUADRON	AIRCRAFT	FIRST OPERATIONS
Little Snoring	23	De Havilland Mosquito	July 1944
Swannington	85	De Havilland Mosquito	June 1944
West Raynham	141	Bristol Beaufighter, De Havilland Mosquito	December 1943
Swannington	157	De Havilland Mosquito	May 1944
Little Snoring	169	De Havilland Mosquito	January 1944
North Creake	171	Short Stirling, Handley Page Halifax	September 1944
Foulsham	192	De Havilland Mosquito, Vickers Wellington Handley Page Halifax	December 1943
North Creake	199	Short Stirling, Handley Page Halifax	May 1944
Sculthorpe, Oulton	214	Boeing Fortress	April 1944
Oulton	223	Consolidated Liberator, Boeing Fortress	September 1944
West Raynham	239	De Havilland Mosquito	January 1944
Foulsham	462 (RAAF)	Handley Page Halifax	March 1945

No. 8 (Pathfinder Force) Group Stations (April 1945)

Sorties: 51,053 Aircraft Lost: 675; Aircrew: 3,700+

Avro Lancaster

WARTIME STATION	COUNTY	SQUADRON
Oakington	Cambridgeshire	7
Graveley	Huntingdonshire	35

WARTIME STATION	COUNTY	SQUADRON
Coningsby	Lincolnshire	83*
Bourn	Cambridgeshire	97*
Upwood	Huntingdonshire	156
Linton-on-Ouse	Yorkshire	405
Little Staughton	Huntingdonshire	582
Downham Market	Norfolk	635

De Havilland Mosquito

WARTIME STATION	COUNTY	SQUADRON
Upwood	Huntingdonshire	105
Little Staughton	Huntingdonshire	109
Warboys	Huntingdonshire	128
Upwood	Huntingdonshire	139
Gransden Lodge	Bedfordshire	142
Bourn	Cambridgeshire	162
Wyton	Huntingdonshire	163
Warboys	Huntingdonshire	571
Downham Market	Norfolk	608
Woodhall Spa	Lincolnshire	627**
Gransden Lodge	Bedfordshire	692

*Squadrons returned to lead No. 5 Group in April 1944

Other Royal Air Force stations used by Bomber Command

STATION	LOCATION
Thurleigh	Bedfordshire
Wittering	Cambridgeshire
Leuchars,	Fifeshire
Beaulieu, Hartford Bridge, Lasham, Odiham, Thorney Island	Hampshire
Hunsdon	Hertfordshire
Eastchurch, Gravesend, Lympne	Kent
Leicester East	Leicestershire

STATION	LOCATION
Kirmington	Lincolnshire
Sydenham	Northern Ireland
Hucknall	Nottinghamshire
Dunsfold, Gatwick	Surrey
Boscombe Down	Wiltshire
Thornaby-on-Tees	Yorkshire

5

BOMBER COMMAND AIRCRAFT AND ENGINES

General characteristics and specifications of aircraft and engines here focus on the European theatre of war and are only to be used as general reader information and are not definitive. Each aircraft and engine came in many marks/series and it is beyond the scope of this book to list each one of them.

The aircraft are the tools of Bomber Command that brought the destruction to the enemy guided by their crews. It is the aluminium, hewn from the earth as bauxite ore, and wood shaped by craftsmen/engineers that defied gravity, the 'ack ack' fire, and the Luftwaffe fighters to deliver the bombs on target. These aircraft took many shapes and sizes during their development from the First World War until the dissolution of Bomber Command in 1968.

During the First World War companies such as De Havilland, Handley Page, and Vickers produced the biplane bomber aircraft. These companies, along with Avro, Boulton Paul, Fairey, and Hawker, designed and produced the aircraft in the peacetime transition during the 1920s from biplane to monoplane aircraft. The Royal Air Force suffered during this period from budgetary constraints as the politicians still favoured the 'Senior Service', the Royal Navy.

In 1934 there was more funding available and Bristol and Armstrong Whitworth joined the previous companies producing bomber aircraft. The Short Stirling and Vickers Wellington were designed and built during the mid-1930s. It was not until 1936 that Britain realised it had neglected its military overall and specifically the bomber force. Suddenly, it was realised that this force was inadequate for the looming war. It would require bigger aircraft to carry heavier payloads longer distances into the heart of industrial Germany. The need would be met initially by the Handley Page Halifax (1939) and Avro Lancaster (1941). These British-designed heavy bombers would serve Bomber Command until the end of the war.

The Bomber Command aircraft that flew above Germany in the 1940s in no way resemble the military aircraft flying today: lack of pressurisation, insulation, and air conditioning immediately come to mind. The Second World War aircraft were extremely noisy, as the manufacturers built heavier aircraft requiring four piston engines instead of two, to carry the ever-increasing payload. Who can forget the sound of Merlins at an airshow when one of the two remaining flying Avro Lancasters takes to the air? The crew lived with that sound for up to twelve hours only separated from the engine and propeller noise by a thin sheet of aluminium, the fuselage.

The Rolls-Royce Merlin had twelve cylinders. The list of engines at the end of this chapter features engines from nine cylinders up to twenty-four cylinders, as in the Hawker Typhoon and Avro Manchester. The total focus was on horsepower and, unfortunately for crew comfort, noise suppression was low on the list of considerations.

The focus of production was on building quickly, cheaply, and for ever larger large payloads. Ergonomics were never a consideration: look inside a Second World War bomber when you get a chance. It was an offensive weapon with some defensive capability that indicated it was not expected to have a long life. The Avro Lancasters that exceeded 100 operations were few and far between and became famous in their own right.

Post-war the piston engine Avro Lincoln and Boeing Washington were the transition bomber aircraft until the turbojet English Electric Canberra joined Bomber Command in 1951. In 1955 the Vickers Valiant initiated the strategic V Bomber Force followed closely by the Avro Vulcan and Handley Page Victor. Bomber Command had joined the nuclear arms club. With the advent of surface-to-air missiles, the previous 'fly faster and higher' philosophy no longer applied. The V bombers then took on a low-level role, which accelerated airframe fatigue. A solution was the nuclear deterrent stand-off role. The aircraft were armed with guided missiles capable of striking targets deep within the Soviet Union. Bomber Command had adopted a new role, being remote from the target after nearly thirty years of the conventional attack mode – over the target and drop the bombs.

A change in defence policy resulted in the merger of Fighter Command and Bomber Command into the newly formed Royal Air Force Strike Command on 30 April 1968. The Avro Vulcan and Handley Page Victor continued to serve Strike Command until 1984 and 1993 respectively.

Bomber Command Aircraft Europe 1939–1945

ARMSTRONG WHITWORTH WHITLEY

- Squadrons: 10, 51, 58, 77, 78, 97, 102, 166
- First Flight: 1937 Number Built: 1,814
- Engine: Armstrong Siddeley Tiger, Rolls-Royce Merlin
- Range: 1,650 miles (2,660km) Service Ceiling: 26,000ft (7,900m)
- Bomb Load: 7,000lb (3,175kg) in fuselage, 4,000lb (1,814kg) in fourteen wing cells

The Whitley was one of four front-line medium bombers at the start of the Second World War. It preceded the Handley Page Hampden and Vickers Wellington and was designed to replace the Handley Page Heyford biplane bomber. It was based on the AW.23 design for a bomber transport aircraft. It initially had the Armstrong Siddeley Tiger radial engine; later models had the Rolls-Royce Merlin engine driving a two-position variable pitch propeller, unique for 1936. The Whitley had the distinction of being the first RAF aircraft with a semi-monocoque fuselage replacing the traditional tubular construction of previous Armstrong Whitworth aircraft.

A verbal order for production was given, which was most unusual, but was a sign of the urgency of the times. The prototype took to the air at Baginton Aerodrome, 3.5 miles (5.6km) south of Coventry, piloted by the Armstrong Whitworth Chief Pilot Alan Campbell-Orde. Further developments included power-operated turrets, increased fuel capacity, modification of tail fins and rudder, leading edge de-icers, hydraulically operated bomb doors, and fuselage extension to improve the rear gunner's field of fire. Initially the aircraft had a manually operated nose and rear turret. These were eventually replaced with a power-operated Nash and Thompson .303in (7.7mm) Vickers K machine gun nose turret and a powered ventral retracting turret. The ventral and tail turrets were eventually replaced with a four Browning .303in (7.7mm) machine gun turret.

The Whitley had a crew of five: a pilot, co-pilot/navigator, a bomb aimer, a wireless operator, and a rear gunner. The pilot and second pilot/navigator sat side by side in the cockpit, with the wireless operator further back. The navigator, his seat mounted on floor rails, slid backwards and swivelled to the left to use his chart table behind him. The bomb aimer, in the nose, had the gun turret above him. The bomb bay divided the fuselage with the main entrance and rear turret aft of it.

AVRO MANCHESTER

- Squadrons: 49, 50, 61, 83, 97, 106, 207
- First Flight: 25 July 1939 Number Built: 202
- Engine: Rolls-Royce Vulture

- Range: 1,230 miles (1,930km) Service Ceiling: 19,200ft (5,853m)
- Bomb Load: 10,350lb (4,695kg)

The Manchester was a British twin-engine medium bomber designed to replace the Armstrong Whitworth Whitley, Handley Page Hampden and Vickers Wellington. The Air Ministry's specification demanded shallow, thirty degrees dive bombing attacks and an 8,000lb (3,630kg) bomb load. It used the Rolls-Royce Vulture engine, which proved to be underpowered and very unreliable. Initial production aircraft had a twin tail, a central fin was used on the prototype only. The aircraft was designed with ease of manufacture and repair as paramount. The fuselage was made of longerons with an external aluminium alloy skin. It had three powered turrets: nose, mid upper, and rear (tail).

The bomb bay was the defining feature of the design covering about two-thirds of the fuselage floor. It had hydraulic bomb bay doors and internal bomb racks. The bomb bay was also capable of carrying torpedoes. The aircraft was considered an operational failure by the Royal Air Force and production was stopped after only a year. The Manchester is best remembered as the aircraft which gave birth to the famous, very successful, Avro Lancaster bomber by having its attributes incorporated into the new aircraft. Those, plus the addition of four Roll-Royce Merlin engines, turned the Manchester's successor into a winning combination.

The Manchester had a crew of seven: a pilot seated on the left side of cockpit, flight engineer next to pilot on folding seat, bomb aimer/nose turret lying down when directing pilot, navigator behind pilot facing port (left side), wireless operator aft of navigator facing forward, mid upper gunner, and rear gunner.

AVRO LANCASTER

- Squadrons: 7, 9, 12, 15, 35, 44, 49, 50, 57. 61, 75, 83, 90, 97, 100, 101, 103, 106, 115, 138, 149, 150, 153, 156, 166, 170, 186, 189, 195, 207, 218, 227, 300, 405, 408, 419, 420, 424, 425, 426, 427, 428, 429, 431, 432, 433, 434, 460, 463, 467, 514, 550, 576, 582, 617, 619, 622, 623, 625, 626, 630, 635
- First Flight: 09 January 1941 Number Built: 7,377
- Engine: Rolls-Royce Merlin
- Range: 2,530 miles (4,073km) Service Ceiling: 21,400ft (6,500m)
- Bomb Load: 14,000lb (6,400kg) normal, 22,000lb (10,000kg) bomb bay doors off

The Lancaster, the 'Lanc', was a British four-engine heavy bomber which arguably was the most famous Second World War bomber. It was developed and in service at the same time as the Handley Page Halifax and Short Stirling. Designed by Roy Chadwick, it had its roots in the unsuccessful, under-powered, and unreliable twin Rolls-Royce Vulture-engined Avro Manchester. Chadwick improved the basic design by using four reliable Rolls-Royce Merlin engines on a new wing centre section. The Merlin is also surely the most famous engine of the war. On 9 January 1941 the prototype went airborne under the control of Avro test pilot H. A. 'Sam' Brown.

The demand for the Lancaster exceeded the Avro capacity and other manufacturers in England produced the aircraft under licence. It was also made in Canada by Victory Aircraft at Malton, Ontario, which used the Packard Merlin engine manufactured in the United States of America. A limited number, 300, of Lancasters had the Bristol Hercules engine. In the latter half of the war it was the principal heavy bomber.

It was a mid-wing cantilever monoplane design with a tailplane consisting of two tall elliptical fins and rudders. The five-piece metal wing and fuselage were manufactured separately and assembled. The hydraulically actuated main landing gear retracted rearwards into the engine nacelle; the tail wheel was fixed. The important and distinctive feature of the Lancaster was the 33ft (10m) bomb bay with removable or modified doors, which allowed a wide variety of weapons to be carried. The Lancaster was famous for the No. 617 'Dam Busters raid' in *Operation Chastise* to destroy the dams of the Ruhr Valley.

The defensive armament consisted of two .303in (7.7mm) Browning Mark II machine guns in the nose, two in the upper turret, and four in the rear turret. The aircraft had a crew of seven: pilot, navigator, flight engineer, bomb aimer/nose gunner, wireless operator, mid upper and tail gunner.

BOEING FORTRESS

- Squadrons: 90, 214, 223
- First Flight: 28 July 1935 Number Built: 12,731
- Engine: Wright R-1820-97 Cyclone
- Range: 2,000 miles (3.219km) Service Ceiling: 35,600ft (10,850m)
- Bomb Load: 4,500lb (2,000kg) 800-mile mission, overload 17,000lb (7,800kg)

The Fortress was a four-engine heavy bomber developed by Boeing in the 1930s for the United States Army Air Corps. It went through many design changes. Boeing chief test pilot, Leslie Tower, flew the Model 299 for the first time on 28 July 1935. He was subsequently killed on the second evaluation flight of the prototype when the crew failed to remove the gust locks. Boeing lost the contract. In 1940 the Royal Air Force ordered twenty Boeing B-17Cs with flush oval-shaped gun blisters out of thirty-eight produced.

The aircraft had a short-lived career as a daylight bomber in 1941 with Bomber Command. By September eight of the twenty had been lost. An example is that it only flew for nine months with No. 90 Squadron against Europe. It needed greater mechanical reliability, improved defences, and more accurate bombing methods with a greater payload. They were transferred to Coastal Command duties and later to 100 Group using the electronic warfare system 'Airborne Cigar'.

Improvements, too late for Bomber Command, to the Fortress included engine turbo superchargers, larger rudder and flaps, gun fairings, extended rear fuselage and larger tail surfaces, and increasing the number of guns, M2 Browning .50in (12.7mm) machine guns, from seven to thirteen. The Wright Cyclone engines were upgraded to cope with the increased weight of the modifications.

The Fortress had a crew of ten: pilot, co-pilot, navigator, bomb aimer/nose gunner, flight engineer/top turret gunner, wireless operator, waist gunners (two), ball turret gunner, and tail gunner.

BRISTOL BEAUFIGHTER

- Squadron: 141
- First Flight: 17 July 1939 Number Built: 5,928
- Engine: Bristol Hercules, Rolls-Royce Merlin, Rolls-Royce Griffon
- Range: 1500 miles (2,414km) Service Ceiling: 29,000ft (8,839m)
- Bomb Load: Two 250lb (110kg)

The British Beaufighter was a twin-engine multi-role aircraft developed from the Beaufort. It was a long-range fighter that also served with Coastal Command as a torpedo bomber. It saw very limited service with No. 100 (Bomber Support) Group as a Radio Counter Measures aeroplane.

The armament consisted of four .787in (20mm) Hispano Mk II cannon in the nose or six .303 (7.7mm) Browning machine guns, four in starboard wing, two in port wing.

The Beaufighter had a crew of two: pilot and observer.

BRISTOL BLENHEIM AND BISLEY

- Squadrons: 13, 15, 18, 21, 35, 40, 57, 82, 88, 90, 101, 104, 105, 107, 110, 114, 139, 218, 226
- First Flight: 12 April 1935 Number Built: 4,422
- Engine: Bristol Mercury
- Range: 1,460 miles (2,350km) Service Ceiling: 27,260ft (8,310m)
- Bomb Load: 1,200lb (540kg) internal/external load

The Blenheim was a British medium bomber that served with Bomber and Fighter Commands; a four-gun pack was installed in the bomb bay. It first flew on 12 April 1935 as the Type 142 and was one of the first

British aircraft to have a stressed metal skin construction, variable pitch propellers, retractable landing gear, and powered gun turret. The Type 142 was created trhrpough the efforts of Lord Rothermere, owner of the *Daily Mail* newspaper, to create the fastest commercial aircraft in Europe to beat German aircraft such as the Heinkel He70.

The military version, the Blenheim, flew a year later in June 1936. It had a three-section light alloy monocoque construction fuselage with a metal tailplane. However, the rudder and elevators were still a fabric-covered metal frame. The ground attack variant had four extra guns in the nose and was called the Bisley.

Ergonomics were not its strong point. The pilot on the cramped left side of the cockpit could not see his flight instruments because of the control yoke and the engine instruments obscured his forward landing vision. Secondary controls were located behind the pilot, selected by feel only! The navigator, alongside the pilot, made use of a sliding seat for bomb aiming duties. The wireless operator/air gunner was located behind the wing at the dorsal gun turret.

There was a minimum of a forward firing .303in (7.7mm) Browning machine gun outboard of the port engine and a rear firing Vickers VGO of the same calibre in the dorsal turret. The Mark IV had two remotely controlled rearward firing .303in (7.7mm) machine guns mounted beneath the nose. The Blenheim had a crew of three: pilot, navigator/bomb aimer, and wireless operator/air gunner.

CONSOLIDATED LIBERATOR

- Squadron: 170
- First Flight: 29 December 1939 Number Built: 18,188
- Engine: Pratt & Whitney R-1830
- Range: 2,100 miles (3,380km) Service Ceiling: 28,000ft (8,534m)
- Bomb Load: 5,000lb (2,300kg) < 800 miles (1,300km)

The American-built Liberator was a four-engine shoulder-mounted wing heavy bomber. The Royal Air Force assigned it to No. 100 (Bomber Support) Group because its spacious fuselage allowed the Radio Counter Measures equipment to be easily installed.

The defensive armament varied as per the model from none on the transport version to ten .50 in (12.7mm) caliber M2 Browning machine guns on the bomber version. The Liberator had a crew of eleven: pilot, co-pilot, navigator, bombardier, radio operator, nose turret, top turret, two waist gunners, ball turret, and tail gunner.

DOUGLAS BOSTON

- Squadrons: 13, 18, 88, 107, 223, 226, 342
- First Flight: 23 January 1939 Number Built: 7,478

- Engine: Wright R-2600-23 Twin Cyclone
- Range: 945 miles (1,521km) Service Ceiling: 23,700ft (7,200m)
- Bomb Load: 4,000lb (1,800kg)

The Boston was an American medium mid-wing bomber that served with several Allied Air Forces. The French Air Force initiated an order for the Model 7B. The aircraft, now DB-7 B-3 (Douglas Bomber 7 Bomber 3 seat) retreated to North Africa before the fall of France and briefly fought against the Allies under the Vichy government! The undelivered aircraft to France were taken up by Britain as the Boston, original name A-20 Havoc. The aircraft were to replace the Bristol Blenheim.

The tricycle landing gear aircraft made takeoff, landing, and ground handling relatively simple. It had an advanced flying control system that made control very light and manoeuvrable at high speeds. It had excellent single engine handling characteristics. It was considered a 'pilots aeroplane'. A negative comment was that the takeoff speed was too high, and the flaps were not very effective, which caused difficulties landing on wet grass airfields.

Its robust construction allowed it to withstand considerable battle damage. The fuselage was semi-monocoque construction of alclad skin over framers and divided into three sections: pilot's compartment, bomb-bay section, and gunner's compartment.

The narrow fuselage isolated the crew from each other, and the bomber version had the nose compartment glazed with room for a bomb aimer and bomb site. The Boston III, the most important version, had four .303in (7.7mm) Browning machine guns, two in each side blister just below and behind the glass nose, two identical flexible .303in (7.7mm) guns in the dorsal position, and one flexible .303in (7.7mm) in the ventral position. The nose had been lengthened as a British requirement. The Boston had a crew of three: pilot, bomb aimer, air gunner.

FAIREY BATTLE

- Squadrons: 12, 15, 35, 40, 88, 98, 103, 105, 142, 150, 207, 218, 226, 300, 301, 304, 305
- First Flight: 10 March 1936 Number Built: 2,201
- Engine: Rolls-Royce Merlin
- Range: 1,000 miles (1,610km) Service Ceiling: 25,000ft (7,620m)
- Bomb Load: 1,000lb (450kg) internally/ 1,500lb (680kg) externally

The monoplane single-engine light bomber Battle was designed by Marcel Lobelle and succeeded the biplane Hawker Hart and Hind. It was the first aircraft in the Royal Air Force to have the new Rolls-Royce

Merlin engine and, during the 'Phoney War', to achieve the first aerial victory. It first flew on 10 March 1936 at Hayes, Middlesex, and, despite some limitations, joined the pre-war expansion production program. It served in many Allied Air Forces.

Its oval shaped fuselage manufactured in two sections resulted in very clean lines. The forward section was a steel tubular structure to support the engine. It was Fairey's first low wing monoplane. All the control surfaces were metal framed with fabric covering, the split trailing flaps were metal. The pilot and gunner sat in tandem; the observer sat below the pilot and sighted the target in prone position through a sliding access panel in the floor.

It had a single .303in (7.7mm) Browning machine gun in the right-hand side wing leading edge operated by the pilot and a trainable pintle mounted .303in (7.7mm) Vickers K machine gun in the rear position. By its introduction it was already obsolete with its lack of armament, self-sealing fuel tanks, and armoured cockpit. In May 1940, the Battle suffered immense losses and was withdrawn from front line service shortly thereafter.

The Battle had a crew of three: pilot, observer/navigator and wireless operator/rear air gunner.

HANDLEY PAGE HALIFAX

- Squadrons: 10, 35, 51, 76, 77, 78, 102, 103, 158, 199, 346, 347, 405, 408, 415, 419, 420, 424, 425, 426, 427, 428, 429, 431, 432, 433, 434, 460, 462, 466, 578, 640
- First Flight: 25 October 1939 Number Built: 6,176
- Engine: Bristol Hercules, Rolls-Royce Merlin
- Range: 1,860 miles (2,990km) Service Ceiling: 24,000ft (7,300m)
- Bomb Load: 13,000lb (5,897kg)

The Halifax was a British four-engine heavy bomber, first flight by Chief Test Pilot Jim Cordes at Royal Air Force Bicester in response to the Air Ministry's Specification P.13/36 using the Rolls-Royce Vulture engine. It was ordered as a backup to the twin-engine Avro Manchester which, as it turns out, was not a success. The Halifax flew with other Allied Air Forces and along with the Avro Lancaster was the backbone of the heavy bomber force.

Uniquely it was assembled at different sites throughout Britain from various completed sub-assemblies. Halifax variants were built with Bristol Hercules and Rolls-Royce Merlin engines. It was a mid-wing stressed metal skin monoplane with twin fins and rudders. The slab-sided fuselage contains a 22ft (6.7m) bomb bay.

The bomb aimer was in the front of the nose with the navigator's table behind. Above the navigator was the forward turret, behind the navigator was the wireless operator. The pilot was above the navigator and sat on the left with the flight engineer/co-pilot on a folding seat to the right. Aft of the flight engineer there were two rest bunks but used for treating wounded crew members. Aft of the bunks was the two-gun dorsal turret with the four-gun turret in the tail of the aircraft. The different models of Halifax used different combinations and numbers of turrets depending upon the requirement, firepower or speed.

B.III armament was eight .303in (7.7mm) Browning machine guns, four in dorsal turret, four in tail turret and .303 (7.7mm) Vickers K machine gun in the nose. The Halifax had a crew of seven: pilot, co-pilot/flight engineer, observer/navigator, bomb aimer, wireless operator/gunner, two air gunners.

HANDLEY PAGE HAMPDEN

- Squadrons: 7, 44, 49, 50, 61, 76, 83, 106, 144, 207, 408, 420, 455
- First Flight: 21 June 1936 Number Built: 1,430
- Engine: Bristol Pegasus
- Range: 1,720 miles (2,768km) Service Ceiling: 19,000ft (5,790m)
- Bomb Load: 4,000lb (1,814kg)

The Hampden was a British twin-engine medium bomber, a companion to the Armstrong Whitworth Whitley, Bristol Blenheim and Vickers Wellington. Piloted by Handley Page Chief Test Pilot Major J. Cordes, the Hampden had its maiden flight at Radlett Aerodrome with Bristol Pegasus engines. The Hampden was also built under licence in Canada and by English Electric at Preston, Lancashire. It served with many Allied Air Forces.

There was a fixed .303in (7.7mm) Browning machine gun in the upper part of the fuselage nose, a .303in (7.7mm) Vickers K machine gun in the curved Perspex nose, and .303in (7.7mm) Vickers K machine guns in the dorsal and ventral turrets.

A split assembly was used where the big three fuselage prefabricated sections were joined in an economic and rapid way. The flush riveted stressed fuselage skin was strengthened by shaped and extruded sections. The navigator sat behind the pilot in an extremely narrow cramped fuselage. Access to the cockpit required folding down the seats. The crews called it the 'Flying Suitcase'.

The highly tapered wing had wingtip slots and hydraulically operated flaps. It flew well at a relatively high speed for the time, but the crew positions were uncomfortable, lacking heat, and some of the controls for systems were not readily to hand. It did have excellent pilot visibility, which contributed to the manoeuvrability of the aircraft. The Hampden had a crew of four: pilot, navigator/bomb aimer, wireless operator/dorsal turret gunner, and ventral gunner.

LOCKHEED VENTURA

- Squadrons: 21, 464, 487
- First Flight: 31 July 1941 Number Built: 3,028
- Engine: Pratt & Whitney R-2800
- Range: 1,660 miles (2,670km) Service Ceiling: 26,300ft (8,020km)
- Bomb Load: 3,000lb (1,400kg)

The Ventura was an American multi role twin-engine aircraft that Bomber Command used as a bomber. Used initially as a daylight bomber it was quickly removed from service as, without fighter protection, it proved too vulnerable to fighter attack. It was eventually replaced with the De Havilland Mosquito. The aircraft were then transferred to Coastal Command.

The Ventura was a development of the pre-war Hudson which, because of the United States neutrality, were flown close to the Canadian border, landed, towed across the border, and put on a ship to Liverpool.

The elliptical cross section fuselage was an all-metal stressed skin construction. The centre section of the wing was an integral part of the fuselage. The large flaps were Fowler type. The twin tail fins were the identifiable Lockheed elliptical shape. The rear fuselage was constructed with a step to incorporate a ventral gun position.

The Ventura had a higher wing loading and some models had a marginal takeoff performance. It did have improved handling performance over the Hudson, but a drawback was more limited range. The aircraft were produced by Vega, a subsidiary of Lockheed, in Burbank, California. It flew with many Allied Air Forces.

The armament consisted of two fixed forward firing .50in (12.7mm) guns in the nose, two flexible .303in (7.7mm) guns in the nose, a dorsal turret with two .303in (7.7mm) guns later increased to four, and two .303in (7.7mm) guns in the ventral position. The Ventura had a crew of four: pilot, bombardier-navigator, radio operator / tunnel gunner, and upper turret gunner.

NORTH AMERICAN MITCHELL

- Squadrons: 98, 180, 226, 305, 320, 342
- First Flight: 19 August 1940 Number Built: 9,816
- Engine: Wright R-2600
- Range: 1,350 miles (2,170km) Service Ceiling: 24,200ft (7,400m)
- Bomb Load: 3,000lb (1,360kg)

The Mitchell was an American twin-engine medium bomber named after Major General (posthumous promotion) William 'Billy' Mitchell, a pioneer of United States military aviation. The NA-40B aircraft was originally designed as an attack bomber for the French and Royal Air

Forces. The French opted out for the Douglas DB-7 and the original design, NA-40B, crashed in April 1939. A revised design, NA-62, was submitted and accepted for production as the B-25. The initial design incorporated a constant angle dihedral, which proved unstable and it was altered to have a slight anhedral outboard of the engines. This gave the aircraft a gull wing appearance.

The B-25 'C' and 'D' models were designated the Mitchell II and the B-25J the Mitchell III. The Royal Air Force used these Mitchells to replace the older Douglas Bostons, Lockheed Venturas, and Vickers Wellington bombers.

The Mitchell III was a cross between the B-25D and B-25H. It either had a 'strafer' nose or a transparent nose. It had tremendous fire power with anywhere between twelve to eighteen forward facing .50in (12.7mm) machine guns. This included two guns in the forward dorsal turret.

The aircraft had a crew of five: pilot, navigator/bomb aimer, turret gunner/engineer, wireless operator/waist gunner, tail gunner.

SHORT STIRLING

- Squadrons: 7, 15, 75, 90, 149, 196, 199, 214, 218, 620, 622, 623
- First Flight: 14 May 1939 Number Built: 2,371 Engine: Bristol Hercules
- Range: 2,330 miles (3,750km) Service Ceiling: 16,500ft (5,000m)
- Bomb Load: 14,000lb (6,350kg)

The Stirling was the first British four-engine heavy bomber to be introduced into service with the RAF. Up until the mid-1930s the focus had been on making the twin-engine bomber more efficient to carry greater payloads. Bigger and bigger engines were being developed for the twins but were not available for production. Short, sometimes referred to as Shorts, was founded in 1908 in London by the Short brothers and was the first company in the world to make production airplanes. One of the first was a glider for Charles Rolls of Rolls-Royce fame.

Russia and the United States of America were both having success with four engines instead of two and so Short responded to the Air Ministry Specification B. 12/36 with the successful Stirling. It would have been more successful if the specification had not the restriction of a 100-foot wingspan which, among other factors, restricted its service ceiling. It was suggested that the wingspan restriction was to fit in with existing 1930s infrastructure, a strange limitation at such a time. The construction was based on their flying boat experience, a two-spar mid-mounted cantilever wing with the alloy aluminium sheeting riveted to the internal ribs and spars for strength.

After the Munich Agreement of 1938 the government greatly increased the order to 1,500 aircraft to meet the evident threat of Nazi expansion. The production was often delayed by Luftwaffe bombing sorties targeting the factories and the emphasis changing to the production of fighters. Finally, after the Battle of Britain, the Stirling had its first operational mission in February 1941. For a heavy bomber it handled well and had a very tight turning radius for defensive manoeuvring. However, it was a tailwheel aircraft which had the associated challenges in taking off and landing, especially for inexperienced pilots. The Stirling had a relatively short operational life being replaced by the more advanced Handley Page Halifax and Avro Lancaster.

The armament was eight .303in (7.7mm) Browning machine guns, two in the nose turret, four in the tail turret, and two in the dorsal turret. The bomb aimer had control of the aircraft autopilot when using the drift sight approaching the target. The aircraft had a crew of seven: pilot, co-pilot, navigator/bomb aimer, front gunner/wireless operator, two air gunners and flight engineer.

VICKERS WELLESLEY

- Squadrons: 223
- First Flight: 19 June 1935 Number Built: 177
- Engine: Bristol Pegasus
- Range: 1,220 miles (1,960km) Service Ceiling: 25,500ft (7,800m)
- Bomb Load: 2,000lb (910kg)

The Wellesley was an early 1930s British designed single-engine medium bomber built at Brooklands, Surrey, by Vickers-Armstrongs. The original specification called for a general-purpose aircraft, but that was changed to bomber after a successful first flight by Vickers Chief Pilot J 'Mutt' Summers at Brooklands on 19 June 1935, and testing revealed its superior performance.

It was a new geodesic design implemented in the fuselage and wings by Barnes Wallis. It had a high aspect ratio wing, manually operated retractable landing gear, and the bomb load was carried underneath the wings in panniers. Initially, the canopy was for the pilot only, but on subsequent models it was extended to include the bomb aimer.

At the outbreak of war, the Wellesley was obsolete for the European theatre but did see service in East Africa. In 1938 the aircraft established a world record for the longest flight, 7,162 miles (11,526), by a single piston engine aircraft.

The armament consisted of a .303in (7.7mm) Vickers machine gun embedded in the right wing and a .303in (7.7mm) Vickers K machine gun in the rear cockpit. The aircraft had a crew of three: pilot, bomb aimer, and rear gunner.

VICKERS WELLINGTON

- Squadrons: 9, 12, 15, 37, 38, 40, 57, 75, 99, 101, 103, 104, 115, 142, 149, 150, 156, 158, 166, 196, 199, 214,215, 218, 300, 301, 304, 305, 311, 405, 419, 420, 424, 425, 426, 427, 428, 429, 431, 432, 458, 460, 466
- First Flight: 15 June 1936 Number Built: 11,461
- Engine: Bristol Pegasus, Bristol Hercules, Rolls-Royce Merlin, Pratt & Whitney Twin Wasp
- Range: 2,550 miles (4,100km) Service Ceiling: 18,000ft (5,500m)
- Bomb Load: 4,500lb (2,000kg)

The Wellington was a British twin-engine long-range medium bomber designed by Vickers-Armstrongs' chief designer Rex Pierson. It was based on the successful Vickers-Armstrongs' geodetic design Wellesley bomber, which had shown superior strength. Wooden battens were screwed on to the metal beams of the structure. Doped Irish linen was attached to these battens and formed the outer skin of the aircraft. The geodesic structure allowed the aircraft to absorb a great amount of enemy damage.

The aircraft was designed with air-cooled Bristol Pegasus and liquid-cooled Rolls-Royce Goshawk engine versions. The final engine selection was the Bristol Pegasus for the first production models. Subsequently, some Wellington versions would have Rolls-Royce or Pratt & Whitney engines. The engines initially had a variable pitch propeller.

Refinements included mid-mounted wings, three Vickers-powered turrets instead of two, and spring-loaded bomb bay doors. The first flight was by Vickers Chief Pilot J 'Mutt' Summers with Barnes Wallis on board. A nose -heavy control problem at high speeds was rectified by modification to the elevator trim tabs. Other changes were a retractable tail wheel and improved constant-speed propellers. The tail had a single tall fin vertical stabiliser.

One Wellington, LN514, was built in 23 hours and fifty minutes at Broughton, North Wales. It flew less than an hour later. The achievement was filmed by the Ministry of Information and was broadcast in Britain and the US. The aircraft was also the most produced British bomber during the war; it included sixteen variants. The aircraft had a crew of five: pilot, bomb aimer, and nose, tail and dorsal gunner.

Fighter/Bomber Europe 1939-1945

DE HAVILLAND MOSQUITO

- Squadrons: 21, 105, 107, 109, 110, 128, 139, 141, 142, 162, 163, 305, 464, 487, 571, 608, 627, 692
- First Flight: 25 November 1940 Number Built: B 1,100+ (7,781 All Models)
- Engine: Rolls-Royce Merlin
- Range: 1,485 miles (2,750km) Service Ceiling: 37,000ft (11,000m)
- Bomb Load: 4,000lb (1,814kg) 'Cookie'

The Mosquito was a British two-seat twin engine fighter-bomber with a frame constructed mainly of wood. It was nicknamed the 'Mossie' or 'Wooden Wonder'. Originally designed as an unarmed fast bomber it evolved into a medium-altitude daytime tactical bomber, high-altitude nighttime bomber, fighter-bomber, and intruder. One intruder raid was to bomb the main Berlin radio station as General Hermann Goring was making a speech. The aircraft had a crew of two, the pilot and bomb aimer/navigator. De Havilland already had experience with fast aircraft in the DH. 88 Comet, so the Mosquito was a natural progression. The test flight was carried out by Geoffrey de Havilland Jr. and John Walker, chief engine installation engineer. Initial airframe buffeting was cured by lengthening the engine nacelles and wing-root fillets. The initial bomb load was increased by a conversion that included modified bomb bay suspension arrangements, bulged bomb bay doors, and fairings. The Strike fighter-bomber versions could have bombs, cannons/Browning machine guns, and/or rockets.

Bomber Command aircraft engines 1939-1945

Armstrong Siddeley

PANTHER

- Type: 14-cylinder, twin row, air-cooled, radial engine
  First ran: 1929
- Displacement: 27L
  Power: 638hp (478kW) @ 2,400rpm with 0.5psi (3.5kpa) boost
- RAF Bomber Aircraft: Fairey Gordon

The Panther was developed from the Jaguar series of engines which were developed from the Royal Aircraft Factory RAF.8. The Jaguar engine was the first production engine that incorporated a geared supercharger and ran seven years earlier in 1922. It was originally called the Jaguar Major engine.

TIGER

- Type: 14-cylinder, twin-row, air-cooled, radial engine
  First ran: 1932
- Displacement: 32.7L
  Power: 907hp (677kW) @2,375rpm for takeoff
- RAF Bomber Aircraft: Armstrong Whitworth Whitley

The Tiger was developed from the Jaguar series of engines which were developed from the Royal Aircraft Factory RAF.8. The Tiger IV engine was the first production engine that incorporated a geared two-speed centrifugal type supercharger.

Bristol

HERCULES

- Type: 14-cylinder, twin-row, single sleeve valve, air-cooled, radial engine
  First ran: 1936
- Displacement: 38.7L
  Power: 1,272hp (949kW) at 2,800rpm for takeoff
- RAF Bomber Aircraft: Handley Page Halifax, Short Stirling, Bristol Beaufighter.

The Hercules engine was designed by Roy Fedden, a very successful engineer who designed most of the Bristol Engine Company's winning piston aircraft engines. It was based on the sleeve valve Perseus engine. The sleeve valve design allowed more efficient intake and exhaust gas flow, which in turn improved volumetric efficiency and higher compression ratios. It was a modular installation that allowed the complete engine and cowling to be installed as a unit. It was considered a very reliable engine of its time with a slight difficulty in maintaining sufficient lubrication of the sleeve and cylinder. There were over 57,000 engines built including post-war production.

MERCURY

- Type: 9-cylinder, single-row, air-cooled, radial engine
  First ran: 1925
- Displacement: 24.9L
  Power: 612hp (457kW) at 2,750rpm for takeoff
- RAF Bomber Aircraft: Bristol Blenheim

The Mercury engine was designed by Roy Fedden to replace the Jupiter, which was at the end of its useful life. Some of the Jupiter parts were used, the block for example, and the smaller Mercury began to achieve ever increasing horsepower. The Mercury XV used 100 octane fuel from the US, which allowed it to run at higher compression ratios and supercharger boost pressures. The Mercury was also the first British engine approved to have a variable-pitch propeller. A total of 20,700 engines were built.

PEGASUS

- Type: 9-cylinder, single-row, air-cooled, radial engine
  First ran: 1932
- Displacement: 28.7L
  Power: 965hp (720kW) at 2,475rpm for takeoff
- RAF Bomber Aircraft: Handley Page Hampden, Vickers Wellesley, Vickers Wellington

The Pegasus engine was a natural evolution by Roy Fedden from the experienced gained by the previous Jupiter and Mercury engines. Both engines displayed improved power-to-weight ratio. The Pegasus laid claim to the 'pound-per-horsepower' laurels and it achieved a higher maximum engine speed, which resulted in more horsepower. It is estimated that 32,000 engines were built. The Pegasus established a height record, first flight over Mount Everest, and in 1938 set a world long distance record.

TAURUS

- Type: 14-cylinder, twin-row, air-cooled, radial engine
  First ran: 1936
- Displacement: 25.4L
  Power: 1,140hp (850kW) at 3,225rpm for takeoff
- RAF Bomber Aircraft: Bristol Beaufort

The Taurus engine was developed from the single row Aquila engine by adding another row of cylinders. The Taurus was a sleeve valve design which resulted in a relatively orderly exterior and low weight for the horsepower generated. It initially proved troublesome and, in spite of some improvements, never left its poor reputation behind.

Pratt & Whitney

R-1830 (TWIN WASP)

- Type: 14-cylinder, twin-row, air-cooled, radial engine
  First ran: 1932
- Displacement: 30.0L
  Power: 1,200hp (895kW) at 2,700rpm for takeoff
- RAF Bomber Aircraft: Martin Maryland

The Wasp series of engines was conceived as a business venture by Frederick Rentschler, George Mead, and some colleagues (all former employees of Wright Aeronautical). Just over 173,000 R-1830 engines were built. The engine was installed in two of the most produced aircraft, the Douglas C-47/DC-3 Dakota and the Consolidated B-24 Liberator. The engine was part of the Wasp series of engines and followed the Wasp (22L) and Wasp Junior (16L) in size.

R-2800 (DOUBLE WASP)

- Type: 18-cylinder, twin-row, air-cooled, radial engine
  First ran: 1937
- Displacement: 46L
  Power: 2,100hp (1.567kW) @ 2,700rpm
- RAF Bomber Aircraft: Lockheed Ventura

The R-2800 presented a design challenge: how to get rid of the heat created by the engine. The solution was machined cooling fins on the cylinder head rather than the standard cast or forged fins. The roots of the fins rose and fell to follow the contour of the cylinder head, which increased the surface area of the fins. The engine was re-rated as higher-octane fuel became available.

Rolls-Royce
MERLIN

- Type: V12, liquid-cooled engine
  First ran: 1933
- Displacement: 27L
  Power: 1,290hp (962kW) @ 3,000rpm for takeoff
- RAF Bomber Aircraft: Avro Lancaster, Handley Page Halifax, Fairey Battle, De Havilland Mosquito, Hawker Hurricane, Bristol Beaufighter

The Merlin engine was arguably the engine that won the war in the air. (See *The Merlin: The Engine that Won the Second World War* published by Amberley Books). Over 149,000 engines in fifty versions were built in Britain and 55,000-plus engines by the Packard Motor Car Company in the US. The engine was built as a development of the very successful Kestrel engine and because of its potential took precedence over the Peregrine and Vulture engines. As with other engines, the advent of 100 octane fuel improved the engine performance. Stanley Hooker re-designed the supercharger and made a good engine a great engine. Not only was the Merlin the mainstay of the Battle of Britain but the Merlin subsequently was the primary engine of the heavy bomber force, Avro Lancaster and Handley Page Halifax, and the lightning strike force, De Havilland Mosquito, in the latter stages of the war when the tide of war had changed, and Britain was on the offensive.

VULTURE

- Type: X-24 cylinder, supercharged, liquid-cooled engine
  First ran: 1937
- Displacement: 42.5L
  Power: 1,780hp (1,327kW) @ 2,850rpm at +6psi (0.4bar) boost
- RAF Bomber Aircraft: Avro Manchester

The Vulture was an unusual four (six cylinder) block configuration joined to a common crankcase. It was derived from the Peregrine engine. The engine's development was halted in 1940 as the production focus was on the Rolls-Royce Merlin to support the Battle of Britain fighter aircraft. This resulted in very poor performance and reliability, big end bearing failures, and heat dissipation problems when installed in the Manchester and production was ceased after 538 engines. The twin-engine Vulture-powered Manchester became the very successful four-engine Merlin powered Avro Lancaster.

Wright

R-1820 (CYCLONE)

- Type: 9-cylinder, single-row, supercharged, air-cooled radial engine
  First ran: 1930s
- Displacement: 29.9L
  Power: 1,000hp (746kW) at 2,200rpm for takeoff
- RAF Bomber Aircraft: Boeing Fortress

The R-1820 was a further development by Curtiss-Wright of the Wright P-2 engine. It was built under licence by Lycoming, Pratt & Whitney Canada, Studebaker Corporation, and in Russia.

R-2600 (TWIN CYCLONE)

- Type: 14-cylinder, twin-row, supercharged, air-cooled, radial engine
  First ran: 1935
- Displacement: 42.7L
  Power: 1.750hp (1,305kW) @ 2,600rpm/3,200ft
- RAF Bomber Aircraft: Douglas Boston, North American Mitchell

Curtiss-Wright developed the R-2600 as a more powerful version of their very successful R-1820 series. The outcome was the 14-cylinder, twin-row configuration.

GR-2600 (TWIN CYCLONE)

- Type: 14-cylinder, twin-row, supercharged, air-cooled, radial engine
  First ran: 1943
- Displacement: 42.7L
  Power: 1,600hp (1,193kW) @ 2,400rpm
- RAF Bomber Aircraft: Martin Baltimore

R-3350 -23 (DUPLEX-CYCLONE)

- Type: 18-cylinder, twin-row, supercharged, air-cooled, radial engine
  First ran: 1937
- Displacement: 55L
  Power: 2,200hp (1,641kW) @ 2,800rpm for takeoff
- RAF Bomber Aircraft: Boeing Washington

The R-3350 continued the development of the successful R-1820/R-2600 Cyclone series with the R-3350. This was a natural evolution for more power and the fact that Pratt & Whitney had started development on the more powerful Double Wasp. Initial development was slow as funds were being directed to the R-2600 and the complexity of the R-3350. The large engine, partially due to the demands of wartime production, tended to overheat and suffered from valve failure. The engine started with carburettors and finished the war with direct fuel injection into the combustion chamber.

6

BOMBER COMMAND AIRCREW

Many of the young men who made up the Bomber Command 125,000 aircrew did not survive the war: over 55,000. Some 9,838 were shot down and became prisoners of war to be released at cessation of hostilities. Some were shot down and escaped or evaded capture and returned to Britain. Some were shot down and lie in marked graves in a foreign land, not forgotten. Some simply went missing, never to be found, and tend to be forgotten except by their families. Some 8,403 were badly injured, survived, and never flew again. Some returned badly injured and did not survive. Some returned injured, survived, but with severe physical handicaps for life. Some returned seemingly unscathed but silently braved their mental anguish. Some could not and took their own lives to escape the torment. Some were killed in training accidents and never saw action.

Stories are told by survivors; so many stories will never be told. Acts of heroism and self-sacrifice which are known are acknowledged by the military, many other stories died with the crews. I am fortunate to have been told three personal stories of Bomber Command aircrew: from a pilot, a bomb aimer, and a wireless operator. Each came from a different background, and each had a unique story. One did not survive the war; two did survive. One became a prisoner of war; he would not talk to me about it.

These men were heroes to face each Bombing Command mission knowing the odds of surviving, even more so surviving unscathed, were against them. Each of them contributed to the efficiency of his crew and had his responsibilities. All were vital 'cogs in the wheel', selected and trained in their 'trade' to fill the required positions in the aircraft. These positions could vary in number from two in the De Havilland Mosquito to ten in the Boeing Fortress. The multi-position aircrew formed a very strong bond of comradeship which, for the survivors, continued for many years in post-war reunions. Their very survival depended on this bonding.

In general terms the aircrew positions were pilot, navigator, wireless operator, flight engineer, bomb aimer, and air gunner. The number of positions required would of course depend on the type of aircraft. Some positions had multi-tasking duties such as a wireless air gunner and he would be trained for both positions. Regardless of position, all the aircrew were volunteers. A civilian volunteered for service and so began the training to convert that person to a way of life that perhaps he knew nothing about. The vast majority had had no previous exposure to the military life to guide them. It was quite a shock at the beginning, and most accepted the routine, rules, and regulations, but there were always the rebels to provide the fun and humour to soften the transition.

The Pilot and Flight Engineer were the ones who flew the aircraft to the mission location and back to home base. The Air Gunners were its defence and the Bomb Aimer was its offence. The Navigator was both, offensive to get it to the target to fulfil its mission and defensive to get it back to base to do it all again another day. The Wireless Operator was the ears of the aircraft, keeping in touch with Bomber Command and passing back enemy information and weather reports.

Successful medical, health, and dental examinations during the interview process at a Recruiting Centre resulted in basic kit being issued and the volunteers went for Basic Training at an Initial Training School. They studied and were subjected to a variety of tests. Theoretical studies included navigation, theory of flight, meteorology, duties of an officer, air force administration, algebra, and trigonometry. Tests included psychological and aptitude tests, the four-hour long M2 physical examination, and a flight test in a Link Trainer.

The military life is based on a hierarchy, so the recruit was instructed on the military organisation and how the command structure worked. This was achieved through such activities as physical training, marching, saluting, and the inevitable barrack and parade inspection. These all led to the military decision as to what the candidate was most suitable for, guided of course by the requirements at the time. At the end of the course the postings were announced. The recruit then would report to a Personnel Despatch Centre to be sent overseas, mainly to Canada. There were different career paths at that stage: Pilot, Navigator, Bomb Aimer, Air Gunner and Wireless Operator/Air Gunner, and Flight Engineer. Most Flight Engineers were trained in Britain, but 1,900 graduates came from Canada after July 1944.

The Pilot went to an Elementary Flying Training School. The course was eight weeks in length and gave the new pilot fifty hours on such aircraft as the Tiger Moth, Fleet Finch, and Fairchild Cornell. Unsuccessful candidates would be assigned other aircrew positions and successful trainees went on to a Service Flying Training School for more advanced instruction. This was also where the group was divided into fighter pilots and bomber, coastal, and transport pilots. This selection process depended on the present wartime requirement, much to the disappointment of some would-be fighter pilots. The course varied from ten to sixteen weeks and seventy-five to one hundred hours flying. The fighter pilots would train on the single-engine North American Harvard, a real rudder plane due to the powerful radial engine, and the bomber, coastal and transport pilots went on multi-engine airplanes, the Avro Anson, Cessna Crane, and Airspeed Oxford.

The Navigator went to an Air Observer School for approximately twenty weeks and a hundred and twenty flying hours in a Navigation Course for Navigators. Ground school consisted of such courses as map reading, plotting courses (true and magnetic tracks), calculating/interpreting wind speed and direction, and meteorology. Flight school consisted of the necessary calculations to fly a predetermined course to arrive at a geographical location at a specific time. The candidate would use such equipment as the Dalton computer and learn such practices as astrograph, vertical line overlap, square search plotting. At night the sextant would be used for navigation using star shots. Successful graduation resulted in a promotion to Sergeant.

The Wireless Operator went to a Wireless School for approximately twenty-eight weeks to learn the intricacies of maintaining and operating radio equipment and how to communicate using Continuous Wave Morse Code. The end of the ground school course consisted of time in an 'airborne aircraft simulator', a cubicle replica of an aircraft installation, whereby the student would communicate with an instructor. This would be followed by actual flight training in such aircraft as the Fleet Fort and later in the North American Harvard. Some bomber aircraft had dual role wireless/air gunner positions with the appropriate training.

The Bomb Aimer initially took courses at an Air Observer School on navigation and map reading before proceeding to a Bombing and Gunnery School. The bombing course was up to twelve weeks in duration and each student dropped up to eighty practice bombs. The school used such aircraft as the Fairey Battle and Avro Anson.

The Air Gunner received twelve weeks of ground training and air gunnery practice. Initially with Vickers guns in an open cockpit, Fairey Battle, and subsequently with twin Browning machine guns in a turret on the Bristol Bolingbroke.

The Pilot went on to an Advanced Flying Unit and the Bomb Aimer/Navigator went to an Advanced Observer School for five weeks of aerial photography, reconnaissance, and air navigation and then to an Advanced Flying Unit. After 1942 the duties of the Air Observer were divided between the Bomb Aimer and Navigator, thus abolishing the observer category. This would be followed by the assembled crew proceeding to an Operational Training Unit and subsequently posting to a squadron.

British Commonwealth Air Training Plan

At the very beginning of the war Britain looked to the colonies to help set up the Empire Air Training Scheme to train aircrew. Britain did not have the room to accommodate both training and operational facilities, which were within the range of enemy fighters and bombers. Canada offered this opportunity to Britain as it certainly had the space, ready access to parts from the US, and its (relative) proximity to Britain. The Canadian Prime Minister, William Lyon Mackenzie King, believed that the British Commonwealth Air Training Plan would be 'the most essential military action that Canada could undertake'. It would be a significant contribution to the war effort without Canadians being in the front lines. That would change as eventually more than 72,000 aircrew went overseas.

The BCATP agreement was signed by the United Kingdom, Australia, New Zealand, and Canada on 17 December 1939. This commitment so early in the war was one of the major decisions which contributed to ultimate success in the air war. The participants agreed on training requirements and their share of the costs. The United Kingdom paid in materials that Canada did not have. By 31 March 1945 the plan had cost $2.2 billion (£118,529,430) for 151 schools, more than 100 airfields and emergency landing fields, and 104,113 ground personnel (men and women) to train 131,553 Air Force crew.

That was an astonishing 2,100 fully trained aircrew per month. The exhaustive classroom curriculum and schedule turned out crews at a fast rate; only the strong would survive. Hence the calibre of aircrew reaching England was extremely high; contrary to what you would expect in a fast-paced training environment. Twenty-nine Elementary Flying Training Schools and all ten Air Observer Schools were run by local companies, airlines, and flying clubs.

To this day when flying in Canada you can see the familiar triangle shape of the wartime runways to ensure the novice trainees could always land into wind on initial training. Some locations have developed into major airports and some are as they were left in 1945. 856 trainees of the British Commonwealth Air Training Plan were killed or seriously wounded, and the Commonwealth War Graves Commission maintains the graves of those Commonwealth trainees who died on Canadian soil.

Canadians took great pride in welcoming the trainees into the community and the social fabric of the area changed. The Schools entertained the community and the community in turned entertained the trainees. Morale for the war effort was very high although tinged with sadness at each graduating ceremony as the trainees left for an uncertain future in the vagaries of war. There also was a demographic change of the local areas as some Canadian wives, nearly 4,000, either left the area to join their husbands after the war ended or the servicemen they married returned to Canada after release from the Air Force.

NATIONALITY	GRADUATES
Royal Canadian Air Force	72,835
Royal Australian Air Force	9,606
Royal New Zealand Air Force	7,002
Royal Air Force which included:	42,110
Poles	448
Norwegians	677
Belgian & Dutch	800
Czechs	900
Free French	2,600
Total	131,553

	ROYAL AIR FORCE	ROYAL CANADIAN AIR FORCE
Pilot	17,796	25,747
Navigator (Bomber)	3,113	5,154
Navigator (Wireless)	3,847	421
Navigator	6,922	7,280
Bomb Aimer	7,581	6,659
Wireless Operator/ Air Gunner	755	12,744
Air Gunner	1,392	12,917

Upon graduation the men were now ready to get 'crewed up' and start training as a coordinated unit. How were these trained individuals assigned to a crew? Simple: the different crew positions were all put in a large hall with pots of tea and biscuits and told to sort themselves into individual crews. The result was that individuals entered the hall and a crew walked out together some time later to commence training! The crew members, most often comprised of mixed nationalities, were referred to as, for example, 'our Aussie Navigator' in veteran interviews.

They mostly stayed together but sometimes due to sickness or crew leave new bodies would fill in as necessary. By staying together, they would all hope to reach their operational tour of thirty trips at the same time. The camaraderie of shared excitement, terror, and even fun at times lasted a lifetime. This was exemplified by the numerous reunions held throughout the post war years with participants willing to travel from all parts of the globe.

A few personal stories, both told in person (the first) and from personal family records will illustrate just what these young men went through in the prime of their lives; stories that perhaps have not been told in seventy-five years.

Flight Lieutenant W. (Bill) E. Pearson

BOMB AIMER

The rest of the crew got the Lancaster safely to the vicinity of the target; now it was the turn of the Bomb Aimer to deliver the ordnance accurately. Initially, area bombing was the norm, but as the bomb sights and aerodynamics of the bomb improved and the Pathfinders were added to the operation, the ability to deliver bombs to a specific target became possible.

The Bomb Aimer crew position was in the very nose of the aircraft, a cold position at the best of times. Returning from a raid on Stuttgart, his thirteenth op, on the night of 21 February 1944 in Avro Lancaster LL785-Freddie, Pearson asked the skipper if he could come up to the cockpit to get warm. Climbing up the stairs he said: 'I saw a flash of a red light and then there was a loud crash and the whole bomb aiming compartment was destroyed – we had been involved in a mid-air collision.' The whole crew were very fortunate to survive the accident; the other aircraft crashed, and when asked about it Pearson said: 'Lucky, just plain lucky.'

Pearson was born in Regina, Saskatchewan, Canada, and two days before the attack on Pearl Harbor he volunteered to serve in the Royal Canadian Air Force. Initial Training School was in Edmonton, Alberta, followed by gunnery training on the Fairey Battle and navigation training on the Avro Anson in Lethbridge, Alberta. He returned to Blatchford Field (Edmonton) for some navigation training but mainly bombing training. By December 1942 he had his Observer wings and commission and in January 1943 he boarded the *Queen Elizabeth* in New York and sailed to Greenock, Scotland, and boarded a train for Bournemouth, England. Pearson then went to the Advanced Flying Unit at Penrhos, North Wales, and flew Bristol Blenheims. 'I never felt so cold in all my life up there next to the Irish Sea.'

Next, he went to the North Luffenham, Rutland, permanent base to get 'crewed up' and start the Operational Training Unit on the Vickers

Wellington bomber. Pearson's first crew consisted of an Englishman, Australian, and Canadian, not an uncommon situation.

> The base was going to be taken over, so they moved us to Bruntingthorpe just outside of Leicester. Our first OTU (Operational Training Unit) trip was a nickel raid, dropping leaflets on our own single aircraft operation to Rennes, France. This is when I had my first mishap in the air. I had relieved the pilot (I could hold it straight level after some basic Link training) while he had a pee, and when he came back, we exchanged seats; I unplugged my intercom and stepped down. The escape hatch release on a Wimpy is on the right side, it is a lever with a red knob on it. I must have inadvertently kicked it and I stepped out in to space. I caught myself on both sides but I was not plugged in so I could not tell anyone. I just screamed my head off and the Wireless Operator heard me and pulled me up.

The crew were then posted to No. 1654 Heavy Conversion Unit Wigsley, Nottinghamshire, to transition to the Lancaster where they picked up a flight Engineer to make up the crew of seven.

> This is where the engineers became indoctrinated – ours became indoctrinated bloody fast. We did an overshoot one day and he lifted the flaps before the undercart (landing gear) and now that was some sinking feeling. He got a certain amount of you know what from the rest of the crew; he never forgot that.

The crew's next posting was to No. 207 Squadron RAF up in Lincolnshire and the pilot, Johnny Kirkup, went on a 'second dickie' familiarisation trip and never came back. The crew were now leaderless but resisted attempts to split them up. Dave Pearce, recovering from a bail out injury, was assigned as the skipper.

> We went to Balderton, Newark on Trent, to do some circuits and bumps, bombing runs, and cross countries with the new skipper before being posted to No 9 Squadron Royal Air Force, code WS, at Bardney, Lincolnshire. Wing Commander Cheshire VC, he had many other decorations also, joined us for a few circuits. While we were at Newark, we saw a Wimpy (Vickers Wellington) with the rear turret removed and a stove pipe stuck out the back. I guess they were doing some secret testing on a jet engine from a guarded hangar at the far end of the field. The second trip at No. 9 Squadron RAF was to Leipzig where we got shot up by an Fw [Focke Wulf fighter]. We had just started our bombing run, dropped our bombs, and cleared target. The elevator was damaged, the mid-upper gunner, an Aussie, was wounded, and I had to help the engineer take the strain [to maintain level flight]. We diverted to an emergency

runway in the south of England. An engineer pushed down on the left elevator and it snapped. The navigator Jim got the DFC (Distinguished Flying Cross) on that trip. All his charts went out the back and he remembered enough of the numbers to get us home. That was our baptism of fire.

The crew was assigned Berlin as a target very many times, which brought them up to March 1944, the infamous Nuremberg raid; more on that later.

We were now the senior crew on No. 9 Squadron with eight trips. Leave was every six weeks and lasted seven to ten days. F/O Dave Pearce got married and completed his tour of thirty trips. I had about twenty-five trips around the same time and my only claim to fame is Lancaster WS-J completed 110 trips and I had two trips in that baby!

The Station Commander, Wing Commander Porter, needed a crew and Pearson's crew all needed a few more trips after Pearce left, to complete their thirty trips. However, Porter had been tagged to the Pathfinder Force and the crew were all sent on end of tour leave.

To me that was a slap in the face as we all wanted to be in on D-Day. The crew decided to do another tour as Pathfinders, and went to RAF Station Coningsby. We did most of our work with No. 97 Squadron aircraft and we were assigned to be Master Bomber on No. 54 Base and 83 and 97 Squadrons. We did some eight to ten trips there and we had some interesting trips. We even had a daylight trip with a bunch of B-17s and marked the target. We got another leave and I came back a day early because I was broke. I flew a couple of trips with different crews and then one day they did not have any qualified visual Bomb Aimers.

This would be my thirty-seventh and a half trip; I flew more than half of it. They said you will volunteer for this, won't you Pearson? The skipper was Squadron Leader Sparks; he had just returned from a bail out and walked back through the Pyrenees. I met the rest of the crew for the first time climbing into the aircraft, OL-C PB249. It was one of the longest raids of the war, Konigsberg, East Prussia. [The city was annexed by Russia and is now called Kaliningrad.] We were deputy one on that trip and we had the markers for marking. Our aircraft had the Semi-Automatic Bomb Sight. We went over; I dropped a marker that I think was pretty good and had just started to peel away when we got nailed by flak. I think we were down between seven and eight thousand, and I think that it was heavy flak that knocked out the port engines, inner and outer. They went on fire and I kicked out the escape hatch, buckled on [the parachute] and hesitated thinking that maybe they will get those fires

> out. Suddenly there was a guy pushing me; it was the Wireless Op. I went out; he went out, and Squadron Leader Sparks followed me out. I got coned part way down, and they were peppering at me, and I landed on a cobbled road near a potato patch on the outskirts of Konigsberg. I didn't even get my harness off before I got bayonets in my face. I was a PoW pretty quick. After some local confinement I was sent to an interrogation camp near Frankfurt, I think, for a couple of weeks. It is where they send all the aircrew. Then I was sent to Stalag Luft 1 at Barth, Pomerania, up on the Baltic coast. The Russians released us on 30 April, 1 May, and 2 May [1945] when they came through. The date [of being shot down] was 29 August 1944. I was flown back to England in a B-17 late May 1945. I was 185 lb when I was shot down and 138 lb when I weighed in. Squadron Leader Sparks was in the same camp; he eventually got there at a different time. He was captured about the same time because I was under guard in a local municipal hall being looked over by the locals when a Luftwaffe car drove up with Squadron Leader Sparks sitting in the back seat with a guard on each side. They brought me outside and shone a light in his face and asked me if I knew this guy. I said no, but good luck guy.

These are the aircraft shot down over Konigsberg that night, 29/30 August 1944: JB593, LL790, LM237, LM267, LM583, LM656, ND331, ND982, PB249 (Pearson's aircraft), PD258.

In many ways the Bomb Aimer was the eyes of the operation. He helped the navigator, when they were flying in visual conditions, to pinpoint their position and guided the pilot in the last few miles to the 'bombs away' point. Together with his duty as the nose gunner on the twin Browning .303 machine guns, the Bomb Aimer was a very busy member of the crew.

The interview with Pearson brought back a flood of memories for him but through it all there was a sense of pride, accomplishment, and even humour. I was visiting Bill in the hospice and was told by the nursing staff that he did not have long to live. I did not know how to say goodbye. I caught his eye as I stood at the end of his bed and saluted him, and I was astonished to see him raise his hand and give me a thumbs up. My friend Bill Pearson passed away on 15 October 2018. I include the interview here, although previously published in my *Lancaster* book, as a mark of my continuing respect for my friend. Rest in Peace Bill.

Pilot Officer Jack W. Shelson

WIRELESS/AIR GUNNER

The Wireless Operator's station in the Avro Lancaster was just in front of the main spar, in the rear part of the cockpit section. In addition to his official duties related to the radio equipment, the Wireless Operator was also expected to have a working knowledge of the navigator's equipment, understand the aircraft's electrical and intercom systems, and administer first aid as necessary. As well, he was generally on duty in the astrodome in the event of contact with enemy fighters and over the target. The astrodome was a dome-shaped piece of perspex which protruded above the aircraft's fuselage in order that the navigator could take star shots. It also provided an excellent viewpoint.

Pilot Officer Jack W. Shelson was born in Toronto, Ontario and volunteered to serve in the Royal Canadian Air Force. Turned down for medical reasons he went overseas with the Canadian Army to serve. He subsequently was able to re-muster to the Air Force and trained as a Wireless Operator/Air Gunner at No. 2 Radio School, Yatesbury, Wiltshire. He successfully completed Course No. 158 at No. 1 (O) Advanced Flying Unit on the Avro Anson. Subsequent service saw him crew on the Handley Page Halifax and Vickers Wellington prior to his first trip on the Avro Lancaster with B Flight No. 419 Squadron Royal Canadian Air Force at Middleton St George, County Durham, on 3 June 1944.

Shelson was operating radar coverage on the night of 12 June 1944. He departed Middleton St George, 'Goosepool', at 2210 in VR-Z, twenty-six minutes later than Pilot Officer Mynarski in VR-A. The No. 419 Squadron Royal Air Force raid was on the rail marshalling yards at Cambrai, France. Shelson returned; Mynarski did not. Mynarski was awarded a Victoria Cross posthumously for that operation (see Victoria Cross recipients following). Shelson completed his tour and had started a second tour when the war ended.

He took his Northampton war bride, Margaret Barrett, back to Canada where he was honourably discharged. Shelson was not alone. Nearly 45,000 brides and 21,000 children came to Canada, some during the war, most after. His daughter Anne made a point of visiting the Bomber Command Memorial in London, England, to remember her father and all those that served in Bomber Command. Anne, and husband, John Allen are our friends.

Flying Officer Bruce A. Grant

PILOT

Grant was born in Regina, Saskatchewan, on 29 February 1922. His declared birth date on his military application was 28 February 1921. The 'extra' year allowed him to volunteer and apply to the Royal Canadian Air Force. He attended Campion College in Regina, which was associated with the University of Saskatchewan. He volunteered for service and by the autumn of 1939 he was serving as a Leading Air Craftsman with No. 120 Bomber Squadron, Western Air Command,

Royal Canadian Air Force at Royal Canadian Air Force Station Coal Harbour (Vancouver, British Columbia).

He re-mustered in September 1941 and attended the Initial Training School in Edmonton, Alberta. In April 1942 he was at No. 18 Elementary Flying Training School, Boundary Bay, British Columbia, training on the De Havilland Tiger Moth. Grant completed his multi-engine training on the Avro Anson before being posted overseas in August 1942. Grant continued his training on the Airspeed Oxford at No. 6 Advanced Flying Unit at Royal Air Force Station Little Rissington, Gloucestershire. In October 1942 he was assigned to Royal Air Force Station Honington, Suffolk, for Beam Approach Training.

In January 1943 Grant commenced his Vickers Wellington training with No. 22 Operational Training Unit, Royal Air Force Station Gaydon, Warwickshire. He was promoted and commissioned from Sergeant in March to Pilot Officer. On 14 March 1943 he did his first local flight with B Flight, No. 420 (Snowy Owl) Squadron, No. 6 Group, Royal Canadian Air Force at Middleton St. George, County Durham. On 28 March Grant and his crew undertook their first night operation on the heavily defended naval base at St. Nazaire, in German-occupied France.

On the night of 29 March 1943 Grant and crew departed Middleton St. George at 19:33 in a Vickers Wellington Mk X, serial number MS484. His target that night was Bochum, North Rhine-Westphalia, a centre of mining and steel production. Grant was one of a hundred and fifty-seven bombers that took part in the raid that night. Twelve aircraft were shot down, Grant's aircraft was one of them.

At approximately 23:15 his aircraft was attacked by *Oberleutnant* Martin Bauer flying a Messerschmitt Bf 110 of the Luftwaffe Night Fighter Wing I/NJG 1 from the air base at Venlo, Limburg, Netherlands. Bauer was guided in the attack by the Wurzburg radar at Rips. The aircraft crashed in a pasture in the district of Wanroij in the province of Noord-Brabant. Grant and three of the crew were killed. Their average age was twenty-three. The Bomb Aimer survived and became a prisoner of war in Stalag Kopernikus.

When I completed my Basic Flying Training in peacetime with the Royal Canadian Air Force, I had 161 hours flying time. I had to complete my Advanced Flying Training next. Grant had 178 hours when he took his heavily laden Wellington bomber into the night skies with his crew on his second mission over enemy territory. We were both the same age with the same number of flying hours; he was a very brave man.

Flying Officer Grant is buried in Groesbeek Canadian War Cemetery. His nieces, Marcia and Deborah, are family friends and allowed me access to their family papers and Grant's logbook. Deborah and Tom Harkin recently had the chance to pay their respects at 'Uncle Bruce's' grave during a visit to Holland. Rest in Peace Bruce.

Decorations

Decorations were awarded for gallantry and meritorious service during the war and are a visible reminder to us of the valour and sacrifice of the recipient. Unfortunately, some are awarded posthumously as in the Victoria Crosses awarded to Pilot Officer Mynarski, the Canadian Warplane Heritage Museum dedicated their flying Avro Lancaster to him, and the Bomber Command Museum of Canada dedicated their ground running Avro Lancaster to Squadron Leader Bazalgette,.

Victoria Cross (VC)

This is awarded to the soldier, sailor, or airman, regardless of rank, of the British or Commonwealth forces for most conspicuous bravery or some daring or pre-eminent act of valour or self-sacrifice or extreme devotion to duty in the presence of the enemy. It is the rarest of all British decorations and takes precedence over all other orders and medals. In the Royal Air Force, the greatest number of Victoria Crosses were awarded to Bomber Command aircrew during the Second World War; a fitting reflection on the Command and its 'against all odds' struggle in the skies above enemy-held territory.

Several extracts from *The London Gazette* have been selected to illustrate the bravery of the holders of this prestigious award. Further information on those awarded the Victoria Cross may be researched under the individual's name. The word Deceased after the name of course indicates that the recipient had made the ultimate sacrifice during the cited event.

Acting Flight Sergeant Arthur L. Aaron, DFM (Deceased)
Royal Air Force Volunteer Reserve, No. 218 Squadron
Pilot Officer Cyril J. Barton, (Deceased)
Royal Air Force Volunteer Reserve, No. 578 Squadron
Acting Squadron Leader Ian W. Bazalgette, DFC (Deceased)
Royal Air Force Volunteer Reserve, No. 635 Squadron

'On 4th August 1944, Squadron Leader Bazalgette was Master Bomber of a Pathfinder Squadron detailed to mark an important target at Trossy-St. Maximin for the main bomber force.

When nearing the target his Lancaster came under heavy anti-aircraft fire. Both starboard engines were put out of action and serious fires broke out in the fuselage and the starboard main plane. The bomb aimer was badly wounded.

As the deputy master bomber had already been shot down, the success of the attack depended on Squadron Leader Bazalgette, and this he knew. Despite the appalling conditions in his burning aircraft, he pressed on gallantly to the target, marking and bombing it accurately. That the attack was successful was due to his magnificent effort.

After the bombs had been dropped the Lancaster dived, practically out of control. By expert airmanship and great exertion Squadron Leader Bazalgette regained control. But the port inner engine then failed and the whole of the starboard mainplane became a mass of flames.

Squadron Leader Bazalgette fought bravely to bring his aircraft and crew to safety. The mid-upper gunner was overcome by fumes. Squadron Leader Bazalgette then ordered those of his crew who were able to leave by parachute to do so. He remained at the controls and attempted the almost hopeless task of landing the crippled and blazing aircraft in a last effort to save the wounded bomb aimer and helpless gunner. With superb skill and taking great care to avoid a small French village nearby, he brought the aircraft down safely. Unfortunately, it then exploded, and this gallant officer and his two comrades perished.

His heroic sacrifice marked the climax of a long career of operations against the enemy. He always chose the more dangerous and exacting roles. His courage and devotion to duty were beyond praise.'

Wing Commander Geoffrey L. Cheshire, DSO, DFC
Royal Air Force Volunteer Reserve, No. 617 Squadron
Acting Wing Commander Hughie I. Edwards, DFC
Royal Air Force Volunteer Reserve, No. 105 Squadron
Flying Officer Donald E. Garland
Royal Air Force Volunteer Reserve, No. 12 Squadron
Acting Wing Commander Guy P. Gibson, DSO, DFC
Reserve of Air Force Officers, No. 617 Squadron
Sergeant Thomas Gray
Royal Air Force Volunteer Reserve, No. 12 Squadron
Sergeant John Hannah
Royal Air Force Volunteer Reserve, No. 83 Squadron

'On the night of 15 September 1940, Sergeant Hannah was the wireless operator/air gunner in an aircraft engaged in a successful attack on an enemy barge concentration at Antwerp. It was then subjected to intense anti-aircraft fire and received a direct hit from a projectile of an explosive and incendiary nature, which apparently burst inside the bomb compartment.

A fire started which quickly enveloped the wireless operator's and rear gunner's cockpits and, as both the port and starboard petrol tanks had been pierced, there was grave risk of the fire spreading. Sergeant Hannah forced his way through to obtain two extinguishers and discovered that the rear gunner had had to leave the aircraft. He could have acted likewise, through the bottom escape hatch or forward through the navigator's hatch but remained and fought the fire for ten minutes with the extinguishers, beating the flames with his logbook when these were empty.

During this time thousands of rounds of ammunition exploded in all directions and he was almost blinded by the intense heat and fumes but had the presence of mind to obtain relief by turning on his oxygen supply. Air admitted through the large holes caused by the projectile made the bomb compartment an inferno and all the aluminium sheet metal on the floor of this airman's cockpit was melted away, leaving only the cross bearers.

Working under these conditions, which caused burns to his face and eyes, Sergeant Hannah succeeded in extinguishing the fire. He then crawled forward, ascertained that the navigator had left the aircraft, and passed the latter's log and maps to the pilot. This airman displayed courage, coolness, and devotion to duty of the highest order and by his action in remaining and successfully extinguishing the fire under conditions of the greatest danger and difficulty, enabled the pilot to bring the aircraft to its base.'

Sergeant Norman C. Jackson
Royal Air Force Volunteer Reserve, No. 106 Squadron
Acting Flight Lieutenant Roderick A. B. Learoyd
Royal Air Force Volunteer Reserve, No. 49 Squadron
Acting Wing Commander Hugh Malcolm (Deceased)
Royal Air Force Volunteer Reserve, No. 18 Squadron
Flying Officer Leslie T. Manser (Deceased)
Royal Air Force Volunteer Reserve, No. 50 Squadron
Flight Sergeant Rawdon Hume (Missing)
Royal Australian Air Force, No. 149 Squadron
Pilot Officer Charles Mynarski (Deceased)
No. 418 Squadron Royal Canadian Air Force

'Pilot Officer Mynarski was the mid-upper gunner of a Lancaster aircraft detailed to attack a target at Cambrai in France on the night of 12 June 1944. The aircraft was attacked from below and astern by an enemy fighter and ultimately came down in flames.

As an immediate result of the attack, both port engines failed. Fire broke out between the mid-upper turret and the rear turret, as well as in the port wing. The flames soon became fierce and the captain ordered the crew to abandon the aircraft.

Pilot Officer Mynarski left his turret and went towards the escape hatch. He then saw that the rear gunner was still in his turret and apparently unable to leave it. The turret was in fact immovable since the hydraulic gear had been put out of action when the port engines failed, and the manual gear had been broken by the gunner in his attempt to escape.

Without hesitation, Pilot Officer Mynarski made his way through the flames in an endeavour to reach the rear turret and release the gunner. Whilst so doing, his parachute and his clothing, up to the waist, were set on fire. All his efforts to move the turret and free the gunner were in vain. Eventually the rear gunner clearly indicated to him that there was nothing more he could do and that he should try to save his own life. Pilot Officer Mynarski reluctantly went back through the flames to the escape hatch. There, as a last gesture to the trapped gunner, he turned towards him, stood to attention in his flaming clothing and saluted, before he jumped out of the aircraft. Pilot Officer Mynarski's descent was seen by French people on the ground. Both his parachute and clothing were on fire. He was found eventually by the French but was so severely burnt that he died from his injuries.

The rear gunner had a miraculous escape when the aircraft crashed. He subsequently testified that had Pilot Officer Mynarski not attempted to save his comrade's life he could have left the aircraft in safety and would, doubtless, have escaped death.

Pilot Officer Mynarski must have been fully aware that in trying to free the rear gunner he was almost certain to lose his own life. Despite this, with outstanding courage and complete disregard for his own safety, he went to the rescue. Willingly accepting the danger, Pilot Officer Mynarski lost his life by a most conspicuous act of heroism which called for valour of the highest order.'

Acting Squadron Leader John D. Nettleton
Royal Air Force Volunteer Reserve, No. 44 (Rhodesia) Squadron
Squadron Leader R. A. M. Palmer, DFC (Deceased)
Royal Air Force Volunteer Reserve, No. 109 Squadron
Acting Flight Lieutenant William Reid
Royal Air Force Volunteer Reserve, No. 61 Squadron
Squadron Leader Arthur S. K. Scarf
Royal Air Force Volunteer Reserve, No. 62 Squadron
Captain Edwin Swales, DFC (Deceased)
South African Air Force, No. 582 Squadron

'Captain Swales was master bomber of a force of aircraft which attacked Pforzheim on the night of February 23rd, 1945. As master bomber, he had the task of locating the target area with precision and of giving aiming instructions to the main force of bombers following in his wake.

Soon after he had reached the target area he was engaged by an enemy fighter and one of his engines was put out of action. His rear guns failed. His crippled aircraft was an easy prey to further attacks.

Unperturbed, he carried on with his allotted task; clearly and precisely he issued aiming instructions to the main force. Meanwhile the enemy fighter closed the range and fired again. A second engine of Captain Swales aircraft was put out of action. Almost defenceless, he stayed over the target area issuing his aiming instructions until he was satisfied that the attack had achieved its purpose.

It is now known that the attack was one of the most concentrated and successful of the war.

Captain Swales did not, however, regard his mission as completed. His aircraft was damaged. Its speed had been so much reduced that it could only with difficulty be kept in the air. The blind-flying instruments were no longer working. Determined at all costs to prevent his aircraft and crew from falling into enemy hands, he set course for home. After an hour he flew into thin-layered cloud. He kept his course by skilful flying between the layers, but later heavy cloud and turbulent air conditions were met. The aircraft, by now over friendly territory, became more and more difficult to control; it was losing height steadily. Realising that the situation was desperate Captain Swales ordered his crew to bale out. Time was very short, and it required all his exertions to keep the aircraft steady while each of his crew moved in turn to the escape hatch and parachuted to safety. Hardly had the last crewmember jumped when the aircraft plunged to earth. Captain Swales was found dead at the controls.

Intrepid in the attack, courageous in the face of danger, he did his duty to the last, giving his life that his comrades might live.'

Squadron Leader Leonard H. Trent, DFC
Royal New Zealand Air Force, No. 487 (R.N.Z.A.F.) Squadron
Flight Sergeant George Thompson (Deceased)
Royal Air Force Volunteer Reserve, No. 9 Squadron
Sergeant James A. Ward
Royal New Zealand Air Force, No. 75 (New Zealand) Squadron

'On the night of 7th July 1941, Sergeant Ward was second pilot of a Wellington returning from an attack on Munster. When flying over the Zuider Zee at 13,000 feet, the aircraft was attacked from beneath by a Messerschmitt 110, which secured hits with cannon shell and incendiary bullets. The rear gunner was wounded in the foot but delivered a burst of fire which sent the enemy fighter down, apparently out of control.

Fire then broke out near the starboard engine and, fed by petrol from a split pipe, quickly gained an alarming hold and threatened to spread to the entire wing. The crew forced a hole in the fuselage and made strenuous efforts to reduce the fire with extinguishers and even the coffee in their vacuum flasks, but without success. They were then warned to be ready to abandon the aircraft.

As a last resort, Sergeant Ward volunteered to make an attempt to smother the fire with an engine cover which happened to be in use as a cushion. At first, he proposed to discard his parachute, to reduce wind resistance, but was finally persuaded to take it. A rope from the dinghy was tied to him, though this was of little help and might have become a danger had he been blown off the aircraft. With the help of the navigator, he then climbed through the narrow astro-hatch and put on his parachute. The bomber was flying at a reduced speed, but the wind pressure must have been sufficient to render the operation one of extreme difficulty. Breaking the fabric to make hand and foot holds where necessary, and also taking advantage of existing holes in the fabric, Sergeant Ward succeeded in descending three feet to the wing and proceeding another three feet to a position behind the engine, despite the slipstream from the airscrew which nearly blew him off the wing. Lying in this precarious position, he smothered the fire in the wing fabric and tried to push the cover into the hole in the wing and on to the leaking pipe from which the fire came. As soon as he moved his hand, however, the terrific wind blew the cover out and when he tried again it was lost. Tired as he was, he was able with the navigator's assistance to make successfully the perilous journey back onto the aircraft.

There was now no danger of the fire spreading from the petrol pipe, as there was no fabric left nearby, and in due course it burnt itself out. When the aircraft was nearly home some petrol which had collected in the wing blazed up furiously but died down quite suddenly. A safe landing was then made despite the damage sustained by the aircraft. The flight home had been made possible by the gallant action of Sergeant Ward in extinguishing the fire on the wing in circumstances of the greatest difficulty and at the risk of his life.'

Distinguished Service Order (DSO)

This is awarded to commissioned officers in the British armed forces, who have been mentioned in dispatches for bravery or for meritorious or distinguished service in the field or before the enemy.

Distinguished Flying Cross (DFC)

This is awarded to British armed forces (after 1942 it was awarded to Commonwealth forces) officers and warrant officers for acts of valour, courage, or devotion to duty performed whilst flying in active operations against the enemy.

Air Force Cross (AFC)

This is awarded for acts of valour, courage, or devotion to duty whilst flying, though not in active operations against the enemy.

Conspicuous Gallantry Medal (CGM)

This is awarded to NCOs (Non-Commissioned Officers) who had shown exceptional gallantry in the face of the enemy. It is second only to the VC and is the NCO equivalent of the DSO.

Distinguished Flying Medal (DFM)

This is awarded to aircrew NCOs for acts of valour, courage, and devotion to duty whilst flying in active operations against the enemy.

Air Force Medal (AFM)

This is awarded to NCOs for acts of valour, courage, or devotion to duty whilst flying, though not in active operations against the enemy.

(Campaign Stars and medals were awarded for different campaigns. A typical Bomber Command set of decorations could have the Air Crew Europe Star, the France and Germany Star and The War Medal, among others.)

Bomber Command Clasp

It is only recently that a Bomber Command Clasp has been presented to those aircrew involved in the bombing campaign – far too late to honour our veterans who survived the carnage and gave their youth for our freedom. Wing Commander A. J. Wright, DFC Royal Air Force (Ret) stated in a letter to the *Oxford Times on* 5 March 2015, that:

> Many eligible BC [Bomber Command] veterans or their next of kin did not apply because they considered the clasp to be an insult to the memory of the fallen [55,805 aircrew and 1,400 ground staff] ... we believe that a campaign medal would have been more honourable and worthy award than the clasp awarded to aircrew only.

We must never forget that there were unsung heroes and their unseen heroic deeds. Actions that were above and beyond the call of the duty and that went unnoticed, unreported and forgotten in the heat of battle. They happened, they were real, and the aircrew involved never forgot them. No medal, no ribbon and no clasp, just the memories of a job well done.

7

BOMBER COMMAND OPERATIONS 1939–1945

In the previous chapters we have looked at the infrastructure of Bomber Command. Behind this vast organisation were the men and women of the British Commonwealth and their Allies. Up until 1939 this vast army of civilians were going about their daily lives until they answered the call to arms for their country.

William (Billy) Davison was one who did and served as an armourer with No. 463 Squadron Royal Australian Air Force at Royal Air Force Station Waddington after a tour of duty in Southern Rhodesia. Vera Dawe was also one. She enlisted in the Auxiliary Territorial Service where she served as a Medical Orderly. Billy was awarded the Defence Medal and they both were awarded the War Medal. They married after the war, and their daughter Lynn, and husband Harold, are our family friends.

From the moment in the morning of 3 September 1939 when Chamberlain told the people that 'this country is at war with Germany' it was clear that Bomber Command would now be required to perform tasks that it had only practised. It had been twenty-one years since Bomber Command had flown in anger. What would be its initial response now as it was guided by its new political and military masters?

At 1203, just over an hour after the declaration of war, a No. 139 Squadron Bristol Blenheim Mk. IV took off from Royal Air Force Wyton on a photo-reconnaissance of German naval ships north of Wilhelmshaven. Shortly thereafter a small force of ten Armstrong Whitworth Whitleys from Nos. 51 and 58 Squadrons dropped 5.4 million leaflets on Germany. This was the start of nearly six years of wartime operations and about 390,000 sorties, the last an attack on Kiel, a port city on the Baltic Sea coast, on the night of 2/3 May 1945 by No. 8 Group and No. 100 Group.

For a day-by-day detailed account of Bomber Command sorties I recommend Martin Middlebrook and Chris Everitt's *The Bomber Command War Diaries* published by Midland Publishing in 2000. Here a 'typical' or generic sortie will be described to illustrate the reality of a mission over enemy territory and the equally hazardous return. The crew were not safe and the operation not complete until the bomber had been parked on the hardstand at home station and the crew had left the aircraft unharmed and were having their cup of tea.

A general synopsis of operations will include some significant occurrences, unusual results, successful raids, and those not so successful to give an understanding of the diversity. The dangers are illustrated by one chilling (and sometimes challenged) statistic: of one hundred Bomber Command crew members on operations, forty-five would be killed, ten seriously wounded and died as a result, three had various degrees of injury, twelve taken prisoner of war, and two were shot down and evaded capture. This was a terrible cull of young men in the prime of their lives.

How would operations be decided upon and who would authorise them? Who was responsible for these day-to-day, or more correctly night to night, operations? How did it all come about? The initial bombing policy directive came from the Chief of the Air Staff at the Air Ministry that was itself advised by the Chiefs of Staff of the three services. The general policy directives would be received by the Commander-in-Chief, Bomber Command, at Bomber Command Headquarters in High Wycombe, Buckinghamshire.

The Commander would then consider the directive and decide on a method, timing, and means of carrying out the directive. These plans would be communicated to the Groups whose commanders were responsible for drawing up the detailed orders for the squadrons. The attacks all essentially worked the same, bomb the target and if unable to do so, attack the secondary target. The commanders of the Groups daily communicated their strength, number of aircraft and crews, to Bomber Command Headquarters.

One of the most important sections in the planning stage is the Intelligence Section. The section must accumulate vast amounts of information hourly to be able to provide the latest information for the 'Target for Tonight', maps, photographs, plans, defences, and a myriad other considerations. The section will gather information from a wide area of sources; the other services, spies and the 'Underground', photo-reconnaissance and even friendly governments.

In the Operations Room at Bomber Command headquarters there are large boards displaying the Order of Battle giving the exact strength of the Groups and the squadron activity. Other boards display current operations, meteorological information, previous operations and a map of Northern Europe showing main targets. There are also liaison contacts with the Army and Navy. A photographic mosaic of the Ruhr Valley and maps with routes to targets are displayed.

The types of targets are already known from the directives, which can change from time to time as the war progresses. The weather is the prime factor and can cancel the operation after all the preliminary preparations have been completed. The Commander-in-Chief, after considering the weather, intelligence reports, and aircraft status decides on the targets. The hours of darkness over the target are calculated to get the aircraft in the bombing stream over the target and to return in darkness. The proportion of incendiary and high explosive bombs will be included in the 'direct' telephone and teleprinter order to the Groups. The direct telephone is a special secure line which does not pass through a civilian switchboard.

Upon acceptance by the Group, there is room for negotiation; the Orders are passed on to the various Stations. The individual Squadrons are then passed their details of the planned raid. A further confirmation is made by Bomber Command during the afternoon and the operational side continues to prepare itself for the planned departure times – the HQ work is over and now it was the turn of 'the pointy end', the Squadrons and their aircraft, to get the job done.

The Night Operation

The Avro Lancaster and Handley Page Halifax in early 1942 became the night owls of the RAF bomber force due to the unavailability of long-range fighter daylight escorts as the targets became deeper in Germany. To cut losses the decision was made to have bomber streams of all aircraft types, very large numbers of aircraft on occasion, attack targets at night and leave enemy territory during darkness. This also had a psychological effect on the German population, with disturbed sleep patterns that affected production.

The crews were always under nervous tension during pre-flight preparation between notification of the raid and the actual departure. Once underway the anxiety sometimes disappeared temporarily, only to return as the target was approached. The tension was always present, and each crew member dealt with it in his own way, some better than others. The Mess and local pub were the scene of many hijinks as crews let off steam to cope with the situation. The station daily routine also continued, which was not conducive to proper rest after a long night airborne. Even training trips were subject to attack from marauding enemy aircraft looking for targets of opportunity over the English countryside. The stations themselves were subject to attack from both fighter and bomber aircraft.

Pre-Departure

A fairly typical day started with the results of the previous night raid, the losses, and whether another operation was scheduled for that night. Group Headquarters would send the operation message to the Intelligence Section who decoded it and sent the information to all the relevant sections. The Station would be locked down to prevent any inadvertent leak of the operation information. Another operation would mean that the whole station became very active for eighteen hours until the last aircraft had landed after the operation. This included the cooks, administrative staff who prepared the briefing, mechanics, armourers, fuel truck drivers, photo section, electronics personnel, and all the support staff including the very important meteorologist.

The crew would inspect their aircraft at the dispersal point with the ground crew and take it for a test flight if necessary. The ground crew would check the electrical, instrument, radar and hydraulic systems. The briefing would be held several hours before the first departure to allow for fueling, arming of the guns, and loading of the bombs. The Ruhr Valley, a trip of under five hours, would allow less fuel load and a large bomb load. A longer trip deep into Germany or Italy would require a larger fuel load and a subsequent reduction in bomb load. A full fuel load for the Avro Lancaster would give approximately a 2,500 miles (4,023km) range with 7,000lb (3,175 kg) bomb load.

Until the advent of H2S, clear weather was critical over the target area, although Gee and Oboe were of great assistance in locating the target. To help with the Dead Reckoning navigation an aircraft would be dispatched on the initial route to check the weather and especially the winds. The weather at home base upon return was a major concern. After surviving the Flak and fighter activity the pilot had to face the English weather to land. Landing aids were primitive during the 1940s and unfortunately fog and low cloud were prevalent during a large portion of the year. The factories were operating at full capacity and contributed to the industrial haze, which further restricted visibility. Extra fuel was carried to allow diversion if needed to other stations experiencing better weather conditions than home base.

Ground Preparation

Lunch was followed by the start of preparations for the raid. The crew briefing, many reported, was the start of the heightening tension and the uneasy feeling in the stomach. The crew gathered in the briefing room with a shrouded map on a raised platform ready for viewing. A roll-call was held to make sure all crews were in attendance. 'Attention' was called and the whole assembly arose to its feet and stood at attention while the briefing party entered. The briefing party were the station, squadron and senior flight commanders who joined the briefing group who were already on the stage.

The squadron intelligence officer opened the briefing by revealing the map with the route to the target marked along with searchlight, fighter activity and Flak locations. Squadron Leader W. E. Jones in his book *Bomber Intelligence* said of his time as the Squadron Intelligence officer:

> Although I had my briefing notes in my hand, I always made sure that I could do the briefing without having to read from them. If you had to read your notes, you couldn't look at the crews and, in any case, it gave the impression that you were simply reading a prepared 'speech'. As I take the platform with my three feet long black pointer in my hand, I give a quick look around. It happens at every briefing – how many of them will return to be interrogated in the early hours of the morning, I wonder? It was always a tremendous responsibility to stand up there in front of those aircrews and to give them the best information possible that would enable them to do their hazardous job as efficiently and hopefully, as safely as possible.

This was followed by the bombing, navigation, signals and meteorological briefing. The Flying Control Officer explained the start-up and marshalling times followed by the runway in use. The crew navigator then plotted the course with the expected winds to give the time, fuel used and ETA at the target.

The pilot next met with all the crew together to go over the details of the entire raid, so everyone was aware of how and when things were going to happen. Everything was planned down to the smallest detail, but planning and reality rarely coincided. However, without planning there would be total chaos. It was not unusual for aircrew to go through 'lucky' rituals and carry lucky charms.

A final meal of the obligatory eggs and bacon, a cup of tea and the crew was on its way to the Locker Room to pick up their parachutes, Mae Wests and, for the gunners, their kapok 'Taylor Suits'. The crew reached their aircraft at the dispersal point on foot if close during the dry summer months or driven in an enclosed van. A final check with the ground crew, a last cigarette and nervous pee and all climbed aboard to make their scheduled take-off time. The uneasy feeling had now turned to a knot in the stomach. There was no getting around this feeling and it seemed to make no difference to the crews whether they were on their first or twentieth tour.

Everyone proceeded to their crew station. Those in the front had to scale the main wing spars which constricted the passageway and resulted in a few skinned shins. That was nothing compared to the gymnastics that the rear gunner went through in his electrically warmed suit to get over the tailplane spar and close the rear doors of the turret after him.

The emergency parachute was hung inside the fuselage. There were also sandwiches and flasks of tea for the return journey.

Pre-start check was followed by communication with the ground crew, clearance to start, and the engine start sequence of the four engines. Engine warm up, magneto check, and propeller check was followed by the take-off throttle position to check boost and rpm. The airfield was a noisy place until all had departed.

Take-Off

Chocks away and the bomber, we will use the Avro Lancaster as an example, would join the stream of aircraft on the perimeter track to the runway. Steered with the outer engines, as much as possible, the visibility over the nose was restricted for the pilot as he taxied in the dark. Pre-take-off check followed by a green light from control and the throttles were advanced to take-off position. Leading the throttles on one side corrected the swing until the flying controls took effect. The Flight Engineer held the throttles in the take-off position during the take-off run. Forward pressure on the control column raised the tail up and then approaching 100mph (161kmh) back pressure was applied to the control wheel and the heavily laden aircraft lifted off.

Safely airborne, the brakes were applied to stop the main wheels spinning, undercarriage (landing gear) retracted, and above 500ft (152m) the flaps were retracted in five-degree increments. Over the 125mph (201kmh) safety speed the throttles were brought back to the climb setting. The navigator handed the course to steer to the pilot to join up at the group's assembly point. A climb was initiated at 165mph (266kmh) until cruising altitude was reached and where the speed was increased to 200mph (322kmh). The radio operator picked up the latest winds from the 'windfinders', the first aircraft in the stream, and passed them forward to the navigator for course adjustments.

Although the aircraft were in a bomber stream, sometimes up to 1,000 aircraft, each navigator plotted his own course to the target. Constant outside vigilance by the rest of the crew allowed the navigator and wireless operator to attend to their respective duties inside the aircraft. They were looking for attacking fighters but collision avoidance with other bombers was no less important. Operation within the bomber stream was extremely hazardous at night, the presence of other aircraft only felt by the turbulence of their slipstream.

In later years Gee kept the aircraft on course above the black-out of occupied Europe. The gunners and Bomb Aimer would inform the pilot of any fighter activity directed at them and call out the evasive action. The corkscrew evasive manoeuvre was standard for the Lancaster as it could take the stresses of twisting, turning and diving. The idea of Flak evasion was discouraged as it caused more problems than it was worth.

Target and Return

Amid the confusion of Flak, searchlights, fighter aircraft, clouds, and other bombers the crew had to remain calm and steady to deliver the bombs on target. Approaching the target, the Bomb Aimer was down in his nose compartment to confirm his bomb dropping settings. The crew were at their most vulnerable flying straight and level illuminated by the fires below and the ever-sweeping searchlights. Confirming that the Pathfinder coloured flares and target identification markers agreed, he then released the bombs – 'Bomb doors open, master switch on, bombs fused and selected', followed by 'Bombs gone, bomb doors closed, let's get the H--- out of here.' The pilot adjusted trim for the weight reduction and closed bomb doors and maintained course for the important photoflash to confirm their bomb drop accuracy. That completed, the navigator passed a new course to the pilot to clear the target area.

The crew were on their way home after having survived the gruelling task of bombing the target. The unspoken question in the aircraft was would they survive the journey home to celebrate? The odds were not in their favour, for now the journey home could involve wounded crew, damaged aircraft, perhaps even loss of one or more engines, uncertain navigation due equipment damage, loss of hydraulic pressure, deteriorating weather conditions, loss of communication, and the ever-present danger of Flak and night fighters. Cloud and darkness were the crews' best friends now. Time passed agonisingly slowly as the aircraft headed for England with the unforgiving sea ahead of them. Fatigue must not be allowed to interfere with the constant visual scan of the night sky for the fighters. Now was the time for the aircraft captain to show his leadership qualities and keep the crew sharp and alert.

Landing and Interrogation

All being well, they would return to their own station, be correctly identified, and join the traffic pattern for the landing. Eyes were still vigilant because it was not unknown for an enemy fighter to join the circuit and shoot the bomber down when it was most vulnerable during the landing approach. Initially flown at 140mph (225kmh) the flaps were lowered in increments, speed reduced, and the undercarriage selected down to cross the "hedge" and runway threshold at 95 mph (153kmh) for touchdown at 90mph (145kmh). The Flight Engineer brought back the throttles to idle as the pilot applied the brakes. Now light, the aircraft could be taxied on the two inner engines to the hardstand.

The whole crew would be debriefed by the Intelligence Officer over a cup of tea as to Flak, fighter activity, and anything witnessed on the raid. These were the last things anybody wanted to talk about when mind were set on getting out of flying gear, maybe grabbing some breakfast, and getting some sleep. 'A fried egg for breakfast that was part of our payment' remembered tail gunner Art Sewel during our interview with a grin. The mission over, it was time to get some rest and repeat, if the weather was suitable, the next night.

The Reality

The above narrative seems so orderly. Reality was not. A few thoughts:

1. The air is a hostile environment to man, especially at night; he cannot see well.
2. Every take-off is governed by the thought that gravity will win eventually, hopefully in a smooth, uneventful landing.
3. Recent events are alive in the minds of the crew prior to every mission: both of their own previous experiences, maybe even the night before, and the knowledge of the ever-increasing number of squadron mates who never came back.
4. The thought of permanently leaving family, friends, comrades, and loved ones.
5. The climb into the claustrophobic fuselage emphasised even more by the bulky flying wear necessary to keep warm.
6. The crew safety, very often, was in the hands of just one man, a single pilot.
7. The take-off in a heavily laden bomber required maximum performance from all parts, human and mechanical.
8. Noise, vibration, oil and hydraulic odours, vibration, heat, cold, cramped space, being joined to other crew members only by intercom. Weather turbulence, icing, rain, cloud, fog, destination known by name only. Causing destruction and death, at the same time fearing for your own.
9. The anti-aircraft guns and searchlights. The noise of the Flak shrapnel hitting the hollow fuselage.
10. The sound of your own guns shooting at an attacking fighter, wondering if you would survive.
11. The violent evasive turns to find darkness and shake the fighter off.
12. The target: the ground lit up by fires, the searchlights, the puffs of Flak, glimpses of other bombers in the light, Pathfinder flares, explosions, and falling, burning, exploding aircraft.
13. The final straight and level run in to the target until 'Bombs Away'.
14. All to be experienced once again on the way back to the home airfield thinking that this time, you just may make it.
15. The relief of crossing the North Sea.
16. The final battle of a different sort. The approach and landing of a damaged aircraft, perhaps with wounded crew needing immediate

attention, and perhaps with dead crew on board. Getting the aircraft down through the clouds and fog to find and land on a runway without crashing or running off the end, perhaps with bombs hung up on the bomb rack.

17. To do it over again, perhaps the next night. That is the definition of courage.

Logbook

A flight time logbook was kept individually by all the crew and submitted to the Flight Commander monthly for examination. Very often notations were added to the basic entries such as 'lost one engine, rear gunner injured, crash landed' which turned the book into a histororical account of wartime experiences. It is an invaluable source for the archivist, historian, and author.

There were five general outcomes to a wartime operational trip.

- The crew survived the trip and returned safely to home base.
- The crew survived the trip and returned with injuries or casualties.
- The crew were shot down, all/some survived; survivors became PoWs held in a Stalag Luft (camp for Allied airmen) or
- Escaped and returned home.
- The crew went missing, their fate, some but not all, discovered after the war ended. The casualties were buried locally, and some were later reinterred in a war cemetery or Commonwealth War Graves Commission site.

The Bombs

The bomber aircraft were designed to carry bombs as numerous and heavy as possible. The bombs varied in size from the mainstay incendiary 4lb (1.8kg) to the sea mine 250lb (113kg) to 22,000lb (9979kg). They were either thin-skinned High-Capacity bombs, designed for their high blast effect, or Medium Capacity thick-skinned bombs, designed for their penetrating power before exploding. They did have a dangerous habit of exploding during a take-off crash.

The family of High-Capacity bombs weighed 2,000lb (970kg), 4,000lb (1,814kg), 8,000lb (3,628kg), and 12,000lb (5,442kg) and were used with incendiary bombs to light the resulting rubble on fire during an Area Bombing operation.

The family of Medium Capacity bombs weighed 500lb (227kg), 1,000lb (453kg), 4,000lb (1,814kg), 12,000lb (5,442kg), and 22,000lb (9,979kg) and were used on strategic targets. They did have some supply and fusing issues.

There were also specialty bombs such as the Barnes Wallis rolling skipping bomb for dam destruction and the high tensile steel bomb for battleships, railway tunnels, and U-boat pens. The bombs would arrive at the aircraft on a trolley and then be winched into the bomb bay. The laborious process of loading the small incendiaries was first of all made easier by using small bomb containers and then finally by faster and easier loading in cluster containers

The Phoney War and Spring 1940

There was an initial period after war was declared when very little happened in Bomber Command, but there was more activity in the land and naval environments. This period, from 3 September 1939 to the German invasion of France and the Low Countries on 10 May 1940, was called the 'Phoney War'. Photo-reconnaissance and leaflet dropping were the main activities of the Command during this time along with the following notable operations.

- 04 September 1939
  Bristol Blenheims and Vickers Wellingtons make first attack on the German fleet at Wilhelmshaven.
- 01/02 October 1939
  Armstrong Whitworth Whitley of No. 10 Squadron flies over Berlin.
- 03 December 1939
  Vickers Wellingtons attack the German fleet at Heligoland.
- 14 December 1939
  German fleet attacked in Schilling Roads, Wilhelmshaven, with loss of five aircraft.
- 18 December 1939
  Vickers Wellingtons attack German fleet at Wilhelmshaven, twelve aircraft lost.
- Due to mounting losses Bomber Command decides not to continue with daylight raids unescorted by fighter aircraft.
- 11/12 January 1940
  Vickers Wellingtons drop leaflets on Hamburg.
- 12/13 January 1940
  Armstrong Whitleys based in France bomb Prague and Vienna.
- 11 March 1940
  Bristol Blenheim, No. 82 Squadron, sinks U-boat off Borkum.
- 19/20 March 1940
  Largest raid so far in the 'Phoney War' sees fifty Armstrong Whitworth Whitleys and Handley Page Hampdens attack the Hornum seaplane base.
- 13/14 April 1940
  First mine laying operation of the war in sea lanes off Denmark by Handley Page Hampdens.

The German forces had invaded Denmark and Norway in early April 1940 followed by the Low Countries on 10 May 1940; the 'Phoney War' had ended. In April Air Marshal, later Air Chief Marshal, Portal was appointed Commander-in-Chief of Bomber Command. He was an advocate of strategic area bombing against industrial areas; he continued to view this as a winning strategy after his promotion to Chief of the Air Staff on 25 October 1940. Portal also advocated the formation of the Pathfinder Force, an astute leader during Britain's hour of need.

The loss of the European mainland to German troops would continue until the evacuation of Allied troops from Dunkirk, France. The remnants of the Advanced Air Striking Force, including Fairey Battles, would join Bomber Command on Britain's mainland in mid-June.

- 11/12 May 1940
  First raid against mainland Germany, Munchengladbach.
- 15/16 May 1940
  The first strategic bombing raid of the war was on Ruhr oil and railway targets. It would be nearly two years until the authorisation of Area bombing, 14 February 1942
- 20 August 1940
  Sir Winston Churchill, Prime Minister, made his famous 'The Few' speech which is remembered for his remarks about the gallantry of the fighter pilots but included in that speech were the words 'On no part of the Royal Air Force does the weight of the war fall more heavily than on the daylight bombers who will play an invaluable part in the case of invasion and whose unflinching zeal it has been necessary in the meanwhile on numerous occasions to restrain.'
- 23/24 August 1940
  'The Big Mistake'. A Luftwaffe bombing formation that had been assigned industrial targets outside London drifted off course and mistakenly bombed the City of London itself.
- 25/26 August 1940
  Portal, with political support, retaliated with an eighty-one-bomber raid on Berlin, Germany's capital. The attack was hampered by bad weather and damage was inconsequential. However, the raid went down in history as the raid that changed the course of the war, in favour of Britain.
- 04 September 1940
  'The Biggest Mistake'.

It was the biggest mistake as Hitler changed his tactics, because of that raid on Berlin, and retaliated with attacks on British cities. This was a case of pride over military thinking. That fateful decision took pressure off the weakened Allied fighter force, the damaged airfields and the damaged radar sites, and allowed them to recover and become operational again and go on to win the Battle of Britain. The German invasion plans were postponed, as it turned out, indefinitely.

Regroup

September 1940 to January 1941
Raid Losses: 1.6 per cent

Britain paused after the summer all-out effort of the Battle of Britain. The invasion was off, and the weather was deteriorating as winter approached. The Air Ministry directive to Air Marshal Sir Richard Peirse specified oil targets and if resources and weather were suitable there was a list of secondary targets, such as railways and Luftwaffe bomber bases. The number of available bombers was reduced as the Bristol Blenheim neared the end of its effective life and the Fairey Battle was now obsolete. Bomber Command was now in the unenviable position of employing small bomb loads directed at hard to find, small targets. The Area Bombing concept had been rejected at this time. Another, perhaps questionable, concept called the 'Circus' sent Bristol Blenheims to targets with a fighter escort that hoped to draw the Luftwaffe fighters up to engage them. It did maintain the presence of Bomber Command if nothing else, during this slow period.

- 23/24 September 1940
  An exception was a large raid on Berlin, Germany with 129 bombers.
- 7/8 October 1940
  Forty-two bombers attacked Berlin, Germany.
- 15/16 November 1940
  A successful two-wave bombing raid was carried out in clear weather on Hamburg, Germany. Many fires were observed and there was damage at the Blohm & Voss shipyard.
- 16/17 December 1940
  In retaliation for bombing attacks on British cities, Coventry and Southampton, Bomber Command was authorised to carry out a unique Area Bombing on Mannheim, Germany. Vickers Wellingtons carried an all-incendiary bomb load to start fires to guide the succeeding bombers. This was the forerunner to the pathfinder concept.
- January 1941
  Multiple attacks made on the battleship *Tirpitz* at Wilhelmshaven.

February 1941 – March 1941

The year had started with the Handley Page Halifax in service. With a new directive to bomb seventeen synthetic-oil targets in Germany,

Bomber Command now mounted a larger number of aircraft raids. Unfortunately, bad weather hid the intended target. Cologne was the alternate target. A large number of aircraft crashed at the home or diversion airfield.

- 10/11 February 1941
  First operational mission of Short Stirling.
- 11/12 February 1941
  Seventy-nine aircraft attacked Bremen, twenty-two crashed in England. 24/25 February 1941 First Avro Manchester operational mission.
- 8 March 1941
  First Handley Page Halifax operation of the war. No. 35 Squadron Handley Page Halifax mistakenly shot down over Surrey, England, by Supermarine Spitfire.

Coastal Command Assistance

March 1941 – July 1941
Raid Losses: 2.5%

The vital ocean links with North America were under constant threat by U-boat attacks, German battleships, and Focke-Wulf Kondor long-range bombers. Churchill was influential in the new directive to attack anything anywhere that had an effect on keeping Britain supplied. That included specifically the U-boat ports, pens, docks, and the home airfields and factories of the Focke-Wulf Kondor. The directive included the surrounding areas to demoralise the population.

- 12/13 March 1941
  First attacks of the directive were by eighty-eight aircraft on the Blohm & Voss U-boat yards at Hamburg and eighty-six aircraft on the Focke-Wulf aircraft factory in Bremen.
- 28 April 1941
  Operation *Channel Stop* inaugurated by No. 101 Squadron Bristol Blenheims with fighter escort to prevent German ships passing through the English Channel.
- 23 May 1941
  Unsuccessful raid by Bristol Blenheims to sink ships in the Kiel Canal and block it.
- 17 June 1941
  Twenty-three Bristol Blenheims on a Circus raid damaged a power station near Bethune, France, but ten escorting fighters were shot down.

- 24 July 1941
  Nos 35 & 76 Squadrons' Handley Page Halifaxes attacked and damaged the German battleship *Scharnhorst* at La Pallice, France. It required four months to repair.

Ruhr and Rhine, the Heartland Again

July 1941 – November 1941
Raid Losses: 3.9 per cent

In July 1941 a new directive instructed Bomber Command to target the inland transportation system and, most importantly, to focus on 'destroying of the morale of the civil population as a whole and of the industrial workers in particular'. The change was initiated by the Air Ministry. There was a ring of designated targets around the Ruhr Valley to disrupt shipping of war materials, major cities situated on the Rhine River to disrupt river traffic, and more distant cities when the Rhine and Ruhr weather was unfavourable. The old bomber aircraft of Bomber Command were carrying on the offensive while the new aircraft were experiencing teething problems; Bomber Command was under strength. That was not the only problem. The Luftwaffe night fighters stationed in Holland, aided by ground radar and now their own airborne radar, were increasingly able to find the night bomber and their success rate increased.

- 11/12 August 1941
  Munchengladbach had two firsts: the first raid on German soil 11/12 May 1940, and now the first raid by two Vickers Wellingtons using the new Gee navigation system.
- 25 September 1941
  The last day operation by Royal Air Force Boeing Fortress bombers. No. 90 Squadron had little success with the type.
- 12/13 October 1941
  A raid on Nuremberg is indicative of the level of accuracy of night bombing in 1941. A similar looking town and village situated on a wide river were bombed extensively in error. These locations were up to 100 miles (168km) east and west of Nuremberg where only a few bombs fell. The attack was a failure.

The Butt Report Pause

November 1941 – February 1942
Raid Losses: 3.0 per cent

There was some doubt creeping in as to the true accuracy of the bomber attacks. Intelligence reports on the raids were generated from crew debriefing, post operation photo-reconnaissance, and bombing cameras fitted to a few aircraft. These 100 reports were analysed and released in the Butt Report of August 1941. The results were shocking:

- One in three attacking aircraft got within five miles, eight kilometres of target
- Over Germany it was one in four, over the Ruhr Valley it was one in ten
- Full moon it was two in five, new moon it was one in fifteen.

Casualties were also shocking, equivalent to the entire front-line strength of Bomber Command being lost in four months of operations. The raid on Berlin on the 7/8 November 1941 was the proverbial straw that broke the camel's back; see below. The War Cabinet decided that it was too costly to sustain the present level of operations. There would be limited raid activity due to the winter weather, and the decision was made by the War Cabinet to debate the future of Bomber Command.

- 7/8 November 1941
  Due to continuing bad weather and the bad press regarding the bombing accuracy of the Command, Sir Richard Peirce decided to mount a large-scale attack on Berlin. Despite a terrible weather forecast, a force of 169 aircraft attempted to attack Berlin. Seventy-three bombers reputedly reached and bombed the Berlin area with mediocre results. The staggering statistic was that twenty-one aircraft were lost, 12.4 per cent. This was totally unacceptable for the Air Ministry and War Cabinet.
- 27 December 1941
  The island of Vaagso, off the coast of Norway, was the location of the first Combined Operation of all three forces on German-held territory The Commandos were landed by the Navy while Bomber Command provided twenty-nine aircraft for supporting operations. The operation was deemed a success. However, Bomber Command losses once again were extremely high at 27 per cent.
- 29/30 January 1942
  Only two out of sixteen bombers reached Trondheim, Norway, to attempt to bomb the German battleship *Tirpitz*.
- 12 February 1942
  The Channel Dash. The German battleships, *Scharnhorst* and *Gneisenau*, and the light cruiser, *Prinz Eugen*, made a lightning dash from Brest, France, through the Dover Straits back to Germany. In a well-orchestrated plan they were concealed by bad weather and had a top cover fighter escort. Bomber Command was unable to get direct hits on the ships, but the battleships were damaged by previously laid mines in the Frisian Islands.

A Change Of Leader

February 1942 – September 1945

Air Marshal, later Air Chief Marshal, Sir Arthur Harris, KCB, OBE, AFC assumed the post of Commander-in-Chief Bomber Command in February 1942 coincidental with the introduction of the Avro Lancaster and the 14 February 1942 British Government's *Area Bombing Directive No. 5*, which ordered Bomber Command to change tactics to now bomb area targets of the German industrial workforce and German cities. It listed areas primarily within 350 miles (563km) from Royal Air Force Mildenhall that were just over the maximum range of the Gee radio navigation aid. A directive, of 8/9 March 1942 specifically mentioned the Ruhr area and Essen, which were to be bombed without restriction. This directive would be amended from time to time with new targets and methods.

I follow in the shadow of many great historians, politicians, academics, and intellectuals who have debated the rights and wrongs of this Directive, area bombing versus strategic bombing. Do I sit on the fencel amid this ongoing military historic controversy, seventy-five years after the cessation of the Second World War, or do I decide where my feelings lie?

I can certainly quote the main political and military figures of the days leading up to the Second World War and how the feelings changed owing to the enemy switching tactics. Britain started out the conflict because of an agreement to come to the aid of a European mainland country; this slowly evolved into the British homeland facing invasion. Quite a change from a somewhat remote war to one which would threaten the very existence of the nation.

The struggle can be divided into many campaigns throughout the world. However, in Europe the phases can generally be described as the initial defensive containment campaign in Europe, the retreat from mainland Europe, the defence of Britain, and, when assets became available with the change in tide of the war, the aerial bombardment of the enemies' resources, both human and physical, followed by the invasion and the ultimate surrender of the enemy. It is the nature of this aerial bombardment that has prompted many questions.

I have made my choice, not without thought and feeling, to support one of the options, Strategic or Area Bombing. Certainly I think that flying fighters in the Royal Canadian Air Force before my writing career had an influence on my thinking. Perhaps if I had been a civilian, I would have thought differently, but that is not the case.

The dictionary says that Area is 'part, zone, extent, and region' and that Strategic is 'planned, tactical, intentional, and calculated'. This would indicate that Area Bombing could be Strategic Bombing and that

Strategic Bombing could be Area Bombing. What would cause these two terms to be used? It was previously established conventions of conducting war by the military and the rules of engagement set by their political masters. These rules, directives, and orders could be, and were, changed by the politicians as they realised that they had restricted the military in their operations to the detriment of the war effort.

The German war machine did not hold back from the very beginning with the invasion of Poland. The Blitzkrieg used lightning speed and surprise so that pressure could then be put on interior defences. Its aim was to create panic among the civilian population. A civil population on the move can be absolute havoc for a defending army trying to get its forces to the war front. Civilians were used from the very beginning as pawns in this terrible World War.

Similar to the debate on whether the US should or should not have used nuclear weapons on Japan, the debate continues over the Area versus Strategic bombing campaign. It is said that the bombing of Hiroshima and Nagasaki saved a quarter of a million American combatants' lives by hastening the end of the Pacific War. Pearl Harbor could certainly be called a Japanese Blitzkrieg for its speed and surprise. An attack of aggression against a sovereign state should be responded to in kind; it just took a few years for the Americans to get to Japan.

The war machine needs support: some civilians become soldiers, sailors, and airmen; civilians make the weapons and ammunition; and civilians provide food and medical support and perform the small tasks and the larger tasks that support the war machine. There is no way of separating those who support the war effort and those that just want to live a life and not get involved.

Countries fight wars; civilians elect politicians who run countries who fight wars. The military are the executive of the politicians' reaction to aggression by other countries run by civilian governments. Unfortunately, the unarmed civilians are the collateral damage; what a term for destroying peoples' lives. It is my opinion that the sooner the conflict is ended, if negotiation has failed, the better. It took a long time for Britain to recover from the six-year Second World War, but it did recover, and it and many Allied countries were able to enjoy their sovereignty that still exists today.

Meet force with force; meet total force with total force. Bomber Command met the threat of total force with the tools it had, the bomber force. Yes, Area Bombing can be defined as Strategic Bombing with the aim to defeat the enemy and end the war sooner.

Scrutiny

Bomber Command was under War Cabinet scrutiny in early 1942 for the following reasons:

1. Bomber Command was unable to protect itself enough in daylight and had to revert to mainly night operations.
2. The Butt Report highlighted the inability of the Command to find and hit the target at night with a reasonable amount of success.
3. The widening gap between effort and result.
4. The increasing aircrew casualties.

The answer to points 1, 2, and 3 was technology, which would eventually lead to an ameliorisation of point 4. Defensive radar, new navigation aids, better landing aids, more advanced aircraft and bombs, and area bombing directives would lead to the rejuvenation of Bomber Command under the leadership of Harris, soon to be known as 'Bomber Harris'. He arrived eight days after the new directive. The basic directive to Bomber Command, supported by the top political and military members of the War Cabinet and Air Ministry, was the destruction of the German economy and the morale of the industrial workers. The gauntlet was thrown down; how would Bomber Command respond?

While the basic strength of Bomber Command had not changed much since the previous year there was one event that would have a significant effect: the arrival of the new Avro Lancaster in February 1942. This aircraft, in addition to the improved versions of the Short Stirling and Handley Page Halifax, would increase the bomb carrying capability of the Command in 1942 and beyond.

Simultaneously, the first of the navigation aids became operational in March 1942. Gee had a range of up to roughly 350 miles (560km). The first operational mission using Gee was on 8/9 March by No. 115 Squadron Vickers Wellingtons leading a 200-bomber attack on Essen in the Ruhr. The attack was a success with a third of the force reaching the target area. Hard to believe what the percentage was before Gee. It was pretty handy on the return journey as well.

Bomber Harris brought new procedures into force immediately. He was a proponent of the station having Wing Commanders in charge of administration, maintenance and operations, giving the younger active experienced pilots the chance to lead their flights into battle. He believed that training of his crews was very very important, from his own previous experience, and operationally that the greater the force applied quickly, in suitable weather, the greater would be the chance of success. He also believed that fires were the obvious marker at night. Incendiary bombs started fires which would keep the fire services busy and could destroy a city. He ensured that these bombs would be more extensively used. They did have a drawback. If the fires were in the wrong place the 'herd instinct' would tend to draw the eye of the crew to the wrong target area. It was critical that the initial bombs were in the correct location.

- 3/4 March 1942
  Within ten days of his appointment Sir Arthur Harris mounts the greatest number of aircraft, 235, on a single target, the Renault factory at Billancourt, France.
- 10/11 March 1942
  First operational attack by the Avro Lancaster.
- 10/11 April 1942
  First 8,000lb (3,629kg) bomb dropped on Essen by No. 76 Squadron Handley Page Halifax.
- 17 April 1942
  Just over a month later Sir Arthur Harris experimented with a daylight raid on the M. A. N. diesel factory at Augsburg using a low-level attack flown by trained Avro Lancaster crews. The attack was successful, but the casualty rate was too high, and that type of attack was not repeated.
- 30/31 May 1942
  Sir Arthur Harris mounted a 'demonstration' raid of 1,047 (1,046 some sources) bomber aircraft in a bomber stream to attack Cologne, Germany. It was the alternate choice due weather to the primary target Hamburg. Every available aircraft and crew was pressed into service. That included the training units, which, in addition to instructors, sent forty-nine pupil pilots. I have no figures for the students' survival rate. Time over target for the stream to pass was organised at ninety minutes. This greatly increased the risk of collision. The raid was deemed a success with incendiary bombs doing more damage than the high-explosive bombs.
- 31 May 1942
  First use of the De Havilland Mosquito to photograph Cologne and drop bombs.
- 1/2 June 1942
  Second 1,000-bomber raid on Essen, Germany, not as successful due a layer of low cloud creating difficulty finding target.
- 25/26 June 1942
  The third, and last, 1,000-bomber raid on Bremen, Germany, was more successful than the previous raid on Essen, but still fell short of anticipated results owing, once again, to cloud cover and the high losses of the Operational Training Units. Something would have to improve the accuracy. That would appear in August.
- 11/12 July 1942
  Low level daylight raid by Avro Lancasters on Danzig, Germany, U-boat yards
- Losses had climbed to 4.3 per cent and accuracy had not improved significantly. Up until now the squadrons had been using 'raid

leaders' who by their experience and skill had an above average record of correctly finding the target. Group Captain S. O. Bufton suggested that these crews should be gathered together as a 'Target Finding Force'. Initially resisted by Sir Arthur Harris, the famous 'Pathfinder Force' was formed on the 15 July 1942. Initially marking the site with flares this developed into distinctly coloured super incendiaries on the ground. Many innovations followed such as lead flare paths and aerial flares.

- 17 August 1942
  Boeing B-17 Fortresses of the Eighth Air Force, United States Air Force became a daylight partner of Bomber Command with a raid on Rouen, France, rail yards. The timing was right as the casualty rate was at its highest, 4.7 per cent, and morale was suffering.
- 18/19 August 1942
  The first Pathfinder led raid had an inauspicious start. The raid on Flensburg, Germany, was blown north and towns north of the target in Denmark were bombed.
- 15/16 August 1942
  First 12,000lb (5,443kg) bombs dropped by No. 617 Squadron Avro Lancasters on the Dortmund-Ems canal, Germany.
- 25 September 1942
  De Havilland Mosquitos attack Gestapo headquarters, Oslo, Norway.
- 17 October 1942
  Despite the previous low-level daylight raid to Augsburg, Harris decided on a similar raid on the Schneider factory at Le Creusot, France. Ninety-eight Avro Lancasters bombed the target area, but subsequent photographs showed little damage to the actual factory.
- 28/29 November 1942
  First 8,000lb (3,629kg) bomb dropped on Turin, Italy.

Technology Improvements and Additional Groups

The end of 1942 saw a second wind for Bomber Command in the new technology available, trained crews from the British Commonwealth Air Training Plan, and the expanding Bomber Command Group structure. The balance of the effort to result ratio was about to change favourably. It had been a long three years of struggle and attrition; technology would initiate the change with navigation aids to allow blind-bombing techniques. This was an important turning point for Bomber Command.

Oboe was the first of the blind-bombing aids used, working on the principle of ground station-transmitted pulses to guide the aircraft to the target being re-transmitted back. The aircraft followed a track and over target, the intersection of two Oboe pulses was a signal to drop its bombs. It did have three main limitations: it was line of sight thus limiting range of operation, each station could only control six aircraft per hour, and the final run-in to the target had to be straight and level leaving the aircraft vulnerable to attack. The high altitude De Havilland Mosquito was an ideal Oboe aircraft as it gave greater line of sight distances. It was a most suitable aircraft for a Pathfinder Force target marker. The Axis were never able to jam Oboe properly, a significant failure. The first operational use of Oboe-aimed bombs was on 20 December 1942 in a raid on the power station at Lutterade, Holland.

H2S, a crude airborne ground scanning radar device, did not have any range limitations. However, in 1942, the picture it displayed to the operator took a lot of skilled interpretation. H2S could distinguish coastlines, major rivers and lakes, and sometimes major cities and it was valuable to the navigator trying to pinpoint his position.

'Mandrel' was a jamming electronic countermeasure used against the German bomber guiding ground radar stations. 'Tinsel' was a noise generating device which could be tuned by the radio operator to drown out the enemy's radio frequencies. These were part of a suite of electronic devices becoming available to Bomber Command.

The Command was gaining technology strength and Group strength. A new marker bomb had been developed for the Pathfinder Force, two new Groups were formed, and the average bomb load had increased due to the number of heavy bombers, particularly the Avro Lancaster.

- 01 January 1943
  No. 6 (Canadian) Group was formed in North Yorkshire and Durham.
- 08 January 1943
  No. 8 (Pathfinder Force) Group was formed.
- 14 January 1943
  Once again a directive altered the focus of the raids for three months; now it was to be Lorient, France, and the other hardened U-boat pens and surrounding area with the tragic loss of French lives. Italy also was included so Germany would be spared, for now.

Return to Target Germany, 1943–1944

On 4 February 1943 A new directive reiterated the Casablanca Conference declaration in January that the primary aim of British and American bomber forces would be:

> The progressive destruction and dislocation of the German military, industrial and economic system, and the undermining of the of the morale of the German people to a point where their capacity for armed resistance is fatally weakened.

On 13/14 February 1943, 466 bombers attack Lorient, France, as per the directive. This year would turn out to be one of mixed results. The best would be the targets within the range of Oboe and the worst would be the targets, especially those with indistinct radar features, that would require the use of H2S. The Oboe navigation system couldo pinpoint targets in the Ruhr industrial area but would just be an en route guide to Hamburg, which would then be found with the aid of H2S.

The capability of the Command to deliver bomb tonnage had increased with the numbers of Avro Lancasters being produced and the improved other heavy bomber, the Handley Page Halifax III, becoming available in greater numbers. The tonnage an aircraft could carry was in inverse proportion to the amount of fuel required. The further the target, the fewer number of bombs and the greater exposure to attack. The Short Stirling would be withdrawn from the longer flights because of its inability to climb to a higher altitude, which made it too susceptible to fighter attack.

TARGET	ROUND TRIP (MILES/KM)	FLYING TIME STRAIGHT LINE*
Berlin	1168/1880	8.5
Bremen	776/1248	6.5
Cologne	712/1146	6.0
Duisburg	664/1070	6.0
Essen	684/1102	6.0
Hamburg	872/1400	7.0
Hannover	866/1394	7.0
Mannheim	934/1504	7.0
Nuremberg	1130/1820	8.0
Stuttgart	1048/1686	7.5

* The actual flying time, when I checked some wartime log books, could be up to three hours longer via routes avoiding fighter and Flak areas, or in damaged aircraft, or with diversion to alternate stations due to local weather.

Over fifty per cent of the objectives in this period would be industrial targets in the Ruhr Valley, followed by Berlin and Hamburg. The greatest challenge of the year was to find targets at night outside the Oboe navigation range. Due to previous bad weather, Hamburg had avoided a planned 1,000-aircraft raid. Now, as the target, it did present a reasonable H2S picture with the River Elbe and its dock basins. Berlin itself was not so distinct a radar picture as a defined coastal target.

The Pathfinder Force was getting better results with the fast, high-flying Mosquito initially marking the target and the Pathfinder 'Heavies' following up with their coloured markers. The unarmed, faster, and even higher flying De Havilland Mosquitos of No. 1409 (Meteorological) Flight would have first checked that the weather was suitable.

Technology was contributing to the positive results. Window (chaff), strips of metallic foil, were air-dropped ahead of the Main Force obscuring the 'view' of the German ground-based Wurzburg radar, which guided the night fighters and anti-aircraft guns. Corona, a ground-based German-speaking Allied controller, and A.B.C., an Allied aircraft-based German-speaking controller, would interfere with the instructions to the Luftwaffe night fighters.

Similar to the Pathfinder Group, a dedicated Group No. 100 (Bomber Support) Group would be formed to join the main force and provide electronic countermeasures. However the 'cat and mouse' electronic games would continue until the end of the war. The Luftwaffe night fighters now homed on the Window cloud knowing that the bomber stream would be somewhere close!

- 12/13 March 1943
  Successful Oboe -marked raid by 457 aircraft on Essen, Germany.
- 27/28 March 1943
  Pathfinder-marked mission to Berlin, bombs fell short of the city, raid a failure.
- 16/17 April 1943
  Successful raid on Mannheim but with high losses, 6.6 per cent.
- 16/17 May 1943
  Departing at 0012 hours Flight Sergeant Ken Brown in Lancaster ED918/G Squadron code AJ-F lifted off from the runway at RAF Station Scampton, Lincolnshire, into the history books. Brown was on the third wave of aircraft to inflict further damage, if needed, to any of the dams. For his bravery that night Brown was awarded the Conspicuous Gallantry Medal and subsequently received his commission as an officer.

Here is a transcribed excerpt, courtesy of the museum, of a speech given to an audience at the Bomber Command Museum of Canada by Ken Brown CGM on the occasion of the raid's fiftieth anniversary:

> We arrived at the Mohne Dam. It had been breached by that time. The gunners were still fairly active. We thought we'd leave them alone and we went over to the Sorpe Dam. The Sorpe was of a different construction

altogether. It was an earthen dam, where you have a solid core and earth on either side, very difficult to breach. This was one thing that they never really took a hard look at with such a dam. But our tactics were to run parallel with the dam and drop our bomb in the middle so that it would explode, wash out the front of it, crack the wall and the water would do the rest. But we needed more than one.

The only problem was the whole damn valley was full of fog. When we arrived there, they told us that there would be a church up on top of the village. We found that all right – but just the spire of the church. So I tried to position myself from the spire. I didn't do too well. I got behind the dam on the first run. When I found myself at ground level, behind the dam I had to climb up roughly eighteen hundred feet. It didn't do my nerves any good at all. Because I was on top of the trees, I had to do a flat turn. I couldn't move the wing down to get around. I had to stand on the rudder to get around and then we were down in the valley again. Well we did quite a number of runs on the dam, before we were able to clear enough of the fog away with the propellers constantly going through it. And I must say, according to the historians today, it was a near perfect drop. And I didn't even write to them about it. However, we were pleased with it and as far as the explosion was concerned, the waterspout went up to about a thousand feet and so did we. I think we ended up about eight hundred.

There was one thing that sort of bugged me. When we went to the Mohne Dam, one of our aircraft [flown by Flight Lieutenant John Hopgood] had been shot down there. And I felt we owed the fellow a visit. So I went back. All the other aircraft had left. But as soon as we came over the Mohne, they were throwing 20mm at us. I think there was some that was 37mm. But I figured that we owed that fellow a visit. So we came real low, below the towers, straight on at them. And I heard this fellow's story about three weeks ago in Germany, and he said – no I won't try his German. Anyhow, we opened up at about five hundred yards and carried in over the tower and the rear gunner depressed his guns and we raked the thing as we went through. Well, there was no firing coming from that tower when we left. We figured we'd done him in, however the fellow got the Iron Cross. So we weren't that successful.

The worst was really yet to come. It was then daylight or just breaking. We had to go across and up the Zeider Zee. There was no horizon – the mud from the Zeider Zee and the sky were all one. So I started across, strictly on my altimeter with my head below the cockpit top at fifty feet and I hung onto it. I'd been told by a famous Wing Commander in the RAF, 'Never, ever pull up. If you're low, never pull up.' So I hoped he was right – because all hell broke loose within a matter of fifteen minutes.

Searchlights, even though it was light, caught us from the starboard side and straight on. There was a lot of light Flak immediately in front of us. The cannon shells started to go through the canopy, the side of the aircraft was pretty well blown out, and there was only one thing to do. That was go lower, so I put her down ten feet. We came across and actually their gun positions were on the sea wall. So they were firing slightly down at us and I guess they couldn't believe we were lower than what they could fire. So in this turmoil with the front gunner blazing away at them, I just got a glance, for a moment, and I could see the gunners either falling off because they were hit from our guns or rather, they were jumping off to save their skin.

I pulled up over top of them and we all gave a great sigh of relief.

- 20/21 June 1943
  The 'Master Bomber' technique was used where a circling bomber visually controlled the following stream after the Pathfinder flares were dropped on Friedrichshaffen. The idea was to prevent 'creepback' of the Main Force. The bombers continued on and landed in North Africa, so avoiding the waiting fighters for their return. These became known as 'shuttle' raids.
- 3/4 July 1943
  First use of the 'Wild Boar' night fighter technique over the Ruhr.
- 24/25 July 1943
  Window was used for the first time in this 791 aircraft raid on Hamburg.
- 27/28 July 1943
  Freak firestorm created in Hamburg, approximately 40,000 people died.
- 2/3 August 1943
  Thunderstorm over Germany caused failure of raids.
- 23/24 August 1943
  Berlin offensive. Partially successful 791 aircraft raid on Berlin.
- 3/4 September 1943
  Handley Page Halifax and Short Stirling removed from Berlin operations, Avro Lancasters only. Bombing short of target, 7.7 per cent loss.
- 7/8 October 1943
  A.B.C. communication jammer first used by No. 101 Squadron during raid on Stuttgart. German night fighter controller confused by diversionary attack on Munich.
- 19/20 November 1943
  First operational use of Fog Investigation and Dispersal Operation.
- 18/19, 19/20, 22/23, 23/24, 26/27 November 1943 'Blitzkrieg' on Berlin.
- 16/17 December 1943
  'Serrate' first used by Bristol Beaufighters and De Havilland Mosquitos of No. 100 (Bomber Support) Group to home in on the

radar emissions of Luftwaffe night fighters and protect the bomber stream.

- 16/17, 23/24, 29/30 December 1943
  Raids continue, a quarter of Berlin homes uninhabitable.
- 2/3, 20/21, 21/22, 27/28, 28/29, 30/31 January 1944
  Attacks continue on the German capital.
- 4/5 January 1944
  Special 'Resistance Operations' dropped agents and supplies.
- 8/9 February 1944
  No. 617 squadron, under Wing Commander Leonard Cheshire, pioneered a new technique of very low-level marking. It was a controversial method which never got acceptance from the Pathfinder Group but would be used successfully by No. 5 Group.
- 15/16 February 1944
  Nearly 900 aircraft dropped a record 2,642 tons of bombs on a partially evacuated city. This was the largest raid on Berlin.
- 24/25 February 1944
  A new tactic was employed attacking Schweinfurt. The Main Force was divided into two streams; one followed the other by a gap of two hours. The later stream had fewer casualties with fewer night fighters attacking it.
- March 1944
  The 800+ bomber raid had become an achievable operation: 15/16 Stuttgart, 18/19 Frankfurt, 22/23 Frankfurt, and 24/25 Berlin.
- 30/31 March 1944
  Nuremburg. Weather, crosswind, moonlight, Pathfinders wrongly marked Schweinfurt, and German controllers that ignored the diversion raids all contributed to Bomber Command's worst losses of the war, 11.9 per cent.

France

Once again, a directive changed the future role of the Command; it was now directed against railway targets inland connected to the planned invasion of the coast of France. The plan was to cut off the supply of Axis troops in German-occupied France. Tragically, there would be French citizen casualties prior to the invasion and liberty, a grim bombing campaign. However, No. 5 Group was operated as an independent force that used the Cheshire very low-level bombing technique and that greatly reduced the citizen casualty rate.

The change of Allied loss rate occurred in early 1944 as the distance to targets in France was very much closer than Germany. This allowed greater fighter escort coverage, time to/from the target was reduced, and there was therefore less vulnerability to night fighter attack. Temporarily, the focus of the main operations would change to France in preparation of the planned foothold on mainland Europe, but the raids would still continue to a lesser degree on Germany. The French targets, mainly railway marshalling yards and stations, are too numerous to list here so a few examples are given. Suffice to say it was a softening up of the infrastructure as well as specific targets in preparation for the retaking of Europe, targets such as troop camps, ammunition depots, and armament factories. A huge responsibility and challenge for Bomber Command.

- 5/6 April 1944
  Raid on aircraft factory at Toulouse, France; low-level marking used successfully.
- 9/10 April 1944
  Raid on freight station in Lille, France; heavy citizen collateral damage.
- 15 April 1944
  Communication targets were added to the main directive.
- 30/01 May 1944
  Successful raid on the Maintenon, France, Luftwaffe bomb dump.

In May French raids further intensified in preparation for D-Day in June; a few examples follow:

- 1/2 May 1944
  Toulouse, St-Ghislain, Malines, Chambly, and Lyons.
- 7/8 May 1944
  Nantes, St-Valery, Salbris, Tours, and Rennes.
- 18/19 May 1944
  Boulogne, Orleans, Amiens, Tours, Le Mans, Le Clipon, Merville, and Mont Couple radar station.

At the end of May and beginning of June coastal batteries and radar stations were priorities. As part of the deception of the D-Day landings in Normandy targets in the Pas de Calais region continued to be heavily attacked. The Normandy installations would only be attacked the night before the landings. A record total of 1,211 sorties were flown in support of the battle for Normandy with a loss rate of 0.7 per cent; a total success for Bomber Command, it had more than played its part. Not only were the attacks to be on the Axis troops, ammunition and oil dumps, rail and road communications, but they would include ports where E-boats had gathered.

- 5/6 June 1944
  At least 5,000 tons of bombs were dropped on Normandy coastal gun emplacements. Bomber support groups engaged in electronic

countermeasures and diversionary raids were carried out on the French coast between Boulogne and Le Havre.

- 8/9 June 1944
  The first 12,000lb (5443kg) bomb was dropped by the specialty No. 617 squadron on the Saumur railway tunnel. This prevented a Panzer unit on a train from getting to the front.
- 12/13 June 1944
  The first raid of the simultaneous synthetic oil campaign was on Gelsenkirchen, Germany. It was a success with production slowed for a few weeks.
- 14/15 June 1944
  Major raid to support the army at Caen, Normandy, to hold their gains.
- 16/17 June 1944
  New directive to attack flying-bomb launch sites with some resources as well as to support the army in Normandy and maintain the oil campaign in Germany. The flying bombs targeted London, not military sites, and were effective until August when the Allied army captured the launching sites.
- 18 July 1944
  Raid supported the British Second Army just east of Caen.
- 14 August 1944
  Raid supported the Canadian Army advancing on Falaise. Confused markers, Pathfinder and the Army markers both being yellow, caused Bomber Command to attack friendly troops. An unfortunate incident in the confusion of war. However, the break-out from Normandy was continuing and now, hard to believe thirty months ago, the attention of Bomber Command could once again focus on Germany itself in what could be described as the prelude to the final campaign.

The Final Nine Months of the Campaign

- 15 August 1944
  1,004 aircraft attacked Luftwaffe night fighter airfields in Holland and Belgium.
- 29/30 August 1944
  189 Avro Lancasters of No. 5 Group successfully bombed the extreme range target of Konigsberg, Germany, now in Russia. Heavy fighter activity caused 7.9 per cent loss rate. My friend Flight Lieutenant Bill Pearson, mentioned in Chapter 6, was shot down and lived to tell the story.
- September 1944
  Sir Arthur Harris was formally released by the Supreme Headquarters Allied Expeditionary Force and Bomber Command and reverted to Air Ministry control.

- 25 September 1944
  A directive put the emphasis on Allied army support and the remaining resources, by another directive, were to attack the oil industry followed by the transport industry and the vehicle production industry. Sir Arthur Harris still favoured Area Bombing and interpreted the directive loosely with specific targets, oil production, having intentionally large collateral damage to the workers and citizens in the belief that Germany would collapse internally. Bomber Command had increased in strength due to the Avro Lancaster being produced at home and in Canada and in operational capability with the newer G-H navigation system.
- 5/6 October 1944
  Saarbrucken bombed on the request of the American Third Army.
- 14 October 1944
  Duisburg, Operation *Hurricane* was a show of strength by Bomber Command's 1,013 aircraft and the American Eight Air Force with 1,251 aircraft escorted by 1,700 fighters.
- 12 November 1944
  Tirpitz attacked at Tromso, Norway. Two Tallboy bombs hit the ship and sink it.
- 31 December 1944
  Twelve De Havilland Mosquitos attack Gestapo Headquarters Oslo, Norway.

Sir Charles Portal had concerns about the direction Sir Arthur Harris took to maintain collateral damage. The war appeared to be coming to an end and Bomber Command continued its offensive unabated. Total war in September 1939 was now being met with total war in 1945.

- 12 January 1945
  Three Tallboy bombs dropped on the U-boat pens at Bergen, Norway.
- 13/14 February 1945
  Hoping to bring the war to an end by two massive raids on the civilian population, Operation *Thunderclap* struck Dresden, Germany, three hours apart and created a firestorm similar to Hamburg previously. Casualties may have exceeded 50,000.
- 12 March 1945
  1,108 aircraft attacked Dortmund and stopped synthetic oil production.

On 21 March 1945 the Gestapo Headquarters in Copenhagen, Denmark, were attacked. This attack was well planned with large-scale models set up of the building and city to familiarise the crews with the objective. The target was a six-storey u-shaped building. The underground had provided information that the entire Gestapo staff for Denmark was housed in the Shellhaus building. A special force of De Havilland Mosquitos from Royal Air Force No. 140 Wing was assigned the raid. The aircraft took off in three waves of six aircraft, which included two De Havilland Mosquitos of the Royal Air Force film unit. The morning raid ensured that the building would be occupied.

Crossing the North Sea, the Wing made landfall on the coast of Jutland and set course for Copenhagen. The Wing was escorted to and from the target by North American Mustangs providing top cover for the low-flying Mosquitos. The first wave attacked at roof-top level and one of the aircraft struck a building and crashed. Photos and reports indicated that the building had been severely damaged by the attack and subsequent fire. Over 150 Gestapo personnel had been killed in addition to some Danish patriots.

The Mosquitos were all FB Mk VIs belonging to No. 487 Squadron, Royal New Zealand Air Force, No. 464 Squadron, Royal Australian Air Force and No. 21 Squadron, Royal Air Force. A fitting raid to show the support and cooperation of the Commonwealth Air Forces and their commitment to the De Havilland Mosquito. Nos 487 and 464 Squadrons were Article XV squadrons formed from the graduates of the British Commonwealth Air Training Plan in Canada under the operational control of the RAF. All three squadron had recently moved to France to keep in touch with the advancing Allied armies and were based at B.87/Rosières-en-Santerre.

There is absolutely no doubt that the 7,700+ Merlin-powered De Havilland Mosquitos contributed significantly to the Allied victory. A De Havilland Mosquito B Mk IX, *LR503* known as F for Freddie, holds the record for the greatest number of missions flown by an Allied bomber. It flew 213 sorties with Nos 109 and 105 Squadrons; quite an aircraft, quite an engine.

- 24/25 April 1945
  Leaflets dropped to PoW camps.
- 25 April 1945
  Raid against Hitler's 'Eagle's Nest' chalet.
- 26 April 1945
  Operation *Exodus* commenced flying prisoners-of-war home
- 2/3 May 1945
  Raid on Kiel, Germany, to prevent German troops boarding ships to Norway to carry on the war there.
- 9 May 1945
  The end of hostilities in Europe, but Bomber Command was already preparing the Tiger Force to carry on the fight in Asia against the Japanese forces.

Sir Arthur Harris would remain in command of Bomber Command until 15 September 1945. He would see the highest average loss rates in the winter of 1942, 4.7 per cent, and the lowest average loss rates, 1.1 per cent, in the winter of 1945. Individual raid losses would vary from very high, see 30/31 March 1944, Nuremburg, to very little and some losses were caused by weather accidents and not enemy action. The average Second World War loss rate was 2.3 per cent. At the start of the bombing campaign, Sir Arthur Harris said, quoting the Old Testament:

> The Nazis entered this war under the rather childish delusion that they were going to bomb everyone else, and nobody was going to bomb them. At Rotterdam, London, Warsaw, and half a hundred other places, they put their rather naive theory into operation. They sowed the wind, and now they are going to reap the whirlwind.

Bomber Harris never wavered in his total commitment to Bomber Command. In October 1943 he issued one of his many statements regarding the Area Bombing versus Strategic Bombing controversy:

> The aim of the Combined Bomber Offensive ... should be unambiguously stated [as] the destruction of German cities, the killing of German workers, and the disruption of civilised life throughout Germany ... the destruction of houses, public utilities, transport and lives, the creation of a refugee problem on an unprecedented scale, and the breakdown of morale both at home and at the battle fronts by fear of extended and intensified bombing, are accepted and intended aims of our bombing policy. They are not by-products of attempts to hit factories.

8

POST-WAR BOMBER COMMAND 1945–1968

The Second World War was drawing to a close. The Allies were united in battle, which would soon be over, but divided in ideology. What would happen when all the victorious countries had no common enemy? They would look to their own future. The US and Britain were looking to a very different future than the one that the Soviets envisioned. The cooling off had begun. The Cold War ideology was actually born in the race to capture Berlin.

It would be a long cold period until reason prevailed, 1947 to 1989. Forty-two years of varying degrees of political tension. The superpowers played an ideological chess game, countries were the chess board. It ranged from local border skirmishes in Germany, the Korean War, and to the near cataclysmic stand-off when Soviet missiles were shipped to Cuba. Bomber Command was part of the standoff and deterrent until 1968.

On 16 October 1962 a Lockheed U2, nicknamed 'Dragon Lady', on a high-altitude surveillance flight had discovered, thanks to initial information from the US spy Oleg Penkovsky, the presence of Soviet missile sites under construction in the island country of Cuba, then governed by the United Party of the Cuban Socialist Revolution (PURSC), which would become the Communist Party of Cuba on 3 October 1965. The island is a mere 93 miles (150km) from the US. After careful and extensive deliberation, a line was drawn in the sand. President Kennedy addressed his nation on the 22 October 1962 and indicated that missiles had been discovered in Cuba and announced a blockade of the island nation. The entire world waited with bated breath to see who would blink first, President Kennedy or Premier Khrushchev? The world was on the brink of a war which probably would be fought with nuclear weapons. Would this be the Third World War? Would it be the final war of the twentieth century or even the last war that the world would ever see, total annihilation?

Tensions were extremely high in the US for the next three days as the Soviet missile supply ships continued to sail towards the blockade. What would Khrushchev do? He, thank goodness for world peace, decided to withdraw the missiles from Cuba and negotiated terms that included a promise that the US would not invade Cuba. Another Cold War crisis had passed peacefully into history.

Post-war, the United States and the Union of Soviet Socialist Republics found themselves as powerful nations with large armies. The difference between the two countries being that the US had industrial might as its mainland had been remote from the war. The Soviet army had been beaten back and their country ravaged, all the way to Stalingrad, before the tide of the war reversed. It had been a long fight back to recover the territory lost and the Soviet countryside and industrial heartland had been devastated.

The Cold War can be defined as an extended period of tension between capitalism and communism that manifested itself in military skirmishes of varying seriousness, political manoeuvring, and manipulation of world economics that changed the very way we lived. The different ideologies were centred the two great powers but affected the entire globe. What side are you on? If you could not make up your mind to join the communist side or tended to the other side then – Hungary in 1956 is an example – you risked being invaded to toe the party line.

Some of the following list of events are well known, and some are not. They all contributed to the political tensions of their time which was reflected in the varying degrees of military preparedness. Military budgets are directly connected to the mental state of the politicians; when détente prevailed the budget was low; when tensions existed the budget was higher.

Cold War world events during the 1940s

- July 1945
  First United States of America atomic bomb tested in New Mexico.
- August 1945
  Two atomic bombs dropped on Japan, Japan surrenders
- March 1946
  Churchill's 'Iron Curtain' speech at Westminster College in Fulton, Missouri, used the term in the context of Soviet-dominated Eastern Europe. 'From Stettin in the Baltic to Trieste in the Adriatic an iron curtain has descended across the Continent. Behind that line lie all the capitals of the ancient states of Central and Eastern Europe. Warsaw, Berlin, Prague, Vienna, Budapest, Belgrade, Bucharest,

and Sofia; all these famous cities and the populations around them lie in what I must call the Soviet sphere, and all are subject, in one form or another, not only to Soviet influence but to a very high and in some cases increasing measure of control from Moscow.'

- July 1946
  First US peacetime atomic bomb test.
- March 1947
  Truman discloses containment document against communist aggression.
- September 1947
  Communist Information Bureau (COMINFORM) established.
- February 1948
  Moscow denounced Tito's Yugoslavian independent communist regime. You are either in or out; no party line variance tolerated.
- March 1948
  Czechoslovakia became a communist regime. The USSR has started pushing the central party communist boundaries outwards from Moscow.
- May 1948
  West German state proclaimed.
- June 1948
  Stalin decides to blockade Berlin in the hope that the Allies will relinquish the city to the surrounding communist sector. Wrong, it triggered a massive airlift of previously unknown proportions that kept the city alive until Stalin relented in defeat.
- October 1948
  East German state proclaimed.
- April 1949
  North Atlantic Treaty Organisation founded.
- May 1949
  Stalin had underestimated the resolve of the Allies; the blockade ends.
- August 1949
  To the surprise of the Americans, they had forecasted a longer time of weapon superiority, the Soviets explode their first atomic bomb.
- September 1949
  Germany divided, East (communist) and West (capitalist)

Cold War world events during the 1950s

- January 1950
  The weapons race gains momentum. The US planned the hydrogen (thermonuclear) bomb to take the deterrence level to a higher level. This did not bode well for world stability as each side probed and manoeuvred.

- June 1950
  The peace bubble burst; North Korea invaded South Korea with communist support, either directly or indirectly, from China and Russia. The first war during the Cold War had begun.
- May 1951
  British diplomats Burgess and Maclean defected to the Soviet Union.
- October 1952
  Britain exploded its first atomic bomb.
- November 1952
  Us explodes its first hydrogen bomb. It is now leading the arms race; how far behind is the Soviet Union?
- June 1953
  The Rosenbergs are executed in the US for atomic espionage activities.
- July 1953
  Korean War ends, stalemate.
- August 1953
  Nine months behind! The Soviet Union exploded its first Hydrogen bomb.
- January 1954
  The Cold War is gathering momentum; US announced the doctrine of massive retaliation. American Cold War advocates proclaim, 'better dead than Red'.
- May 1955
  The Warsaw Pact formed in opposition to North Atlantic Treaty Organisation.
- January 1956
  First Lockheed U-2 spy plane mission over the Soviet Union.
- October 1956
  Soviet army suppressed the revolt against communism in Hungary. The free world watched.
- August 1957
  Soviets launch first Inter-Continental Ballistic missile.
- October 1957
  Soviet Union launched the first earth orbit satellite (Sputnik 1). There was no doubt who was leading the race now, the Soviet Union. It had taken the race into space, the new frontier.
- November 1957
  Britain exploded its first hydrogen bomb.
- November 1957
  Soviets orbit a dog, Laika, in space. The Soviet Union has the attention of the world media as communist prowess is demonstrated.

- January 1958
  The US finally has its first successful satellite launch.
- November 1958
  Khrushchev issues first Berlin ultimatum giving the Western powers six months to agree to withdraw from Berlin and make it a free, demilitarized city. The Cold War was heating up with this first ultimatum; the Allies replied that they would remain in Berlin. The ultimatum was withdrawn, and a conference was held by Premier Khrushchev and President Eisenhower to discuss the situation.
- January 1959
  Castro takes power in Cuba; where would his loyalties lie?

Cold War world events during the 1960s

- February 1960
  France joined the nuclear club, explodes first atomic bomb.
- May 1960
  US U-2 spy plane shot down over the Soviet Union, which had now demonstrated its ability to protect its territory. The United States no longer enjoyed the advantage of undetected surveillance by high-flying aircraft.
- January 1961
  First United States of America Inter-Continental Ballistic missile test.
- April 1961
  Soviet Union put first man in earth orbit.
- May 1961
  United States put first American astronaut in space.
- August 1961
  The Berlin Wall was constructed to stop the flow of citizens from the eastern communist sector to the western sectors. The two sides faced off with each other and, at one time, armed tanks were separated by 656ft (200m) at the Brandenburg Gate. President Kennedy ordered troops to West Germany and mobilisation of Reserve troops in the US. The two sides paused.
- October 1961
  Soviet Union flexed its muscles by conducting the largest ever atmospheric nuclear test. When was this escalation going to end? The situation was building to an event of epic proportions; what and where in the world would it be?
- October 1962
  The Cuban Missile Crisis was the event that brought the world to the brink of nuclear holocaust. This was the discovery of a Soviet supplied missile site in Cuba. Castro had obviously decided what

team he was on. President Kennedy established a blockade around Cuba and now it was up to Premier Khrushchev to decide what to do as his ships steamed towards the blockade. The ships turned back and the world's population collectively breathed more easily; the crisis had been averted. Vasily Kuznetsov, Soviet First Deputy Foreign Minister, negotiated the end of the crisis at the United Nations, and he remarked 'Well, Mr. McCloy (John J. McCloy, Presidential advisor and chief negotiator on the Presidential Disarmament Committee), you got away with it this time, but you will never get away with it again.' The Soviets vigorously pursued nuclear parity with the US and essentially achieved it, at great cost, around 1970.

- June 1963
  President Kennedy made a famous speech to Berliners to say that the US through NATO was fully behind preserving Berlin in the 'West'. His oft quoted line, 'Ich bin ein Berliner' was received with tumultuous applause.
- April 1963
  A Soviet Union – US hotline was established, the famous red phone.
- October 1964
  Khrushchev lost leadership less than one year after the death of Kennedy. The Soviet Union Politburo thought that Khrushchev was weak in backing down during the 'Caribbean Crisis' but he had in fact prevented the invasion of Cuba. It was learnt, after his death, that he was instrumental in preventing NATO missiles from being installed in Turkey. Whether this was a US bluff is debated.
- October 1964
  The first Chinese atomic bomb test. A new member for the group of nuclear nations.
- March 1965
  The United States bombings of communist North Vietnam began.
- July 1965
  US troops deployed to South Vietnam
- June 1967
  Middle East embroiled in Six-Day War.
- December 1967
  In thirteen years the US has gone from a doctrine of massive retaliation to the brink of an escalating nuclear war, to a doctrine of flexible response. The Soviet Union and the US are now wondering about the aims and ambitions of China. A brand of communism which showed no desire to align itself with Moscow.
- January 1968
  United States offensive began in Vietnam

Commanders Post-War

The Commanders of Bomber Command had new tasks. One was deterrence by a show of offence. It would be twelve years after the Second World War that Britain would first explode its own hydrogen bomb. It had now joined the nuclear club although it had the capability of using American nuclear weapons, Project E, before that if required. Project E were nuclear weapons provided by the United States to Bomber Command until sufficient British weapons became available. US personnel retained custody of the weapons and maintained them in readiness. The first bomber to be equipped with these weapons was the English Electric Canberra. It was a new era of warfare to which the following Bomber Command commanders had to adapt.

Air Marshal Sir Norman Howard Bottomley, KCB, CIE, DSO, AFC
15 September 1945
Educated at the University of Rennes, France, he was commissioned with the East Yorkshire Regiment in1914. He transferred to the Royal Flying Corps in 1915 and became a pilot with No. 47 Squadron. Between the wars he served in the Middle East, commanded No. 4 (AC) Squadron in 1928, and No. 1 (Indian) Group from 1934. At the outbreak of the Second World War he was Senior Air Staff Officer at Bomber Command Headquarters until November 1940 when he was appointed Air Officer Commanding No. 5 Group. A year later Bottomley was moved to Deputy Chief of the Air Staff followed by Assistant Chief of the Air Staff (Operations) in 1942 before reverting to Deputy Chief of the Air Staff in 1943 and taking over Bomber Command after the cessation of hostilities.

Air Marshal Sir Hugh Saunders, GCB, KBE, MC, DFC & Bar, MM
16 January 1947
Saunders, a South African, served with the Witwatersrand Rifles Regiment in 1914 and subsequently enlisted in the Royal Flying Corps and was a pilot with No. 84 Squadron. He was credited with fifteen victories, a triple ace, during the war, and in 1932 was appointed Officer Commanding No. 45 Squadron. His service continued as Chief of Staff of the Royal New Zealand Air Force before becoming Air Officer Administration at Headquarters, Fighter Command, during 1942. By the end of 1942 Saunders was the Air Officer Commanding No. 11 Group and finished the war as Director-General of Personnel at the Air Ministry. Next assignment was as Air Officer Commanding Burma after peace was declared.

Air Marshal Sir Aubrey Beauclerk Ellwood, KCB, DSC, DL
8 October 1947
Educated at Marlborough College, he joined the Royal Naval Air Service in 1916. A Sopwith Camel pilot, he scored ten victories in the First

World War and was subsequently awarded a permanent commission in 1919, one of the first in the new Royal Air Force. In 1932 he was Officer Commanding No. 5 Squadron in India and by 1937 was a member of the Directing Staff of the Royal Air Force Staff College. During the Second World War he was Deputy Director of Bombing Operations, Air Officer Commanding No. 18 Group, Senior Staff Officer at Headquarters, Coastal Command and finally Director-General of Personnel.

Air Marshal Sir Hugh Pughe Lloyd, GBE, KCB, MC, DFC
2 February 1950
Lloyd was the last of the First World War veterans to lead Bomber Command. He joined the Royal Engineers initially before transferring to No. 52 Squadron in the Royal Flying Corps. With a permanent commission he was appointed Officer Commanding No. 9 Squadron in 1939, command of RAF Marham as a group captain, on staff of No. 3 Group and by May 1940 was Senior Air Staff Officer at No. 2 Group. A year later in June 1941 he was appointed Air Officer Commanding in Malta during the island's long siege. In 1942 he was in the Middle East Headquarters followed by the Mediterranean Allied Coastal Air Force in 1943. In preparation for the attack on Japan he was appointed commander designate of a Commonwealth bomber force called Tiger Force; it was disbanded after the successful nuclear bomb attacks by the United States which effectively ended the war in Asia. Lloyd became an instructor at the Imperial Defence College and Air Officer Commanding Air Command Far East.

Air Chief Marshal Sir George Holroyd Mills, GCB, DFC
9 April 1953
Mills was an early graduate of the newly formed Royal Air Force College at Cranwell. He flew with Nos. 8 and 100 Squadrons before attending Staff College in 1935. In 1939 he commanded No. 115 Squadron followed by the Air Staff at Headquarters, Bomber Command. Mills was Station Commander at RAF Watton, Director of Policy (General) at the Air Ministry in 1943 and finished the war as Officer Commanding Balkan Air Force. Subsequent positions were Director of Plans at the Air Ministry, Air Officer Commanding No. 1 Group, and Air Officer Commanding Air Headquarters Malaya in 1952.

Air Marshal Sir Harry Broadhurst, GCB, KBE, DSO & Bar, DFC & Bar, AFC
22 January 1956
He started his military career with the Royal Artillery and then transferred to the Royal Air Force in 1926. Two years later he was with

No. 11 Squadron in India returning to No. 41 Squadron in Britain. He established a reputation as an aerobatic pilot. Broadhurst served in the Royal Air Force Staff College in Andover before assuming command of No. 111 Squadron in 1939. Further promotion saw him appointed station commander at RAF Coltishall before joining No. 60 Wing in France. He continued to be an active pilot even as Officer Commanding RAF Wittering and while commanding the Hornchurch Sector of No. 11 Fighter Group. By 1942 he was Senior Air Staff Officer No. 11 Group and had been credited with 13 enemy destroyed when he was posted to the Middle East as Senior Air Staff Officer in the Desert Air Force. He is credited with developing ground support fighter-bomber operations with the Eighth Army. Returning to Britain he commanded No. 83 Group and at the end of the war became Air Officer Administration at Royal Air Force, Fighter Command. In 1946 he became Air Officer Commanding No. 61 Group followed by a posting to the Imperial Defence College. By 1949 he was Assistant Chief of the Air Staff (Operations) followed by Commander-in-Chief of the Second Tactical Air Force in 1953.

Air Marshal Sir Kenneth Brian Boyd Cross, KCB, CBE, DSO, DFC
20 May 1959
He joined the Royal Air Force in 1930 and served with No. 25 Squadron, the Cambridge University Air Squadron, and as Auxiliary Liaison Officer at headquarters, No. 12 Group, Fighter Command. In 1939 he was Officer Commanding No. 46 Squadron; Cross was one of only forty-four survivors of the sinking of HMS *Glorious* and her two escort ships. He was then appointed Officer Commanding Nos. 252 and 258 Wing in the Middle East. This was followed by Air Officer Commanding No. 212 Group, No. 242 Group, and then Air Commodore, Training at Headquarters, Allied Expeditionary Force in 1944 and then Director of Overseas Operations (Tactical). After the war he became Director of Weapons in the Air Ministry, Director of Operations (Air Defence), and in 1956 Air Officer Commanding No. 3 Group.

Marshal of the Royal Air Force Sir John Grandy, GCB, GCVO, KBE, DSO, KStJ
1 September 1963
Educated at the University College School, London, he joined No. 54 Squadron of the Royal Air Force in 1932. He completed the Instructor's Course at the Central Flying School before being appointed Adjutant, University of London Air Squadron. In 1940 he commanded No. 219 Squadron, No. 249 Squadron, and then was assigned to the Air Staff, Headquarters, Royal Air Force Fighter Command. By 1941 Grandy oversaw Flying Operations and subsequently all operations at RAF

Duxford. In 1943 he was with No. 210 Group in Libya and No. 73 Operational Training Unit in Egypt and in 1944 he was Officer Commanding No. 341 Wing fighting the Japanese forces. He finished the war as Senior Air Staff Officer at Headquarters, No. 232 Group. Subsequent positions held after the war ended were Deputy Director of Operational Training; Air Attache in Brussels; Officer Commanding, Norther Sector, Fighter Command; Air Staff in the Operations Directorate, Headquarters, Fighter Command; and in 1954 was Commandant of the Central Fighter Establishment. These positions were followed by attending the Imperial Defence College and in 1957 he was Commander of Operation *Grapple*, the hydrogen bomb testing program. The next year Grandy was Assistant Chief of the Air Staff (Operations) and in 1961 he became Commander-in-Chief of RAF Germany.

Air Chief Marshal Sir Wallace Hart Kyle, GCB, KCVO, CBE, DSO, DFC
19 February 1965
Kyle was born in Australia and attended the Royal Air Force College Cranwell in 1928. His postings were No. 17 Squadron, No. 442 Squadron Flight Fleet Air Arm, No. 820 Squadron Fleet Air Arm, and Central Flying School. He returned to Australia on exchange before returning as Squadron Commander, No. 3 Flying training School. During the war he was appointed to the Air Staff, Headquarters, Training Command, Station Commander at RAF Marham, and RAF Downham Market and to the Air Staff, Headquarters, Bomber Command in 1944. Subsequent positions after the war ended included Directing Staff at RAF Staff College, Bracknell; Air Plans at Headquarters; RAF Mediterranean & Middle East; and Aide-de-Camp to the King and Queen until 1956. These were followed by Assistant Commandant, Royal Air Force College Cranwell and and Director of Operational Requirements (Air) at the Air Ministry in 1952. In 1955 Kyle was Air Officer Commanding at Air Headquarters, Malaya, followed by Assistant Chief of the Air Staff (Operational Requirements); Air Officer Commanding-in-Chief, Technical Training Command; and in 1962 Vice-Chief of the Air Staff. Kyle became the first Air Officer Commander-in-Chief of the merged Fighter and Bomber Command named Strike Command on the 30 April 1968.

V-Force

Immediately after the ceasefire the RAF started to replace the aircraft that had served it so well but were now obsolete. The two heavy bombers, Avro Lancaster and Handley Page Halifax, were slowly replaced by the Avro Lincoln, which itself was an improved version of the Avro Lancaster. The Lincoln continued to be manufactured after hostilities ceased and filled the transition from piston aircraft to the jet aircraft in the short term, along with the Boeing Washington allocated under the Mutual Defence Assistance Program.

The Lincoln was put into operational service against the Communist terrorists in Malaya and the Mau-Mau in Kenya but lacked the capability of penetrating deep into the USSR, the perceived new threat. It gained notoriety by becoming a casualty of the Cold War when on 12 March 1953 Lincoln *RF531* 'C' was shot down by Soviet Mig-15 fighters near Luneburg, Germany, with the loss of seven lives. The Boeing Washington had the range but was not nuclear-capable.

With the development of the first Royal Air Force jet bomber in the 1950s, the English Electric Canberra, the nuclear age could now replace the old Second World War bombs with bombs capable of even greater mass destruction. The Canberra first flew in 1951 and later bomber variants were certified to carry tactical nuclear weapons internally, such as the American Mk 7 'Thor' fission bomb, B28 thermonuclear bomb, B57, and the first British tactical nuclear weapon the 'Red Beard'. By 1955 the Canberra's short but effective high-level nuclear deterrent bomber role was phased out, but it would continue nuclear bomb service using a Low Altitude Bombing System.

By 1952 Britain had its first atomic test; in 1956 it air-dropped its first bomb, and in 1957 its first H-bomb was successfully tested. The Government and famous aircraft industry leaders, Avro, Handley Page, and Vickers, embarked upon a program to develop aircraft capable of delivering the new weapons. The result, in the mid 1950s, was the service entry of the Vickers Valiant in 1955, the Avro Vulcan in 1956, and Handley Page Victor in 1957. These aircraft were Britain's strategic nuclear strike force.

They were collectively known as the 'V Force' or Bomber Command Main Force and this Force was at its maximum strength in 1964 with fifty Vickers Valiants, seventy Avro Vulcans, and thirty-nine Handley Page Victors. Due to the improved capabilities of the Soviet fighters, improved versions of the Avro Vulcan (higher altitude capability) and the Handley Page Victor (improved engines), electronic countermeasures, and inflight refuelling probes were developed. Bomber Command was assigned designated targets in the USSR, such as cities, long-range aviation bases, and air-defence sites.

The Vickers Valiant retired from Bomber Command in 1965 due to premature fatigue, brought on by role change to low-level bomb delivery, and corrosion in the wing spar attachments. The Vulcan and Victor continued serving until 1984 and 1993 respectively.

The V Bombers

SQUADRON	AIRCRAFT	BASE
7	Vickers Valiant	Honington, Suffolk
9	Avro Vulcan	Coningsby, Lincolnshire
10	Handley Page Victor	Cottesmore, Rutland
12	Avro Vulcan	Coningsby, Lincolnshire
15	Handley Page Victor	Cottesmore, Rutland
18	Vickers Valiant	Finningley, Yorkshire
27	Avro Vulcan	Scampton, Lincolnshire
35	Avro Vulcan	Coningsby, Lincolnshire
44	Avro Vulcan	Waddington, Lincolnshire
49	Vickers Valiant	Wittering, Northamptonshire
50	Avro Vulcan	Waddington, Lincolnshire
55	Handley Page Victor	Honington, Suffolk
57	Handley Page Victor	Honington, Suffolk
83	Avro Vulcan	Waddington, Lincolnshire, Scampton, Lincolnshire
90	Handley Page Victor	Honington, Suffolk
100	Handley Page Victor	Wittering, Northamptonshire
101	Avro Vulcan	Finningley, Yorkshire, Waddington, Lincolnshire
138	Vickers Valiant	Gaydon, Warwickshire, Wittering, Northamptonshire
139	Handley Page Victor	Wittering, Northamptonshire
148	Vickers Valiant	Marham, Norfolk
199	Vickers Valiant	Honington, Suffolk
207	Vickers Valiant	Marham, Norfolk
214	Vickers Valiant	Marham, Norfolk
543	Vickers Valiant	Gaydon, Warwickshire, Wyton, Cambridgeshire
	Handley Page Victor	Honington, Suffolk
617	Avro Vulcan	Scampton, Lincolnshire

Post-War Europe Bomber Aircraft 1945–1968

AVRO LINCOLN

- Squadrons: 7, 9, 12, 15, 35, 44, 49, 50, 57, 58, 61, 75, 83, 90, 97, 100, 101, 115, 116, 138, 148, 149, 151, 192, 207, 214, 527, 617
- First Flight: 9 June 1944 Number Built: 604
- Engine: Rolls-Royce Merlin
- Range: 2,800 miles (4,500km) at 15,000ft (4,600 m) Service Ceiling: 30,500ft (9,300m)
- Bomb Load: 14,000lb (6,400kg) normal, or one 22,000lb (10,000kg) Grand Slam bomb

The Lincoln was a British four-engine heavy bomber developed from the Avro Lancaster and was the last piston engine bomber operated by the Royal Air Force. The war ended before the Lincoln could assume its role in the Tiger Force against Japan. Its improved Merlin engines, greater wingspan, and enlarged fuselage gave it a higher service ceiling and operational range than its predecessors. It retired in March 1963 after being replaced by jet bombers.

The armament was two 0.5in (12.7mm) M2 Browning machine guns or a Boulton Paul Type F nose turret, two 20mm (0.79in) Hispano Mk. IV cannon or Hispano Mk. V cannon in a Bristol B.17 dorsal turret and two 0.5in (12.7mm) M2 Browning machine guns in a Boulton Paul Type D tail turret. The Lincoln had a crew of seven or eight: pilot, flight engineer/co-pilot, navigator, wireless operator, bomb aimer/nose gunner, dorsal and tail gunner.

BOEING WASHINGTON

- Squadrons: 15, 35, 44, 57, 90, 115, 149, 192, 207
- First Flight: 8 May 1944 Number Built: 3,970
- Engine: Wright R-3350 Duplex Cyclone
- Range: 3,250 miles (5,230km) Service Ceiling: 31,850ft (9,710m)
- Bomb Load: High Altitude 5,000lb (2,300kg) Lower Altitude 20,000lb (9,100kg) shorter range

The Washington was an American four-engine heavy bomber loaned to the Royal Air force and known as the Superfortress in the United States Air Force. It dropped the atomic bombs on Japan. One of the largest aircraft in the Second World War it had a pressurised cabin, dual-wheeled landing gear, and an analog computer system for a fire control officer to operate four remote-controlled guns. It had initial problems with the very complicated 'many moving parts' Duplex Cyclone engine. It served for four years from 1950 to 1954 and was part of the transition to the jet bomber aircraft.

The armament was eight or ten .50in (12.7mm) Browning M2/Ans in remote controlled turrets and two .50 (12.7mm) Browning machine guns in the tail. The Washington had a crew of eleven: pilot, co-pilot, bomb aimer, flight engineer, navigator, radio operator, radar operator, right and left gunners, central fire control and tail gunners.

ENGLISH ELECTRIC CANBERRA

- Squadrons: 3, 6, 7, 9, 10, 12, 13, 14, 15, 16, 17, 18, 21, 27, 31, 32, 35, 39, 40, 44, 45, 50, 51, 57, 58, 59, 61, 69, 73, 76, 80, 81, 82, 85, 88, 90, 97, 98, 100, 101, 102, 103, 104, 109, 115, 139, 149, 151, 192, 199, 207, 213, 245, 249, 360, 361, 527, 540, 542, 617
- First Flight: 13 May 1949 Number Built: 1,352
- Engine: Rolls-Royce Avon
- Range: 810 miles (1,300km) Service Ceiling: 48,000ft (15,000m)
- Bomb Load: 8,000lb (3,628kg) internally/wing hardpoints

The Canberra was a British first-generation jet-powered medium bomber designed as a successor to the piston de Havilland Mosquito. It was most successful and established an altitude record in 1951 (70,310ft, 21,430m) and was the first jet aircraft to make a non-stop transatlantic flight. In the 1970s while flying the Avro CF-100 in Electronic Warfare missions for the Canadian Armed Forces my United States Air Force counterparts were flying the Martin B-57 Canberra. It retired from the Royal Air Force in 2006, fifty-seven years after its first flight.

Designer W. Petter focused on accommodating the bomb load, two powerful jet engines, compact aerodynamic fuselage, and to save weight no defensive armament. Roland Beamont flew the prototype with the Avon engines and the first production standard aircraft a year later. In May 1951 it entered service.

The tubular fuselage had a mid-wing low-aspect ratio wing with split flaps and speedbrakes above and below the wing. The width and length of the Canberra are practically the same. The engines were started with Coffman engine starters, large blank cartridges containing Cordite connected to a piston and screw thread which turned the engine over.

The Canberra had a crew of three which included bomb aimer in the nose with optical bomb sight before the H2S automatic radar bombsight. Then it was a tandem layout crew of two in a fighter style cabin. The cabin layout was modified throughout the life of the aircraft. The armament was only on the bomber interdictor model, a ventral pack housing four 20mm (0.79in) Hispano cannons.

AVRO VULCAN

- Squadrons: 9, 12, 27, 35 ,44, 50, 83, 101, 617
- First Flight: 30 August 1952 Number Built: 134

- Engine: Bristol Olympus
- Range: 2,265 (2,607km) Service Ceiling: 55,000ft (17,000m)
- Bomb Load: 21,000lb (9,525m)

The Vulcan was a British jet-powered tailless delta wing high altitude strategic bomber in service from 1956. It was part of Britain's independent nuclear deterrent and carried Britain's first nuclear bomb, the *Blue Danube* fission gravity bomb. It carried a series of nuclear bombs as development of these weapons continued during the Cold War. It also had a secondary conventional bombing role.

Four years later the B.2 featured more powerful engines, larger wing, improved electronic package, and electronic countermeasures and could carry the *Blue Steel* missile. The design was initiated by Roy Chadwick and Stuart Davies. It was continued by Sir William Farren after Chadwick's death in an aircraft accident. A one-third scale Avro 707 flew in September 1949 but crashed later that month. In September 1955 test pilot Roly Falk amazed crowds at the Farnborough Air Show by performing a barrel role in the second production aircraft.

The centre section contained the bomb and engine bays between the front and rear spars and the wing transport joints. The engine intakes were in the centre fuselage. Fuel was carried in fourteen bags, four in the forward fuselage and five in each of the outer wings. Inflight refuelling capability was added in 1959. The B.2 had eight elevon controls, three position speedbrakes, and a brake parachute (drag chute) in the tail cone.

The Vulcan had a crew of five: pilot, co-pilot, navigator plotter, navigator radar, and air electronics officer in a two level pressurised cabin. The armament consisted of twenty-one 1,000lb (454kg) conventional bombs or one of a variety of nuclear or thermonuclear gravity bombs or *Blue Steel* missile.

HANDLEY PAGE VICTOR

- Squadrons: 10, 15, 55, 57, 100, 139, 543
- First Flight: 24 December 1952 Number Built: 86
- Engine: Armstrong Siddeley Sapphire
- Range: 5,217 miles (6,004km) Service Ceiling: 56,000ft (17,000m)
- Bomb Load: 35,000lb (15,876kg)

The Victor was a British jet-powered strategic bomber and part of the V bomber Force of Britain's nuclear deterrent. Handley Page's Dr Gustav Lachmann and Geoffrey Lee developed a crescent-shaped swept wing. The aircraft first flew at Royal Air Force Boscombe Down with test pilot Hedley Hazelden. The initial prototype was lost due to a tailplane failure (subsequently re-engineered). In June 1956 the sound barrier was inadvertently broken during a test flight, confirmed by a sonic boom.

The four jet engines were buried in the thick wing roots of a 'space-age' looking aircraft. The streamlined shape had a highly swept T-tail with pronounced dihedral and a chin bulge that contained targeting radar and the Bomb Aimer's position. The B.2 had more powerful engines, bigger engine intakes, and extended wing tips. A further development converted some Victors to aerial refuelling capability to replace the Valiant that was withdrawn from service in 1964.

The Victor had a crew of five: pilot, co-pilot, navigator plotter, navigator radar, and air electronics officer in a single level compartment. The armament consisted of a conventional bomb load of up to thirty-five 1,000lb (454kg) or one *Yellow Sun* free-fall nuclear bomb.

VICKERS VALIANT

- Squadrons: 7, 18, 49, 90, 138, 148, 199, 207, 214, 543
- First Flight: 18 May 1951 Number Built: 107
- Engine: Rolls-Royce Avon
- Range: 4,500 miles (7,200km) Service Ceiling: 54,000ft (16,000m)
- Bomb Load: 21,000lb (9,525kg)

The Valiant was the first of the British V bombers. It was a high-altitude strategic jet bomber and part of Britain's nuclear deterrent force. It was the only one of the V bombers to drop a nuclear bomb, albeit a de-rated *Blue Danube* weapon, in 1956 at an Australian test range. The Valiant was used for conventional bombing missions during the 1956 Suez Canal crisis. The shooting down of a US Lockheed U-2 in 1960 forced the V-Force to adopt low-level delivery tactics. Wing spar corrosion shortened the expected operational life of the Valiant in 1965.

It had a shoulder-mounted wing with the four engines in the wing roots. While aerodynamically clean the 'buried' engine concept used by all the V bomber Force made it susceptible to engine damage from an adjacent uncontained engine failure and complicated maintenance and repair. The centre fuselage was built around an extremely strong backbone to support the two widely spaced wing spars. Five fuel cells were located in the upper portion of this section. Unfortunately, the aircraft was made of DTD683 aluminium alloy, which shortened its service life.

The wing itself, designed by Elfyn Richards, was a compound sweep design. The inboard and outboard double-slotted flaps were unusually driven electrically as was the undercarriage. Some Valiants had engines with water injection to add thrust.

The Valiant had a crew of five: pilot, co-pilot, navigator plotter, navigator radar, and air electronics officer in a two level pressurised compartment. The armament consisted of twenty-one 1,000lb (454kg) bombs or one 10,000lb (4,540kg) *Blue Danube* nuclear bomb or one *B28* nuclear bomb.

Bomber Command aircraft engines 1945-1968

Armstrong Siddeley

SAPPHIRE

- Type: 14 Stage compressor 2 stage turbine axial flow turbojet First ran: 1 October 1948
- Weight: 3,050lb (1,383kg) Power: 11,000lbf (49kN) at sea level at 8,000 rpm
- RAF Bomber Aircraft: Handley Page Victor B.1

The Sapphire was a direct competitor of the Rolls-Royce Avon. It took over development of the Metropolitan-Vickers A S Sa.2 and achieved higher thrust ratings than the comparable Avon at that time. It did not use variable inlet guide vanes or bleed valves. It did suffer from compressor case shrinkage when flying through thick, moist cloud, which caused blade rub and subsequent engine failure. This was called 'centre-line-closure'. The Sapphire was built under licence in the United States by Wright Aeronautical as the J65 engine.

Rolls-Royce

AVON

- Type: 15 stage compressor 2 stage turbine axial flow turbojet First ran: 1947
- Weight: 2,890lb (1,310kg) Power: 12,690lbf (56.4kN) with reheat 16,360lbf (72.8kN)
- RAF Bomber Aircraft: English Electra Canberra, Vickers Valiant

The Avon engine was the first axial flow engine produced by Rolls-Royce and was the company's most successful immediate post-Second World design. It used principles from the previous centrifugal Rolls-Royce Nene engine and Stanley Hooker, later of Bristol Engines, spearheaded the design team. It went through various improvements such as increasing the number of compressor stages, installing compressor bleed valves, adding another turbine stage, and two position inlet guide vanes.

MERLIN

- Type: V12 liquid cooled engine First ran: 1933
- Displacement: 27L Power: 1,290hp (962kW) @ 3,000rpm for takeoff
- RAF Bomber Aircraft: Avro Lincoln

Over 149,000 engines in fifty versions were built in Britain and more than 55,000 engines by the Packard Motor Car Company in the US. The engine was built as a development of the very successful Kestrel engine and because of its potential took precedence over the Peregrine and Vulture engines.

Similar to other engines, the advent of 100 octane fuel improved the engine performance. As we have seen, the Merlin more or less won the Battle of Britain and was the mainstay engine of the heavy bomber force. It is fitting that the RAF's last piston-engined bomber was powered by the Merlin.

OLYMPUS

- Type: 6 Stage compressor 8 stage turbine axial flow turbojet First ran: 1950
- Weight: 3,615lb (1,640kg) Power: 11,000lbf (49kN)
- RAF Bomber Aircraft: Avro Vulcan

The Olympus was originally developed by Bristol Aero Engines, later taken over by Rolls-Royce, as the Bristol B.E.10 with a two-spool compressor, each driven by its own single-stage turbine. The concept was to achieve a previously unheard of 9:1 pressure ratio. The combustion system was unique in that it was a cannular design, a combination of separate flame cans joined with flame tubes. The engine was flight tested in an English Electric Canberra in August 1952.

Wright

R-3350 -23 (DUPLEX-CYCLONE)

- Type: 18-cylinder, twin-row, supercharged, air-cooled, radial engine First ran: 1937
- Displacement: 55L Power: 2,200hp (1,641kW) @ 2,800rpm for takeoff
- RAF Bomber Aircraft: Boeing Washington

The R-3350 continued the development of the successful R-1820/R-2600 Cyclone series with the R-3350. This was a natural evolution for more power and the fact that Pratt & Whitney had started development on the more powerful Double Wasp. Initial development was slow as funds were being directed to the R-2600 and because of the complexity of the R-3350. The large engine, partially due to the demands of wartime production, tended to overheat and suffered from valve failure. The engine started with carburettors and finished the war with direct fuel injection into the combustion chamber.

CONCLUSION

The aim of this book has been to introduce the readers to the complex story of Bomber Command and perhaps kindle an interest in further research into a particular aspect that interests them. The Bomber Command airfields are a prime example. There are walking tours of abandoned Second World War airfields in England that include derelict watch towers but also some towers and buildings that are fully restored. Some abandoned airfields have established museums on the original location. The Lincolnshire Aviation Heritage Centre at East Kirkby, Lincolnshire, is one. In addition to restoring original buildings and artefacts the museum operates a restored Avro Lancaster that offers taxy rides to the general public on part of the former Royal Air Force Station.

Perhaps the interest is more in the individuals, from the Commander-in-Chief himself to the Group Commanders, the Squadron Leaders, the Flight Commanders and the individual aircraft crew commanders, the pilot. It is a fascinating array of individual stories. The unsung daily heroes doing their duty and the more visible deeds rewarded with medals. The ultimate reward for bravery in the face of the enemy, the Victoria Cross, was awarded to more members of Bomber Command than any other command. The following statistic is probably the most telling of how brave the crews of Bomber Command were: there were more casualties sustained during the night raid on Nuremburg, Germany on 30/31 March 1944 than were sustained by Fighter Command during the entire Battle of Britain.

The number of Royal Air Force Stations created to accommodate the many squadrons is hard to believe. The logistics of building the airfield in open ground with the accompanying infrastructure was a challenge. Its effect on the local community, some good, some bad, was noticeable. The citizens of Britain were well aware of their responsibility to support the local airfield and its wartime demands. The flow of goods to the station to sustain the operation was a twenty-four hour commitment that benefitted the local community financially but certainly disturbed the day-to-day life of the surrounding area. The stations, although scattered for security reasons, were in the eastern half of the country and some were so close together that their departing and landing traffic patterns overlapped and had to be coordinated.

Some of the bomber squadrons in their wartime lifetime moved many times. They had a variety of roles and aircraft that they had to adapt to. Some were specialty squadrons, such as No. 617 Squadron, and some squadrons were assembled into new groups, such as No. 100 (Bomber Support) Group. The squadrons were what Bomber Command was all about, the aircraft and men that would bring the war to the enemy. The camaraderie of the men and women, aircrew and groundcrew, who supported or made up the squadron as it went out nightly on operations, was a unique experience never to be forgotten by the participants.

The reader's interest may lie in the aircraft in Bomber Command's arsenal. Different manufacturers all trying to 'reinvent the wheel' and build the perfect machine to carry the explosives to the target, from the fast and high flying Mosquito to the brute force of the Avro Lancaster, the reliable Rolls-Royce Merlin at work. These aircraft, were the product of the unsung heroes, men and women, working under trying conditions in the factories.

Post-war, aircraft would be capable of bringing nuclear bombs and air launched nuclear tipped missiles to targets in the Soviet Union. This new Bomber Command was the nuclear deterrent force that prevented further political and military expansion of the Soviet Union during the 1950s and 1960s until 1968, when it formed part of Strike Command.

Bomber Command, with all its spectacular successes and failures, played a vital part in bringing victory to the Allied forces. We all owe a huge debt to the aircrew who gave their lives to protect our freedom, those who were wounded, those who endured being prisoners of war, and the men and women of all ranks, organisations, and occupations who supported them through five years of wartime struggle and hardship. Let us, the benefactors of these selfless acts, never forget their sacrifice.

'We Will Remember Them'

APPENDIX

The following statistics, taken from various trusted sources, are for the duration of the war unless stated otherwise.

- Avro Lancaster 156,192 sorties 3,345 lost 2.14%
- Handley Page Halifax 82,773 sorties 1,833 lost 2.21%
- Vickers Wellington 47,409 sorties 1,332 lost 2.80%
- De Havilland Mosquito 39,795 sorties 254 lost 0.64%
- Short Stirling 18,440 sorties 606 lost 3.29%
- Total aircraft lost 12,330
- Total wounded in aircraft returning from operations 4,200
- 1939 591 sorties 31 tons of bombs
- 1940 22,473 sorties 13,033 tons of bombs 762 mines laid
- 1941 32.012 sorties 31,704 tons of bombs 1,055 mines laid
- 1942 35,538 sorties 45,561 tons of bombs 9,574 mines laid
- 1943 65,068 sorties 157,457 tons of bombs 13,834 mines laid
- 1944 166,844 sorties 525,518 tons of bombs 17,500 mines laid
- 1945 67,483 sorties 181,740 tons of bombs 4,582 mines laid
- Highest tonnage dropped in one month 67,637 tons March 1945
- 1943 Troops & Defences 670 tons Oil targets 54 tons
- 1944 Troops & Defences 93,854 tons Oil targets 48,043 tons
- Highest tonnage dropped in one night 14/15 October 1944, over 10,000 tons
- Germany tons of bombs dropped 657,674
- France, Low Countries tons of bombs dropped 284,500
- Italy tons of bombs dropped 9,089
- Total tons of bombs dropped 1,000,000+

BIBLIOGRAPHY

Allward, Maurice, *Hurricane Special,* Shepperton: Ian Allan Ltd 1975

Armitage, M. J., *The History of the Royal Air Force,* London: Weidenfeld & Nicholson Ltd. 2000

Armstrong, David, *How Not to Write a Novel,* Brixton: Allison & Busby Limited 2003

Ashton, J. Norman, *Only Birds and Fools,* Shrewsbury: Airlife Publishing Ltd. 2000

Barker, Ralph, *The Hurricats,* London: Pelham Books Ltd 1978

Barnes, C. H., *Bristol Aircraft since 1919,* London: Putnam & Company Ltd 1964

Barris, T., *Behind the Glory,* Toronto: Macmillan Canada 1993

Bercusson, T. J., *Maple Leaf against the Axis:Canada's Second World War,* Toronto: Stoddart 1995

Bingham, Victor, *Merlin Power,* Shrewsbury: Airlife Publishing Ltd. 2003

Birrell, D., *Baz:The Biography of Ian Bazalgette VC,* Nanton: The Nanton Lancaster Society 2014

Birrell, D., *FM159: The Lucky Lancaster,* Nanton: The Nanton Lancaster Society 2015

Birrell, D., *People and Planes: Stories from the Bomber Command Museum of Canada,* Nanton: The Nanton Lancaster Society 2011

Birrell, D., *People and Planes: Stories from the Bomber Command Museum of Canada,* Nanton: The Nanton Lancaster Society 2011

Birrell, D., *Johnny: Canada's Greatest Bomber Pilot,* Nanton: The Nanton Lancaster Society 2018

Bishop, P., *Bomber Boys: Fighting Back 1940-1945,* UK: Harper Collins Publishers 2008

Bowman, Martin W., *100 Group (Bomber Support): RAF Bomber Command in World War II*, Barnsley: Pen & Sword Books Limited 2006

Bowman, Martin W., *The Mosquito Story,* Stroud: The History Press 2011

Bowyer, Chaz, *History of the RAF*, London: Hamlyn Publishing Group Ltd. 2002

Bowyer, Chaz, *RAF Operations 1918-1938,* London: William Kimber & CO. Limited 1988

Braddon, Russell, *Cheshire V. C.*, London: Evans Brothers Limited 1954

Chisholm, Anne & Davie, Michael, *Beaverbrook A Life,* London: Pimlico 1993

Chorlton, Martyn, *The RAF Pathfinders:Bomber Command's Elite Squadrons,* Newbury:Countryside Books 2012

Christie, C. A., *Ocean Bridge: History of RAF Ferry Command,* Toronto: University of Toronto Press 1997

Cotter, J., *Battle of Britain Memorial Flight: 50 Years of Flying,* Barnsley: Pen & Sword 2007

Cotter, J., *Living Lancasters,* Stroud: Sutton Publishing Limited 2005

Deighton, Len, *Fighter: The True Story of the Battle of Britain,* New York: Alfred A. Knopf,.Inc. 1977

Delve, K., *RAF Bomber Command 1936-1945: An Operational and Historical Record,* UK: Pen & Sword 2006

Edwards, Richard & Edwards, Peter, *Heroes and Landmarks of British Military Aviation: From Airships to the Jet Age,* Barnsley: Pen & Sword Books Limited 2012

Duke, Neville, *Test Pilot,* Plymouth: Latimer, Trend & Co. Ltd 1953

Embry, Sir Basil, *Mission Completed,* London: Methurn & Co Ltd 1957

Falconer, J., *Bomber Command Handbook: 1939-1945,* Stroud: Sutton

Publishing Limited 2003

Forczyk, R., *Bf 110 vs Lancaster:1942-1945*, Oxford: Osprey Publishing 2013

Francis, Paul, Flagg, Richard, Crisp, Graham, *Nine Thousand Miles of Concrete*, Historic England/England Heritage 2016

Garbett, M & Goulding, B., *Lancaster at War,* Shepperton: Ian Allan 1971

Garbett, M & Goulding, B. *Lancaster at War 2,* New York: Charles Scribner's Sons 1980

Garbett, M & Goulding, B. *Lancaster,* Enderby: Promotional Reprint Company 1992

Gibson, G., *Enemy Coast Ahead,* London: Michael Joseph Ltd 1951

Gould, J., *RAF Bomber Command and its Aircraft 1941-1945*, UK: Ian Allan Publishing 2002

Goulding, B. & Garbett, M. & Partridge, J., *Story of a Lanc': NX 611* Lincoln: Keyworth & Fry 1974

Gunston, Bill, *Rolls-Royce Aero Engines*, Wellingborough: Patrick Stephens, 1989.

Halliday, Hugh A., *Woody,* Toronto: CANAV Books 1987

Harker, Ronald W., *Rolls-Royce From the Wings,* Oxford: Oxford Illustrated Press 1976

Harker, Ronald W., *The Engines Were Rolls-Royce*, New York: Macmillan Publishing Co., Inc 1979

Harris, A. T., *Despatch on War Operations: 23 February 1942 to 8 May 1945*, London: Frank Cass & Co. Ltd. 1995

Harvey-Bailey, Alec, *Hives' Turbulent Barons,* Paulerspury: Sir Henry Royce Memorial Foundation 1992

Hastings, Max, *Bomber Command: The Myths and Reality of the Strategic Bombing Offensive 1939-1945* New York: The Dial Press 1979

Henshaw, Alex, *Sigh for a Merlin,* Reading: Cox & Wyman Ltd 1980

Holmes, H., *Avro Lancaster*, UK: The Crowood Press Ltd 2005

Holmes, H., *Avro Lancaster: the Definitive Record*, UK: Airlife Publishing Limited 1997

Hotson, Fred W., *De Havilland in Canada*, Toronto: CANAV Books 1999

Hotson, Fred W., The *de Havilland Canada Story*, Toronto: CANAV Books 1983

Iveson, T., *Lancaster: The Biography,* London: Carlton Publishing Group 2011

Jackson, A. J., *British Civil Aircraft since 1919 Vols 1, 2, 3*, London: Putnam &Co 1973/1974

Jones, W. E., *Bomber Intelligence*, Earl Shelton: Midland Counties Publishing 1983

Kennedy, Paul, *The Rise and Fall of British Naval Mastery*, New York: Penguin 2004

Killen, John, *A History of the Luftwaffe*, New York: Muller, Blond & White, Ltd. 1986

Kirk, P., Felix, P., Bartnik, G., *The Bombing of Rolls-Royce at Derby,* Derby: Rolls-Royce Heritage Trust 2002

Kostenuk, S. & Griffin, J. *RCAF Squadron Histories and Aircraft 1924-1968,* Toronto: Samuel Stevens/Hakkert 1977

Lavigne, Michael & W/C Edwards, James F., *Hurricanes over the Sands Part One,* Victoriaville: Lavigne Aviation Publications 2003

Lloyd, Ian, *Rolls-Royce: The Merlin at War* London: The MacMillan Press Ltd 1978

Ludvig, Paul A., *P-51 Mustang,* Hersham: Classic Publications 2003

Lumsden, Alec, S. C., *British Piston Aero-Engines and their Aircraft,* Shrewsbury: Airlife Publishing Ltd 1994

Mason, Francis K., *The Hawker Hurricane,* Bourne End: Aston Publications Limited 1987

McInstry, Leo, *The Hurricane,* London: John Murray Publishers Ltd 2010

McIntosh, Dave, *Terror in the Starboard Seat*, Don Mills: General

Publishing Co. Ltd. 1980

McKinstry, L., *Lancaster: The Second World War's Greatest Bomber,* London: John Murray 2009

Middlebrook, Martin & Everitt, Chris, *The Bomber Command War Diaries: An Operational Reference Book 1939-1945*, Earl Shilton: Midland Publishing 2000

Mikesh, Robert C., *Excalibur III,* Washington D.C.: Smithsonian Institution Press 1978

Milberry, Larry, *Canada's Air Force at War and Peace,* Toronto: CANAV Books 2000

Mollison, J. A., *The Book of Famous Flyers*, Glasgow: William Collins & Sons 1935

Motiuk, Laurence, *Thunderbirds at War*, Nepean: Tri-Graphic Printing

Moyes, P., *Bomber Squadrons of the RAF and their Aircraft,* London 1998: Macdonald & Co. (Publishers) Ltd 1964

Neillands, Robin, *The Bomber War*, London: John Murray Pubs Ltd 2001

Nesbit, Roy Conyers, *RAF an Illustrated History*, Stroud: Sutton Publishing 1998

Nockolds, Harold, *The Magic of a Name,* London: G. T. Foulis & Company Ltd. 1961

Overy, Richard, *Bomber Command 1939-1945*, London: Harpercollins Publications Ltd. 1997

Page, B., *Mynarski's Lanc: The Story of Two Famous Canadian Lancaster Bombers KB726 & FM213*, Erin: Boston Mills Press 1989

Panton, K., *Fred Panton: Man on a Mission,* Leeds: Propagator Press 2012

Peden, M., *A Thousand Shall Fall,* Toronto: Stoddart 1988

Probert, H. *Bomber Harris: His Life and Times,* London: Greenhill Books 2003

Pugh, Peter, *The Magic of a Name: The Rolls-Royce Story,* 3 vols, Cambridge: Icon Books Ltd 2000, 2001, 2002

Radell, R., *Lancaster: A Bombing Legend,* UK: Chancellor Press 1997

Ramsey, Winston G., *The Battle of Britain Then and Now,* London: Battle of Britain Prints International Limited 1980

Rawlings, John, *The History of the Royal Air Force*, London: Hamlyn Publishing 1984

Richards, Denis, *RAF Bomber Command in World War Two,* London: Penguin Classics 2001

Rolls-Royce Group plc., *Rolls-Royce 1904-2004: A Century of Innovation,* London: Rolls-Royce Group plc 2004

Sarkar, Dilip, *The Last of The Few*, Stroud: Amberley Publishing 2011

Sharpe, Michael, *History of the RAF*, Bath: Parragon Plus 2002

Stokes, P. R., *From Gypsy to Gem,* Derby: Rolls-Royce Heritage Trust 1987

Sweetman, J., *Bomber Crew: Taking on the Reich,* London: Abacus 2005

Sweetman, W., *Avro Lancaster,* New York: Zokeisha Publications 1982

Swift, D. *Bomber County: The Lost Airmen of World War Two,* London: Penguin Group 2010

The Air Ministry Account of Bomber's Command Offensive against the Axis, London: HMSO 1941

The Greater Vancouver Branch of The Aircrew Association, *Critical Moments,* Vancouver: self-published 1989

Thompson, J. E., *Bomber Crew,* Canada: Trafford Publishing 2005

Thompson, Scott, *Douglas Havoc and Boston,* Ramsbury: The Crowood Press Ltd 2004

Turner, P St. John, *The Vickers Vimy*, Sparkford: Patrick Stephens Ltd 1969

Wilson, G. A. A., *Lancaster Manual 1943*, Stroud: Amberley Publishing 2013

Wilson, G. A. A., The *Lancaster,* Stroud: Amberley Publishing 2015

Wilson, Gordon A. A., *The Merlin*, Stroud: Amberley Publishing 2018

Logbook, Flight Lieutenant William Pearson . (Courtesy of William Pearson)

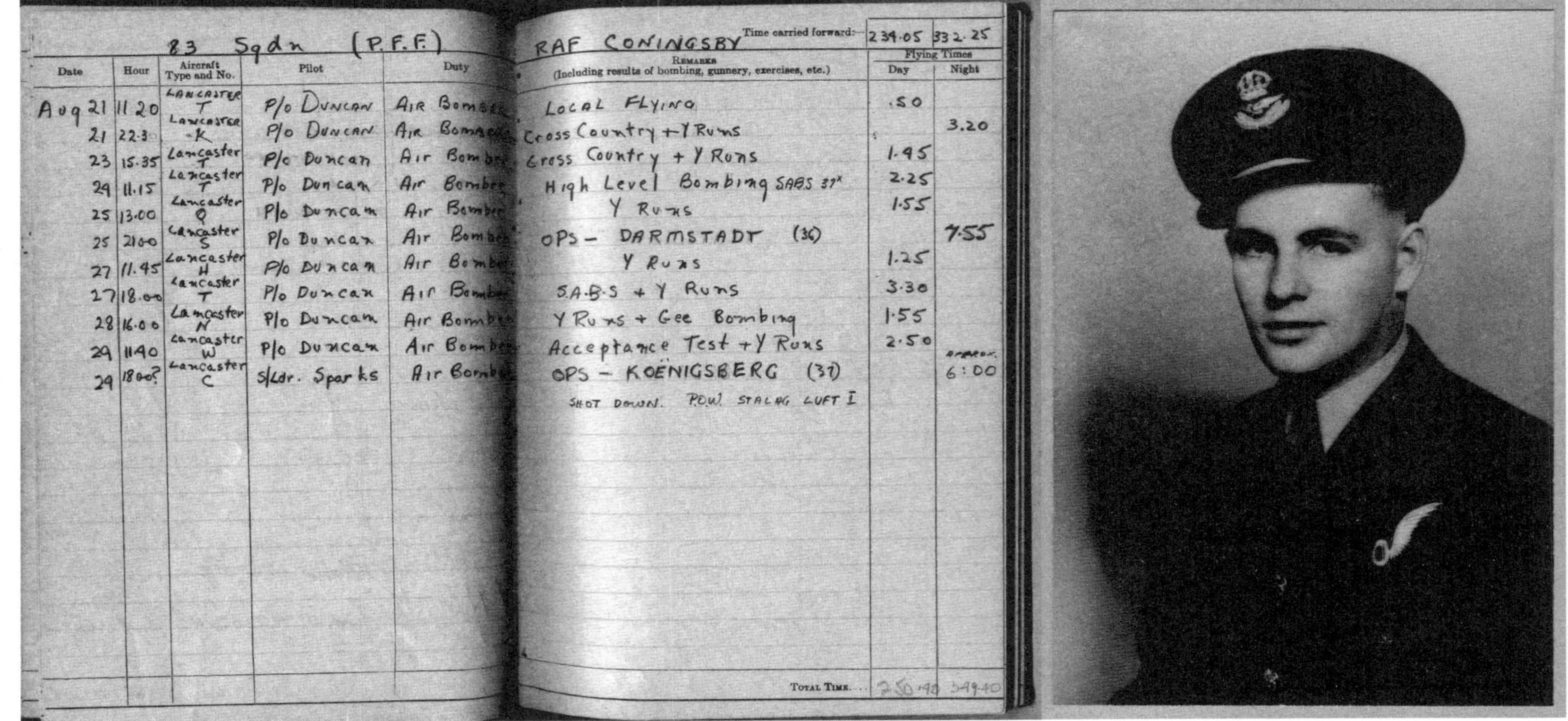

83 Sqdn (P.F.F.) RAF CONINGSBY

Date	Hour	Aircraft Type and No.	Pilot	Duty	Remarks (Including results of bombing, gunnery, exercises, etc.)	Flying Times Day	Flying Times Night
					Time carried forward:—	234.05	332.25
Aug 21	11.20	Lancaster T	P/o Duncan	Air Bomber	Local Flying	.50	
21	22.3	Lancaster K	P/o Duncan	Air Bomber	Cross Country + Y Runs		3.20
23	15.35	Lancaster T	P/o Duncan	Air Bomber	Cross Country + Y Runs	1.45	
24	11.15	Lancaster T	P/o Duncan	Air Bomber	High Level Bombing SABS 37x	2.25	
25	13.00	Lancaster Q	P/o Duncan	Air Bomber	Y Runs	1.55	
25	2100	Lancaster S	P/o Duncan	Air Bomber	OPS – DARMSTADT (36)		7.55
27	11.45	Lancaster H	P/o Duncan	Air Bomber	Y Runs	1.25	
27	18.00	Lancaster T	P/o Duncan	Air Bomber	S.A.B.S + Y Runs	3.30	
28	16.00	Lancaster N	P/o Duncan	Air Bomber	Y Runs + Gee Bombing	1.55	
29	1140	Lancaster W	P/o Duncan	Air Bomber	Acceptance Test + Y Runs	2.50	
29	1800?	Lancaster C	S/Ldr. Sparks	Air Bomber	OPS – KOENIGSBERG (37)		approx. 6:00
					SHOT DOWN. POW STALAG LUFT I		
					Total Time...	250.40	349.40

Anne Allen (*née* Shelson) at Bomber Command Memorial, London. (Courtesy of John Allen)

Dedication

If the peak of courage is number ten,
Then this shall be given to stout-hearted men
Of the Bomber Command in World War Two,
Who fearlessly flew, not knowing who
Will return unscathed from this terrible war,
That young men had undauntingly signed up for.
Let us not forget all those who were lost,
And those who returned but suffered the cost
Of sorrowful memories of comrades now gone
And are striving to show peace must carry on.

Sheila Jakus

INDEX